Business Plan Pro®
Manual

Palo Alto Software, Incorporated, 144 E. 14th Avenue, Eugene, Oregon 97401, USA

First Printing: Version 7.0 – July 2003

Part Number: PA-1123 (7/03)

About this Manual

This manual is one of two books included with Business Plan Pro®. It is designed to provide an overview about the software. In this manual, some details are obvious: installation, for example. However, it also includes chapters that take you further than ever before:

- The guided tour takes you through the main points and highlights of developing a plan.
- Separate chapters offer details on working with text, tables, charts, and printing. The chapter on tables covers every one of the standard tables in detail – what it does, what inputs it expects, and why.
- A complete chapter on advanced spreadsheet work covers functions and blank worksheets that you can add to your plan.
- Separate chapters on working with Microsoft Office®, Quicken®, and QuickBooks®, including how to import and export, what to expect, when and why to move to or from Business Plan Pro.

This manual is also in electronic form (pdf) and is integrated into the software. The Instructions window for each topic and table include links to content-specfic sections within this manual.

The other book is 'Hurdle: The Book on Business Planning.' which provides general information on business planning. The Hurdle book is also provided in pdf format and is referred to as a resource within the software.

Other Help Resources

Special "tips" describe key points about the current section.

? For More Information...

References on how to search the Help Index (built into the software) for step-by-step procedures on using a menu command. There is also context-sensitive help, text, table, and chart instructions and examples, and row-by-row table help, also built into the product.

Online Changes and Additions List

Once the book goes to print, we will find corrections to make. So, to help our customers update their printed manual, we have created "changes and additions" pages on our website. The list of changes will include the date the correction was made. The additions list will include larger section changes or new information not previously included in the manual. These changes and additions can be found online at:

http://www.paloalto.com/su/bp/mc/

Acknowledgements

This manual was coordinated by Teri Epperly, documentation manager, who also co-authored much of the content with Tim Berry, principal author of Business Plan Pro.

The documentation team also included Cale Bruckner, director of product development, and editors Steve Lange and Jacqueline Mansfield. Steve did most of the design layout and implementation of this manual, and Jacqueline developed the Help files.

Business Plan Pro vs. Business Plan Pro PREMIER

This manual was written for both Business Plan Pro and Business Plan Pro PREMIER. Features specific to PREMIER have "PREMIER version" added to the title. The following chart gives a comparison between the two versions:

Which Business Plan Pro has what you need?	Standard	PREMIER
Research it		
More than 400 complete sample plans	x	x
Thousands of industry profiles	x	x
Marketing research tools	x	x
Venture Capital database	x	x
Build it		
Complete text editing	x	x
3-dimension automatic charting	x	x
Complete Microsoft Excel®-like financials	x	x
Import from QuickBooks® 2002 or newer	x	x
Build an Organization Chart		x
Collaborate with a team		x
Detailed sales forecast		x
Detailed personnel planning resources		x
Detailed profit and loss statements		x
Import from Excel		x
Investment analysis		x
Quarterly reports		x
Second year of monthly data		x
User defined tables		x
Distribute and Deliver		
Export to Microsoft Office®	x	x
Publish your plan to SecurePlan.com	x	x
Alternate table styles	x	x
Present your plan using Microsoft PowerPoint® templates	x	x
Use the Report Writer to print multiple plan documents	x	x
Preferred format, respected by banks, lenders, and the SBA	x	x
Save your business plan as a template		x
Distribute plan components for import into other plans		x
Make it Happen		
Legal tools and resources provided by Nolo.com	x	x
Funding tools and resources	x	x
Tools		
Plan Activities	x	x
Forecaster	x	x
Advanced Cash Planning using the Cash Pilot		x

For information on PREMIER upgrades, visit our website at: http://www.paloalto.com/store/bpdupgrade.cfm, or contact the Sales office of Palo Alto Software, Inc. at 1-800-229-7526 Monday through Friday from 8:00 a.m. to 5:00 p.m. Pacific Time.

Table of Contents

Chapter 11: Working with Quicken

Chapter 12: Working with QuickBooks

Appendix A: Range Names

Appendix B: Collaboration

Appendix C: Import and Export Components

Index

Installation

CHAPTER 1: INSTALLATION

This chapter describes how to install Business Plan Pro® *and activate the program, your registration options, and how to obtain product updates from our website.*

Once you have completed this chapter, we recommend you continue with Chapter 2: Getting Started, which gives you an overview of the working screens in the program and its resources.

Also, Chapter 3: Guided Tour, walks you through the process of creating a business plan for a hypothetical graphics company. It gives you a chance to try the features of the program before you start your own plan.

Installation

The DemoShield installation process starts automatically once the CD is inserted into your computer. Follow the DemoShield screen prompts to begin the installation.

Download installation requires a double-click of the Setup.exe file to begin the install.

Check for Microsoft® Internet Explorer®

The InstallShield Wizard checks to see if Internet Explorer (6.0 or higher) is already installed on your computer. If you do not have Internet Explorer, the InstallWizard asks if you wish to install. (NOTE: CD-ROM install only; download install provides instructions on downloading Internet Explorer 6.0. Internet Explorer must be installed before Acrobat Reader.)

- If you answer Yes, the InstallWizard starts the Internet Explorer installation. Follow the screen prompts to complete this install. Once completed, your computer re-boots automatically and the DemoShield InstallWizard re-starts automatically.
- If you answer No, the InstallWizard installation stops.

 TIPS   **What is Microsoft Internet Explorer used for?**

Business Plan Pro uses specific components of Microsoft Internet Explorer to display information and to manage Internet updates.

Check for Adobe® Acrobat® Reader

Adobe Acrobat Reader (4.0 or higher) is also required to complete the Business Plan Pro installation. Acrobat Reader is required before the Business Plan Pro installation can continue. If you do not have Acrobat Reader, the InstallWizard asks if you wish to install. (NOTE: CD-ROM install only; download install provides instructions on downloading Acrobat Reader 5.0. Internet Explorer must be installed before Acrobat Reader.)

- If you answer Yes, the InstallWizard starts the Acrobat Reader 5.0 installation. Follow the screen prompts to complete this install. Once completed, your computer re-boots automatically and the DemoShield InstallWizard re-starts automatically.
- If you answer No, the Business Plan Pro InstallWizard installation stops.

TIPS   **What is Adobe Acrobat Reader used for?**

Acrobat Reader is used by Business Plan Pro to display electronic documentation in portable document format (.pdf). This includes sample plans in the Sample Plan Browser, the product manual, and Hurdle: The Book on Business Planning.

After Internet Explorer and Adobe Acrobat Reader installations are confirmed:

1. The Setup Welcome screen displays:

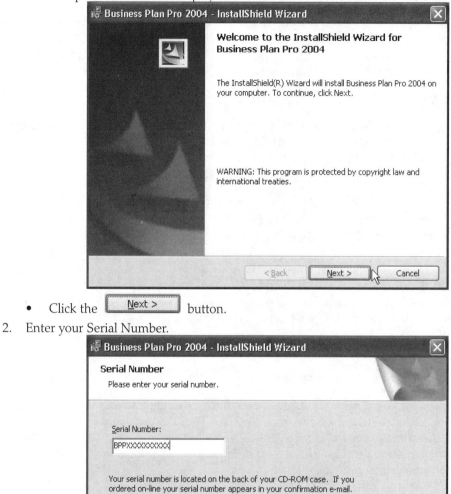

*   Click the [Next >] button.

2. Enter your Serial Number.

*   Type the serial number. Use no spaces when typing; capitalize the first three letters; type the number 0, not the letter O.
*   If you purchased from our online store, the serial number was sent via your order confirmation email. If you purchased from a retail store, your serial number is located on the back of the CD-ROM case
*   Click the [Next >] button to continue.

3. The Electronic License Agreement screen displays:

- If you accept, click the [Next >] button.

4. The Destination Folder screen displays:

- Click the [Next >] button to continue.

5. Add a desktop shortcut.

*   Click the [Next >] button to continue.

6. The Ready to Install the Program screen displays:

*   Click the [Install] button to begin.

7. The program files are copied to your computer:

8. Once the files have been copied, the Installation Completed screen displays:

- Click the [Finish] button to close the screen.

Installation of the Sample Plan Library from CD is discussed in Chapter 4: Starting a Plan.

Activate Your Software

The final step in the installation process is software activation. Palo Alto Software's Activation Wizard is designed to verify the software license and prevent the spread of software piracy. Reduced software piracy makes it possible for us to invest more in product development, quality, and support. In the end, the customer benefits from better software and innovation.

Activation also prevents unsuspecting customers from installing counterfeit software that could be missing key features and resources. The Activation process is simple and private; no personal information is exchanged during the process.

The Activation Wizard gives you three options.

Activate by Using the Internet

If you have an Internet connection, the Activation Wizard confirms your product serial number and Activation ID automatically and completes the process in minutes. No personal information is transferred during activation.

Activate by Using the Telephone

Telephone activation is also provided. Keep your screen open; call the phone number shown on your screen; the activation agent asks you to confirm your serial number and the program generated Activation ID shown in the dialog box. Once confirmed, the agent provides you with a Confirmation ID, which you type into the activation dialog box on your screen.

Click the **Next >>** button to continue and complete the activation.

Activate Later

If you are unable to activate by Internet or telephone at this time, this option lets you postpone activation. You can open and use the software up to 10 times before activation is required.

Once activation is completed, you are given the option to register your product, as described in the next section.

Help Click the dialog Help buttons for more information.

Registration

Once your software is activated, you are given the option to register online (you need an Internet connection to use this function):

Follow the prompts and fill in the requested information.

- Fill in your Name, Company Name (if applicable), email address, etc. Required fields are in **Bold**.
- If you want to receive emails about product updates and news, check that box.
- Click the | Next >> | button to continue.

Your product Registration is complete.

Registration   [?][X]

Registration Complete

Thank you for registering your software.

[Help]   [Cancel] [<< Back] [Finish]

- Click the [Finish] button.

Please register your software. The benefits of registration include notification of software updates, access to special offers, free technical support, and restoration of your serial number if you lose it.

TIPS   **Registration Options**

You can access the Register function at any time from the Help > Registration Wizard command. In addition to online registration, you can also send it either as a fax or by mail. See the contact information on the Technical Support page at the end of this chapter.

Monthly Product Update

Periodically, we create updates to our program's current version. Updates are free to all registered users. When you install Business Plan Pro (and each month thereafter), the Update Product screen asks if you want to download the update file:

Update Product   ? X

Update your software

We're constantly improving the software and yes sometimes we're even fixing minor problems. We suggest that you update your product at least once a month. We'll remind you from time to time to do this. Updating frequently insures that you will have the most current content available.

Click "Next" to check for an update now. NOTE: An Internet connection is required to proceed.

| Help | | Cancel | << Back | Next >> |

- Click the **Next >>** button to continue.

The installed version is compared to the latest update:

Update Product   ? X

Download the update

An update has been found and is 39.9MB in size.

Click "Next" to update now.

| Help | | Cancel | << Back | Next >> |

- Click the **Next >>** button to continue.

A Progress screen displays showing how much of the download has been completed.

Once the update file has been downloaded, the following screen displays:

Update Product

Install the update

The update download is complete. Please click "Finish" below to exit the software and install the update. You will need to restart the software when the update is complete.

| Help | | Cancel | << Back | Finish |

- Click the [Finish] button.

The update file opens, and executes the update of your program. We recommend you perform an update each month to ensure that you have the latest update for your version.

 Special Notes about Product Update:

- This function can be accessed at any time from the Tools > Update Product command.
- Product Updates are different from Upgrades. Updates deal with optimizing the current version. An Upgrade is a new version of the program.

Technical Support

We make every effort to provide prompt, professional support for our registered users. Telephone support is available from 8:30 a.m. to 4:30 p.m. (U.S. Pacific time) on normal business days. Email messages and faxes are usually answered within a single working day.

Telephone: **1-541-683-6162**

Please be at your computer when you call, have your system on, and be ready to work with the software. Have your serial number available.

Fax: **1-541-683-6250**

Please make sure your fax number is plainly visible on your fax to us. Unless you specify some other fax number, our responses are sent to the fax number that sent the original message.

Email:

Internet: **help@paloalto.com**

America Online: **Pasware**

Internet Technical Support

Answers to our most common technical questions can be found at:

http://www.paloalto.com/support

> **TIPS** **Online Technical Support**
>
> The Help > Palo Alto on the Web > Technical Support command provides a direct link to the online Technical Support database, as well as our other website resources.

Support Policies and Philosophy

Our product support offers registered users professional answers, to the best of our ability, to questions regarding the installation, use, and normal operation of our software. Support focuses mainly on operating the software, such as and including installation, opening, saving, and printing. Support does not deal with the contents of a business plan.

Getting Started

CHAPTER 2: GETTING STARTED

This chapter introduces you to the EasyPlan Wizard®, Text and Table screen modes that you work in, and other resources available in the program.

Business Plan Pro® provides help in many forms throughout the program. These are described.

Starting Business Plan Pro

During installation, you had the option of having a shortcut icon stored on your computer Desktop area. Additionally, a menu link is created from the Start button. Choose either method to start the program:

Shortcut Icon   Business Plan Pro 2004

Double-click the Business Plan Pro icon from the Desktop.

Start menu

1. Click the Start button.
2. Highlight and Click Programs > Business Plan Pro 2004.

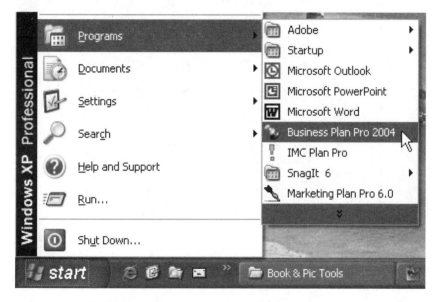

You can use the Windows Start button to access the program menu.

Opening Screen

You start with the opening screen, shown in Figure 2-1.

FIGURE 2-1: START A PLAN SCREEN

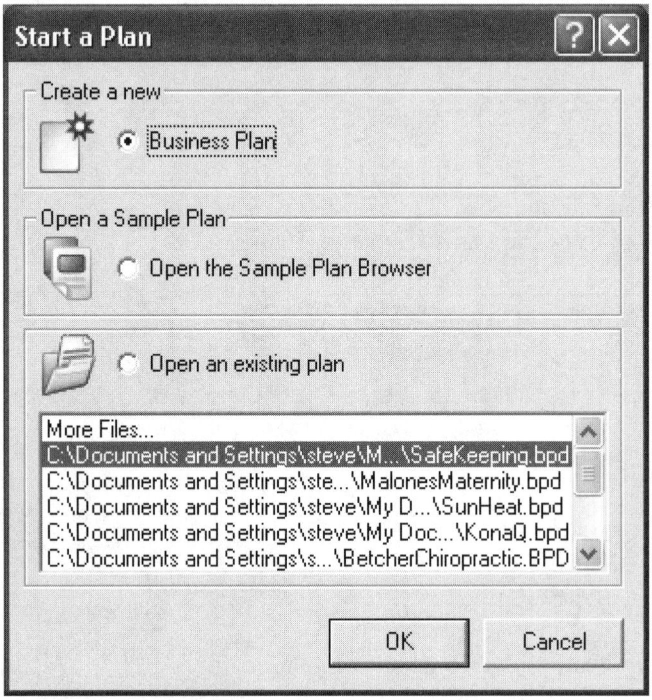

From the opening screen, you can create a new plan, or open a sample plan or an existing plan.

TIPS

When you're first getting started...

Choose Create a new Business Plan and let the EasyPlan Wizard walk you through each step of the planning process.

Start Options from the Open Screen:

1. **Create a new Business Plan**: Starts a new plan using the EasyPlan Wizard.
2. **Open a Sample Plan**: Lets you choose from over 400 sample plans using the Sample Plan Browser. You can view plans in pdf format, and then download and open them in Business Plan Pro.
3. **Open an existing plan**: Lets you choose from your previously-created and saved plan files. A list of files displays in the dialog box. The More Files... option lets you search for files in other directories.

EasyPlan Wizard

The EasyPlan Wizard is designed to lead you through the entire process of writing your plan. From writing your topics to entering numbers into the tables, the EasyPlan Wizard tasks provide a step-by-step process, plus instructions and examples. Figure 2-2 shows the Plan Setup screen.

FIGURE 2-2: EASYPLAN WIZARD PLAN SETUP SCREEN

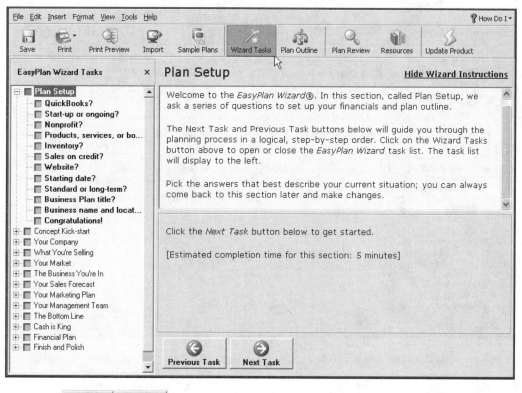

Use the *buttons to move through the tasks.*

TIPS

EasyPlan Wizard - Put it to work for you!

From start to finish, the EasyPlan Wizard is with you all the way. Its screens ask questions, give suggestions, provide Instructions and Examples, as well as feedback as you complete a section of your plan. Think of the EasyPlan Wizard as your personal assistant.

NOTE: Additional information on the EasyPlan Wizard is also found in Chapter 4: Starting Your Plan.

Writing Your Topics

Much of your business plan is text. The text is organized into topics. You work on text from the Topic screen, shown in Figure 2-3.

FIGURE 2-3: TOPIC SCREEN

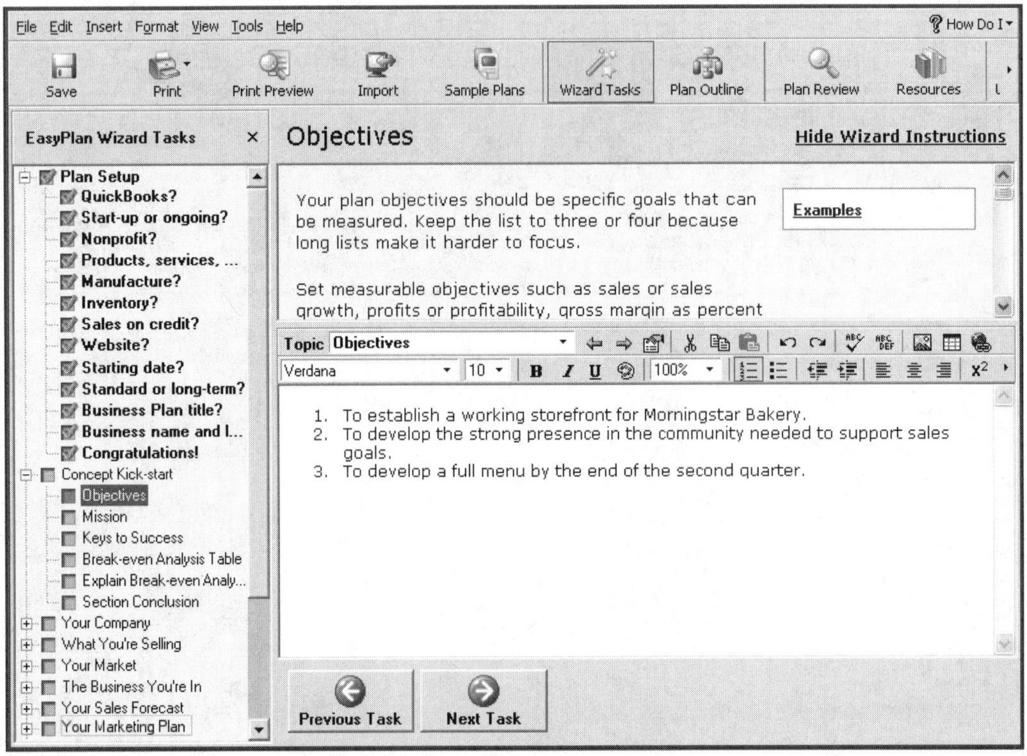

This example shows Wizard Tasks, Instructions and the text window for the Objectives topic.

TIPS

Instructions and Examples

Instructions for the current topic display automatically. Click the Examples link to show text for the same topic from a completed plan. Example text can also be copied into the current topic.

Working in Tables

The Table screen is a spreadsheet format, with columns, rows, and formulas to automatically calculate totals as you enter your numbers. An example is shown in Figure 2-4.

FIGURE 2-4: TABLE SCREEN

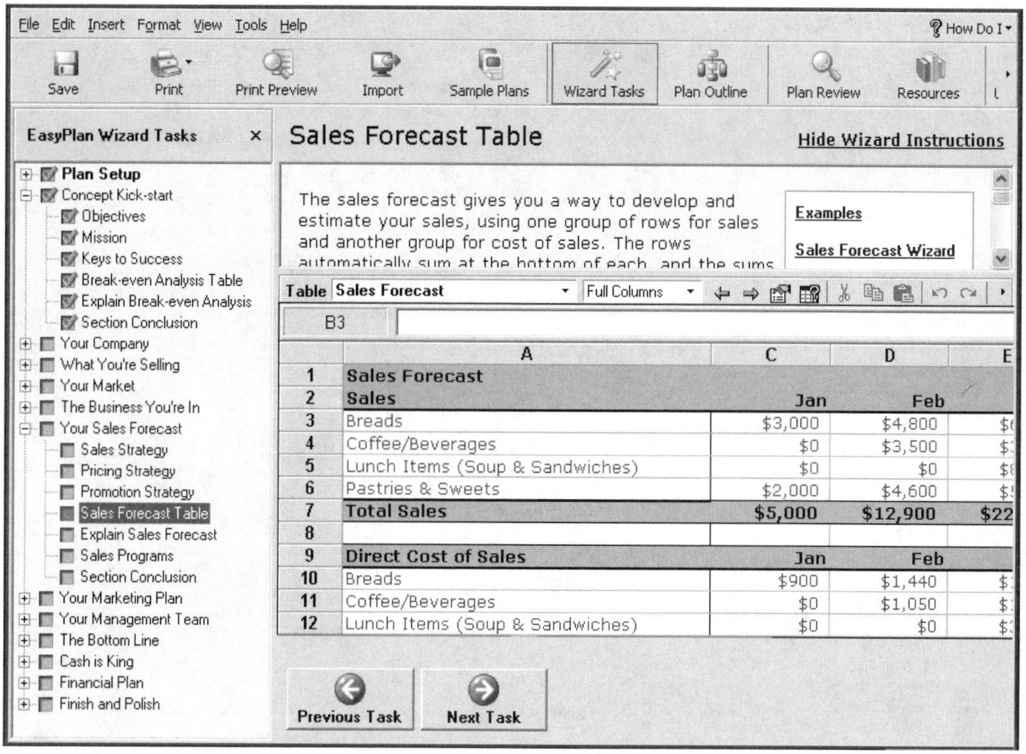

Here the EasyPlan Wizard Tasks and Instructions display in the table screen for the Sales Forecast.

TIPS

Instructions and Examples

Instructions for the current table display automatically. Click the Examples link to show the same table from a completed plan.

Charts are Automatic

All of the charts in Business Plan Pro are automatically linked to tables. As you fill in your tables, your charts start to show data.

FIGURE 2-5: CHART SCREEN

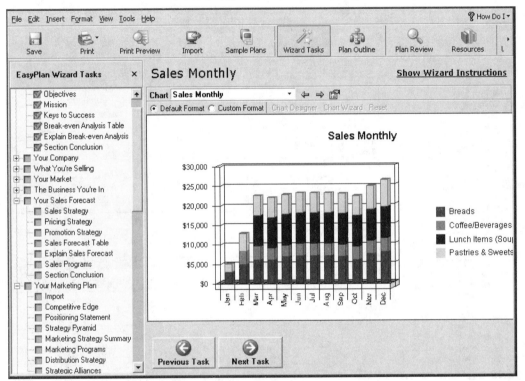

An example of the Sales Monthly chart, created automatically from the Sales Forecast table.

Printing is Automatic

Business Plan Pro prints out a plan with an automatic format.

- It merges the text in topics, the tables, and charts into a professional-looking format. This includes automatic indenting of paragraphs and formatting of topic titles. Bullet points and numbered lists can be added to your text through the formatting toolbar.
- It prints the monthly tables as Appendices.
- It creates a Table of Contents.
- It has a standard cover sheet that you can customize with a company logo and standard text formatting.
- An optional Legal page can be included. Basic text on confidentiality is provided with the template.
- A Print Preview option lets you see the plan document before you print.

For more details on your Print options, please see Chapter 8: Print and Publish, in this manual.

Getting Help

- ## EasyPlan Wizard

  These screens have built-in "help" throughout. Follow the sequence of steps and let the Wizard show you the way.

- ## Context-Sensitive Help

  - Click on a row in a table, then click the ▦ button to see row-specific definitions.
  - When viewing a table in the Table screen, press the F1 key to see help on working in tables.

- ## How do I? Help

  In the top right corner of your screen is the ❓ How Do I ▾ button. Click this button and a list of common questions displays. Select a question and a special window pops-up the answer.

- ## What's This? Help

  In the top right corner of select dialog screens is the ❓☒ Help button. Click this button and a cursor with a question mark displays. Click on an object or text in the dialog, and a special window pops-up the answer.

- ## Business Plan Pro Manual

  Throughout the topic and table instructions, there are links to chapters and specific sections of the electronic version of this manual. This Portable Document Format (pdf) version opens in Acrobat Reader, and includes full-color graphics.

- ## Hurdle: The Book on Business Planning

  Throughout the EasyPlan Wizard screens, there are a number of links to the electronic version of the Hurdle book. This pdf file displays the book in a separate window on your screen as an additional reference tool for you.

- ## Business Planning Resources

  Business Plan Pro has other integrated planning tools and also provides links to Internet resources to help you in developing your plan. Use the Tools > Resources menu or click the button to access these features.

FIGURE 2-6: RESOURCES PAGE

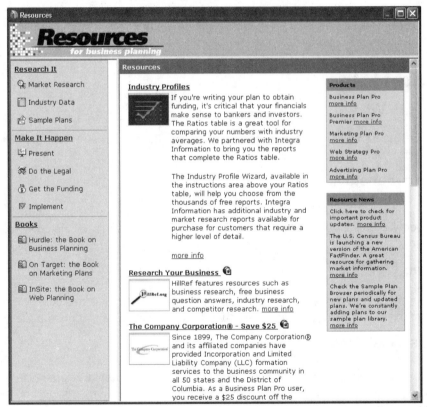

The Resources Page gives you access to many additional tools for building your plan.

Guided Tour

CHAPTER 3: GUIDED TOUR

This Guided Tour develops a business plan for a hypothetical graphics company. The Tour gives you practice in how to input your text and tables. It also demonstrates the importance of reviewing your numbers as you develop your plan and making modifications as necessary.

Tour Overview

So, you are just starting Business Plan Pro® for the first time? This chapter helps get you started. The first section is a general overview of the working screens (Topic, Table, and Chart). Our Guided Tour walks you through an example of how to create a business plan. The Tour hits the highlights to get you started.

TIPS

Who should take the Tour?

This step-by-step Tour introduces you to the basics of the program and the process of writing a business plan. If you prefer to start immediately on your own plan, please go to Chapter 4: Starting a Plan.

If you take the Tour, you work with the following features:

1. Starting Business Plan Pro
2. Starting a Plan
   - Introduction to the EasyPlan Wizard®
   - Saving your plan to file
3. Working with Topics
   - Navigate between topics
   - Choose a topic from the Plan Outline
   - View Instructions and Examples for a topic
   - Type text for a topic
   - Overview of text formatting
4. Working in Tables
   - Show Row and Column Headings
   - Edit Row Labels
   - Enter numbers in key tables
   - Copy cells across columns
   - View linked tables

As you create a plan for this hypothetical graphics company, you see how (and why) it is important to make adjustments to your table numbers as you develop your plan.

For purposes of this Tour, start a new plan using the default EasyPlan Wizard settings.

1. Start Business Plan Pro.
2. Choose Create a new > Business Plan from the Opening dialog screen.
3. Click on the Wizard Tasks button to display the EasyPlan Wizard in the left column.

Your screen should look like Figure 3-1.

FIGURE 3-1: TOUR: SET VIEW SETTINGS

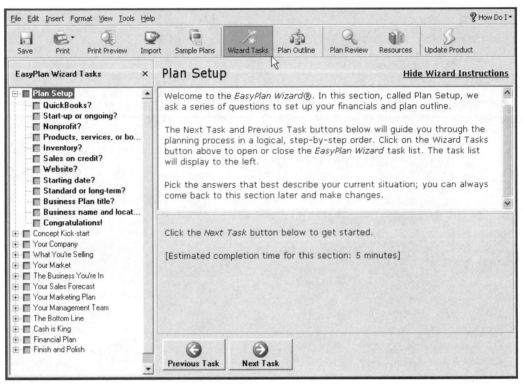

As part of this Tour, we work with the EasyPlan Wizard and the Plan Outline screens. The tool buttons at the top of the screen let you switch between the Wizard Tasks or the Plan Outline while you work.

TIPS

Start a New Plan—Follow the EasyPlan Wizard

For the purpose of this Tour, we jump from text to tables to demonstrate each. However, when you start your plan, we recommend that you follow the sequence of the EasyPlan Wizard Tasks.

Choose default settings for Plan Setup

Each question in the Plan Setup section of the EasyPlan Wizard has a "default" answer. For the purpose of this tour, accept all but one of these default settings. The Starting Date becomes January, 2004.

- Click the Plan Setup check box in the EasyPlan Wizard list. This shortcut automatically chooses the default answer for each question.
- Then, select the **Starting Date** question and choose **January, 2004**.
- Click the ![Next Task] button through the remaining steps.

The final screen describes your business classification and lets you save your Plan Setup answers. There should now be check marks for each topic in the Plan Setup, as shown in Figure 3-2.

FIGURE 3-2: ACCEPTING DEFAULT SETTINGS

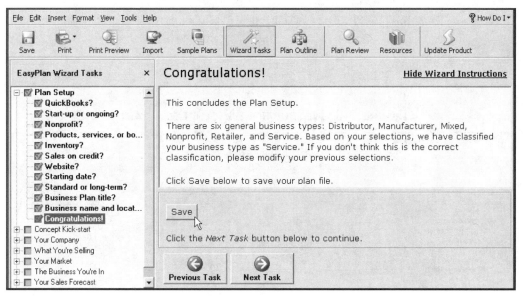

Check marks show that each question in the Plan Setup section has been answered.

- Click the **Save** button to save your new plan file. For this Tour, accept the default filename of "My Plan Title."

Customized vs. Default EasyPlan Wizard Questions

When starting your own plan, we recommend you read each question and choose the answer that best fits your business type, so the EasyPlan Wizard can create a customized outline and tables. Choose the default if you are not sure how to answer. You can change it later.

Practice Working in Topics

We now type text for the Objectives topic and create a standard paragraph and a numbered list.

View Instructions and Examples for this Topic

1. Check to be sure the EasyPlan Wizard Tasks display in the left column. If they do not, click the [Wizard Tasks] button.

2. Click on the **Concept Kick-start** step and choose **Objectives**.

The Instructions/Examples frame should now display, as shown in Figure 3-3.

FIGURE 3-3: INSTRUCTIONS/EXAMPLES FRAME

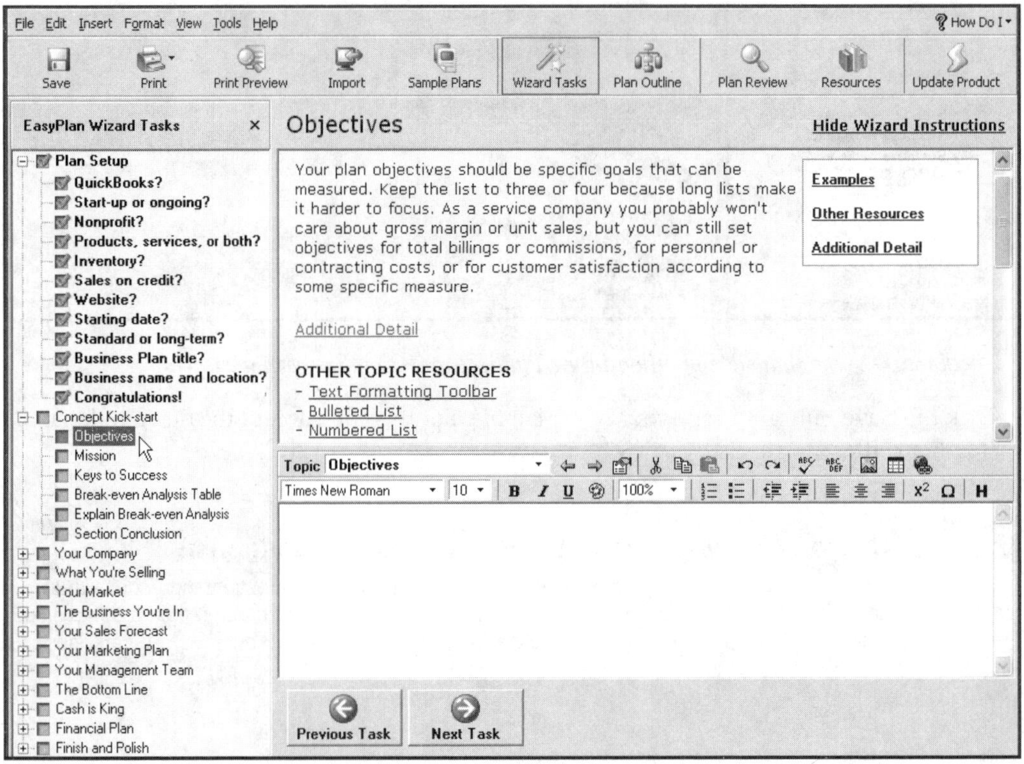

Instructions and examples are automatically displayed for each topic, table, and chart.

3. Click on the Examples link to see an example from a completed plan (for the Tour, we do not use the "paste into your plan" option).

TIPS

For more information:

Please review Chapter 5: Your Plan Text, to learn more about working with text.

Type into Topic Screen

We now type text for our Objectives topic. Once completed, it looks like Figure 3-4.

FIGURE 3-4: TYPING INTO A TOPIC SCREEN

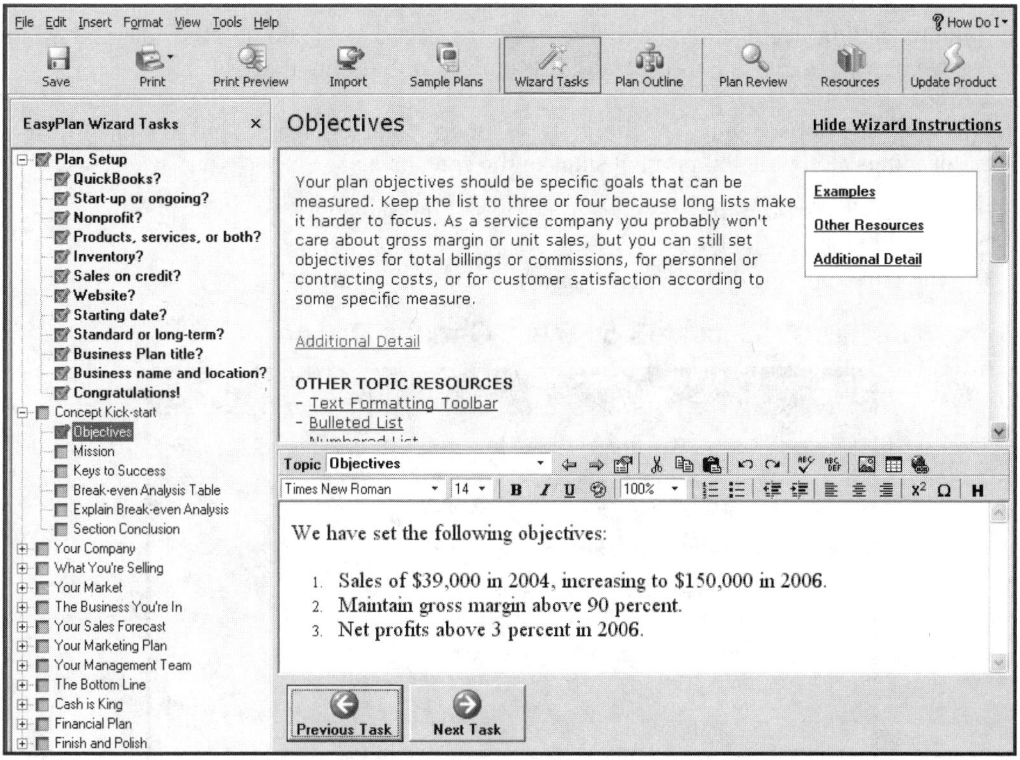

Let the built-in formatting handle your paragraphs. Use the bullet list and numbered list tools from the toolbar.

Click the mouse inside the text window and create the following text with a numbered list:

1. Type: We have set the following objectives:
2. Press the Enter key.

3. Click the numbered list ⊞ tool from the toolbar and type the following:
   1. Sales of $39,000 in 2004, increasing to $150,000 in 2006. Press Enter.
   2. Maintain gross margin above 90 percent. Press Enter.
   3. Net profits above 3 percent in 2006.

   Click the [Previous Task] [Next Task] buttons to move along in your plan.

[Help] For step-by-step procedures, click the dialog Help buttons or the Help menu.

Practice Working in Tables

In the next portion of our Tour, we work in the financial tables. Follow along with the examples here for an overview of how the tables work.

Set Table Options

The column headings (A, B, C, etc.) and row headings (1, 2, 3, etc.) should be visible. If they are, jump to the next page, **Sales Forecast**, and continue with the Tour.

If the headings are not showing, use the Tools > Options > Tables... command to show row and column headings along the top and left sides of the spreadsheet.

1. Click on Tools from the menu list at the top of the screen.
2. Select Options > Tables...
3. The Table Options dialog box displays, as shown in Figure 3-5.

FIGURE 3-5: TABLE OPTIONS DIALOG

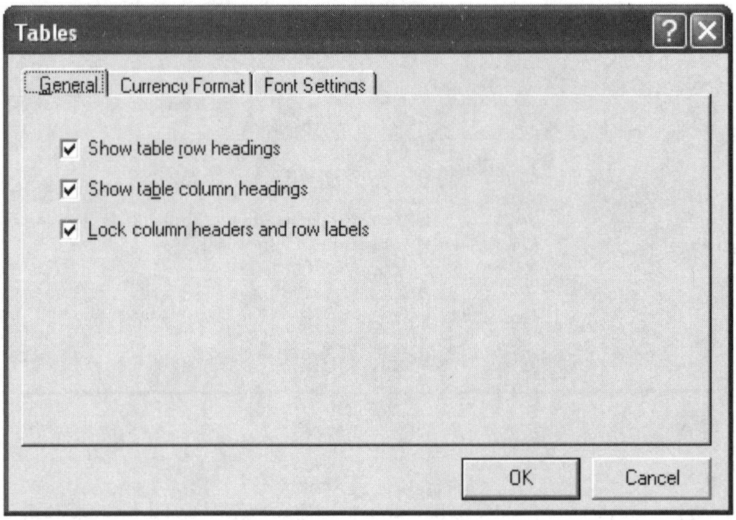

Showing Column and Row headings displays the cell locations when working in the tables.

4. Check the boxes to show table row and table column headings.
5. Click the ⬚ OK ⬚ button to save the setting change.

▮TIPS   **Other Table Options**

Currency Format: Select currency type and apply to table and chart formatting.
Font Settings: Lets you change the font style and size for cell input in your table.

Sales Forecast

In the Sales Forecast table, you learn to create a row label, type in a cell value, and copy that cell number across the row. Click View > Tables > Sales Forecast to open the Sales Forecast table.

TIPS

Sales Forecast Wizard (with Forecaster Tool)

The Sales Forecast Wizard dialog displays whenever you select the Sales Forecast table. It includes the Forecaster tool, which lets you click the mouse to draw a line for your monthly forecast, instead of typing numbers into the cells. For the purpose of this tour, we enter numbers manually (See the Help file for more information on the Sales Forecast Wizard).

The Sales Forecast table should now display, as shown in Figure 3-6.

FIGURE 3-6: TOUR - SALES FORECAST IN TABLE VIEW

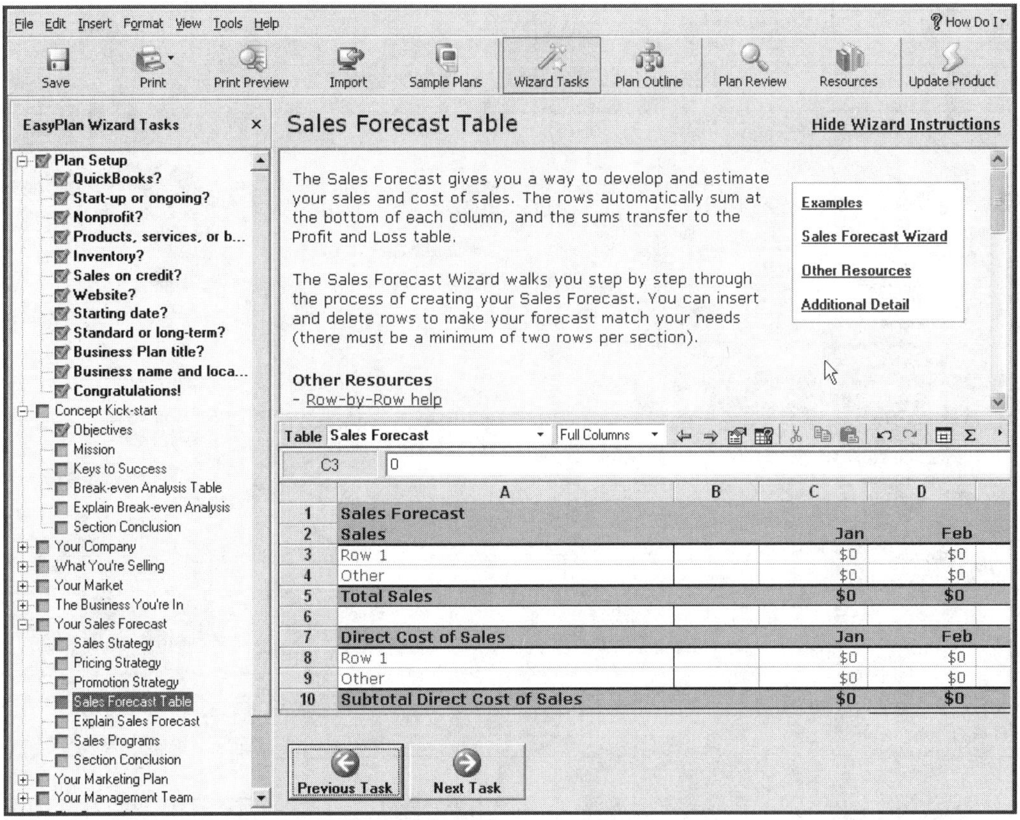

You can also use the Wizard Tasks. Click the Your Sales Forecast section and select Sales Forecast Table as shown in this illustration. Once in Tables, the list of tables can be accessed directly from the Table toolbar.

Type Row Labels

1. Select the first monthly column, January (Jan), of sales. Click the mouse inside that cell (C3).
2. Click on the Edit > Row Label command. A dialog box displays.
3. Type Graphic Services as the row label (as shown in Figure 3-7). Click the OK button.

FIGURE 3-7: ROW LABEL DIALOG

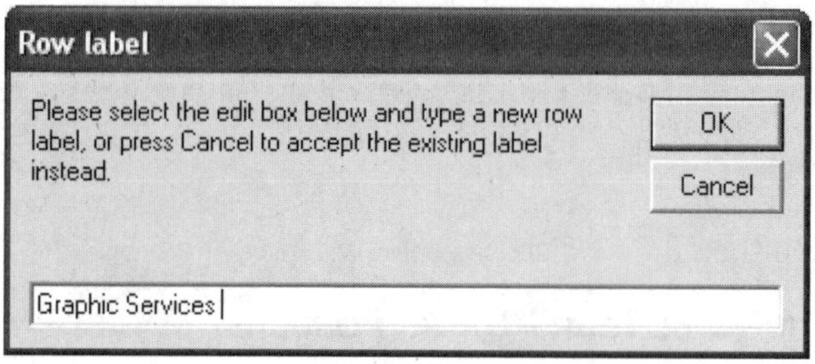

Use the Row Label command to create row labels.

FIGURE 3-8: SALES ROW LABEL

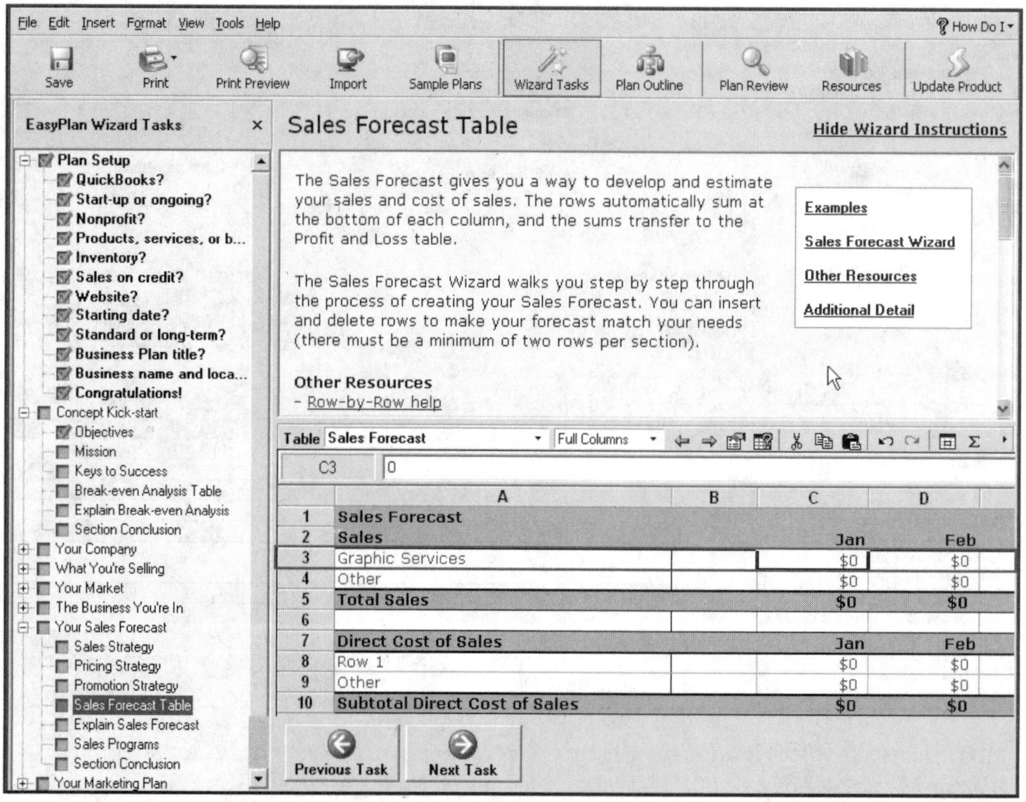

The row label displays in column A, Graphic Services.

Type in a Cell Value

For the purpose of this Tour, we enter sales and costs of sales numbers for our newly-titled row, Graphic Services. The company is estimating a 20% increase in sales each month. Their cost of sales is set at 5% of their sales for each month.

To create this Sales Forecast, we enter the first month's sales number, then use the Edit > Fill > Series command to automatically increase sales by a factor of 1.2 across the row. For our estimated cost of sales, we use a formula to calculate 5% of the monthly sales. Then we use the Edit > Fill > Right command to repeat this formula across the row.

TIPS **Fill > Series**

The Edit > Fill > Series command gives you an easy way to fill in a whole row of numbers with a simple growth rate. Try it!

Input Sales Numbers

1. Click on cell C3, type January's sales value as 1000, and press the Enter key.
2. Use your mouse to highlight the monthly cells in that same row (cells C3 through N3).
3. From the Edit menu, choose Fill > Series command. A dialog box appears. Figure 3-9 shows the dialog box asking for Series Growth Factor:

Figure 3-9: Fill > Series with Growth Factor of 1.2

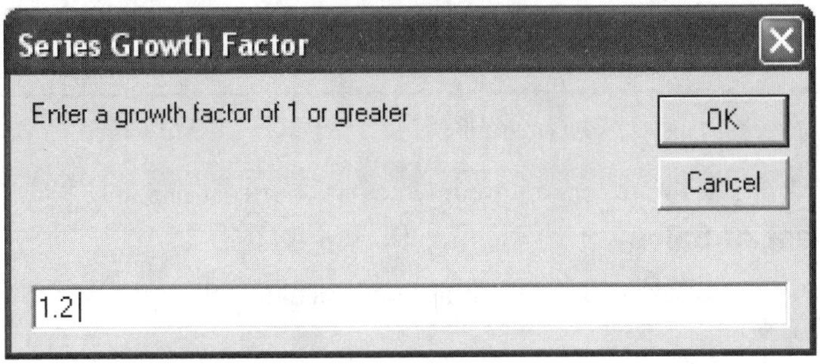

This growth factor creates a formula that automatically increases monthly sales by 20%.

4. Set that growth figure as 1.2
5. Click button.

Your Graphic Services sales row should show that sales for each month increased by 20% from the previous month. February is $1,200, March is $1,440, etc., across the row.

Figure 3-10 shows the final input to the row.

FIGURE 3-10: SALES INPUT WITH GROWTH FACTOR

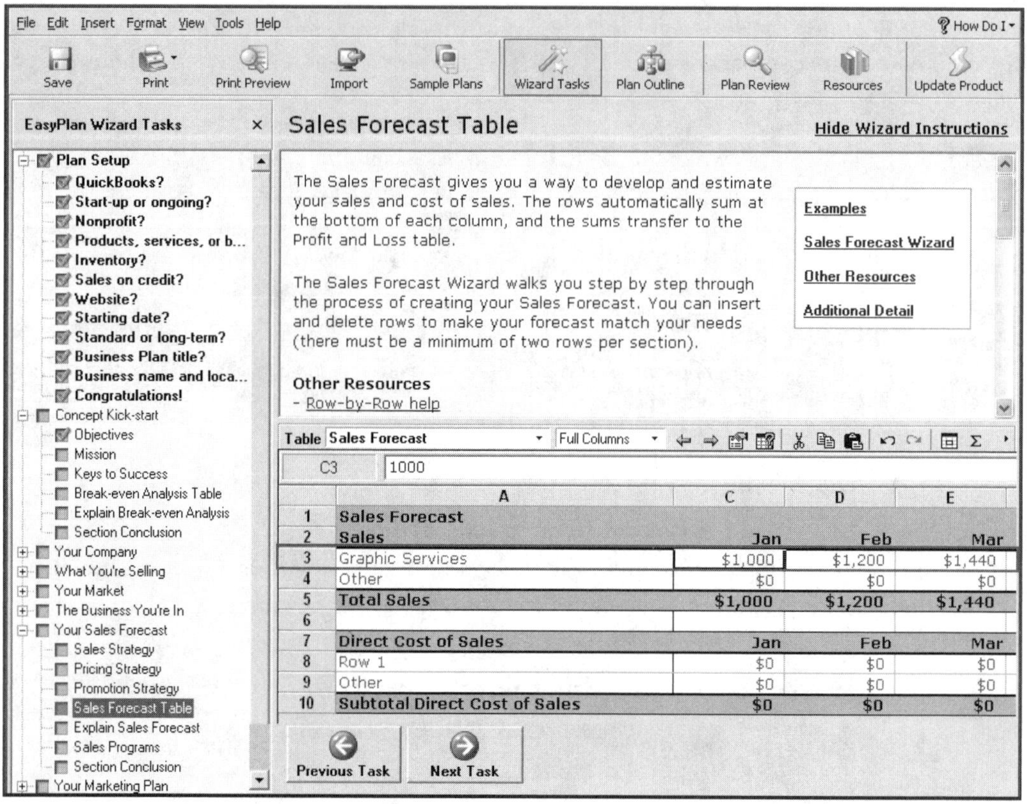

A simple sales forecast has one row each for Sales and Direct Cost of Sales.

Now that we have our sales numbers entered, we create our cost of sales.

Input Cost of Sales

For Cost of Sales, we use a spreadsheet formula that calculates the cost to be 5% of the sales for that month. The formula is: =.05*C3

This formula multiplies the January sales number in cell C3 ($1,000) by .05. The cost of sales for January calculates to be $50 (cell C8).

To create this formula and repeat it across the row:

Under the section, Direct Cost of Sales:

1. Click on cell C8, use the Edit menu > Row Label and type Graphic Services.
2. Type =.05*C3 into cell C8 and press Enter. Cost of Sales for January should show as $50.
3. Highlight cells C8 through N8.
4. Use the Edit > Fill > Right command to repeat this cost of sales formula for each month.

Now, check your Cost of Sales numbers for Graphic Services. January should be $50, February is $60, March is $72, etc., as shown in Figure 3-11.

FIGURE 3-11: COST OF SALES INPUT

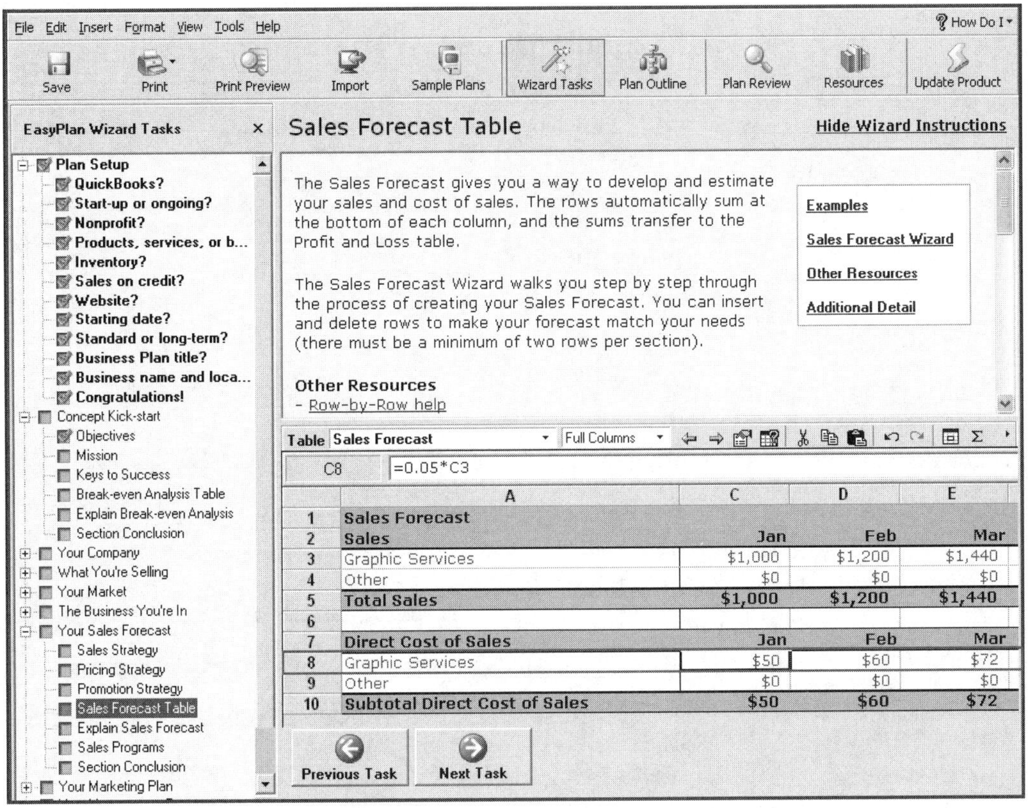

The formula in cell C8 shows in the edit bar portion of the screen.

You have now successfully created a sales forecast for your Graphic Services row.

⚲ TIPS   Do You Know Spreadsheets?

The financials in Business Plan Pro are built on the foundation of a powerful computer spreadsheet built into the application, rather than a simple template. If you know how to use spreadsheets, you will be happy to discover how much Business Plan Pro has in common with Microsoft Excel®.

Use the Tools > Options > Tables settings to set row and column headings so they show, and discover compatibility with more than 100 Excel functions.

Personnel

Now we enter numbers into the Personnel table. To move from the Sales Forecast to Personnel table, use the pull-down menu located on the left side of the toolbar, as shown in Figure 3-12.

FIGURE 3-12: PULL-DOWN LIST FOR TABLES

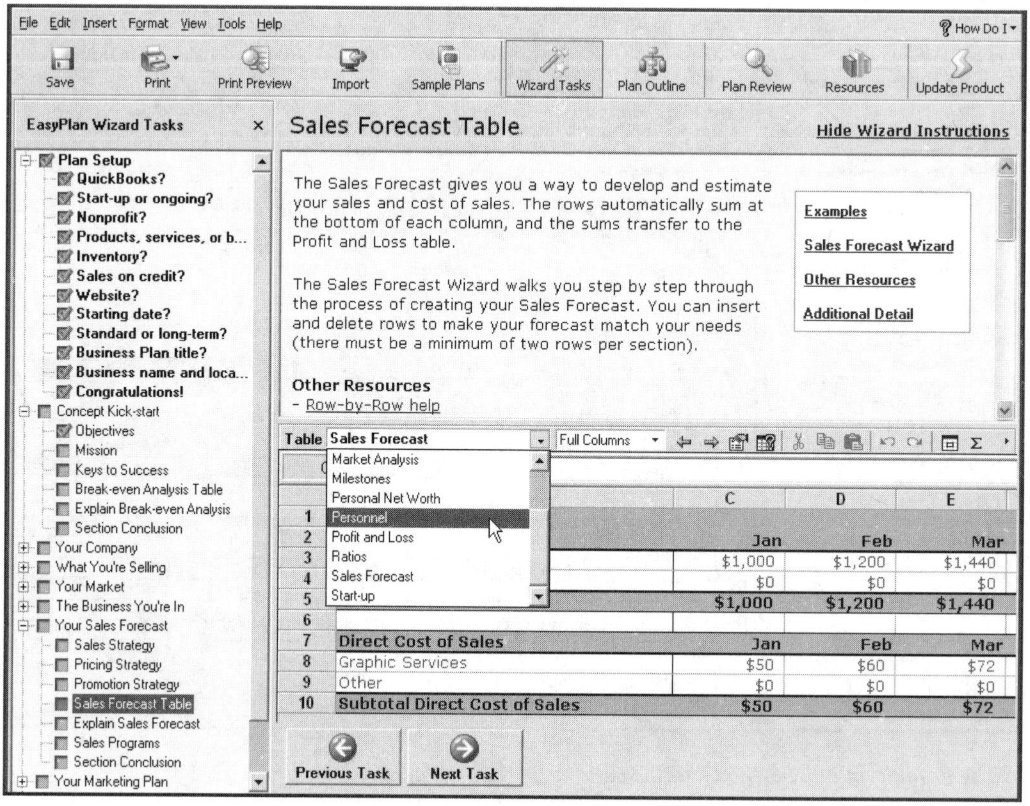

When working in tables, the pull-down list on the toolbar is a quick way to move from one table to another.

TIPS

Payroll Tax Percentage is Automatic

Payroll Taxes are automatically calculated in the Profit and Loss table. The tax percentage has a default setting of 15% but you can change that to reflect your real tax rates by typing the new value into the Payroll Taxes row.

Personnel Options (PREMIER version)

Chapter 6: Your Plan Tables, has details on the different options for personnel tables. You can have a lot more detail in your personnel plan if you want.

In the Personnel table, we create a row called "Main Person," enter a salary amount, and copy it to all remaining months:

1. Use the pull-down table list (shown in Figure 3-12) and choose the Personnel table.
2. Position your cursor on cell A7.
3. Use the Edit menu > Row Label, type "Main Person," and press Enter.
4. Click on Cell C7, and type 3000 as a first-month salary. Press Enter.
5. Highlight the cells C7 through N7.
6. Use the Edit > Fill > Right command to repeat the number across the row.

You should now show a salary of $3,000 for each month of the row, as shown in Figure 3-13.

FIGURE 3-13: PERSONNEL TABLE

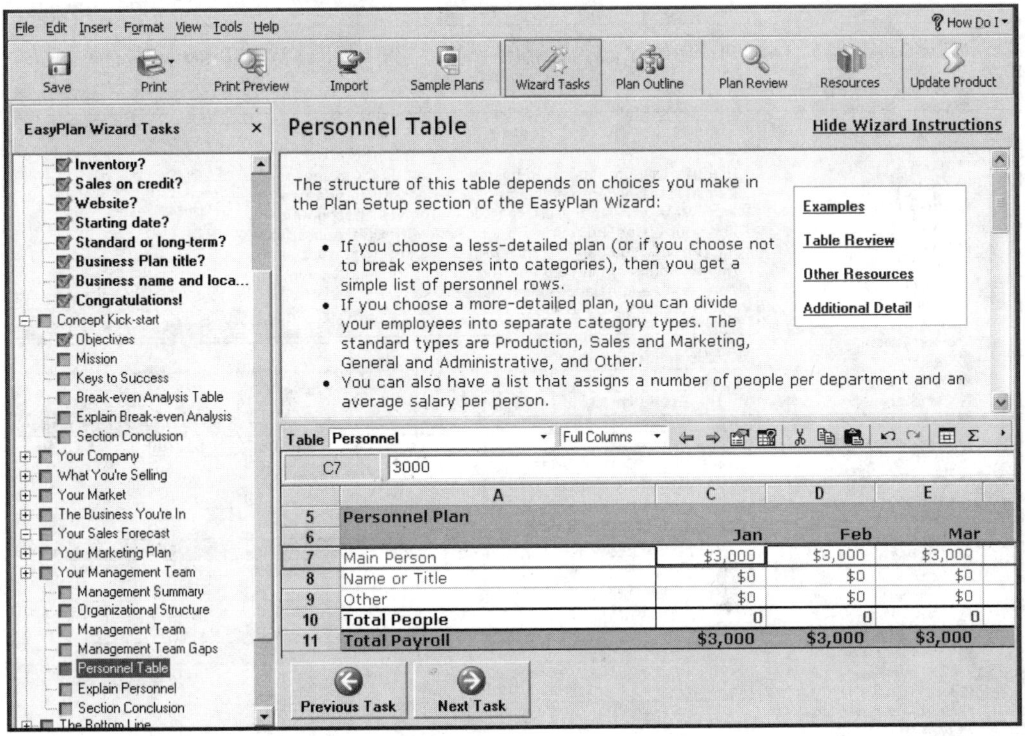

Fill in your personnel table with some simple personnel numbers.

Profit and Loss

Now move on to the next table, Profit and Loss.

- Use your pull-down list from the toolbar and select Profit and Loss.
- The Instructions and Examples in the EasyPlan Wizard window have switched to Profit and Loss.

Look first at the top of the table, and you see that Sales and Cost of Sales numbers are already there. They came directly from your Sales Forecast. It should look like Figure 3-14.

FIGURE 3-14: PROFIT & LOSS TABLE

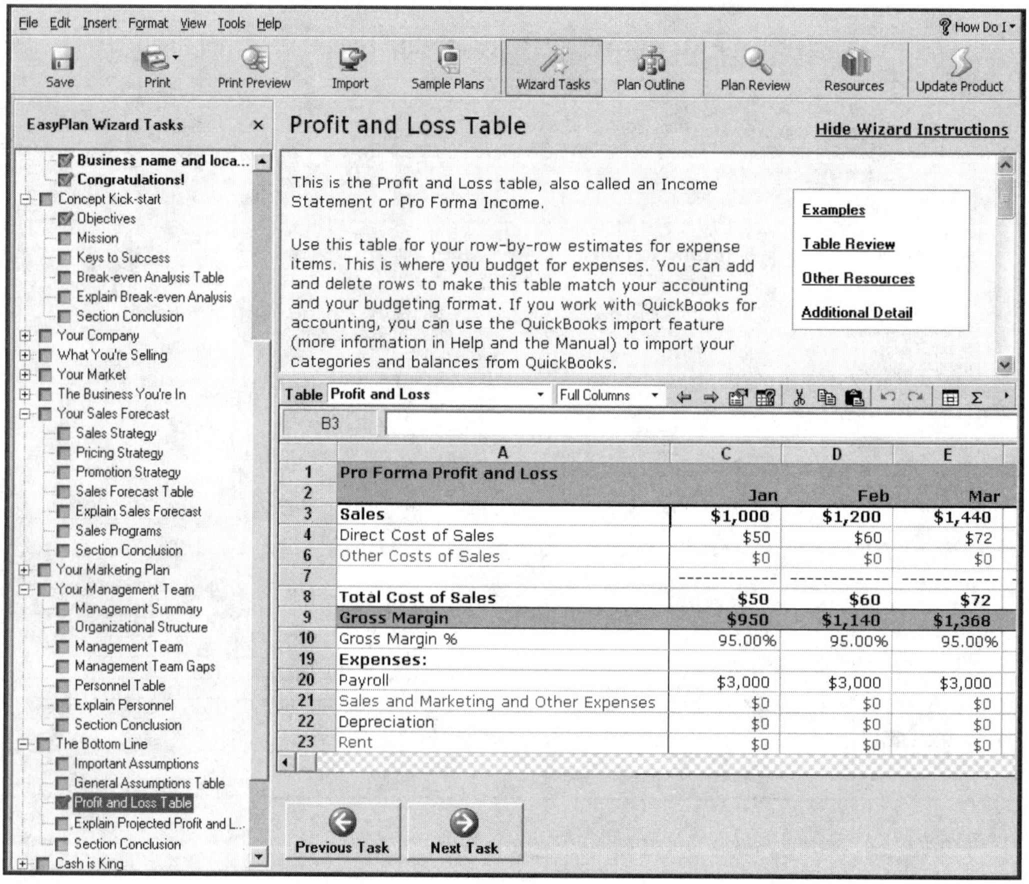

The Profit and Loss table absorbs sales and personnel information, plus assumptions for expenses, to calculate profits.

The Profit and Loss table contains a section for expenses. Several common expense items are automatically listed in this section. Let us rename a row, delete a row, and insert a new row.

Rename a Row

For this Tour, we use the Edit > Row Label command to rename a row.

- Find the row named Rent and rename it Building Lease.

Insert a Row

In addition to the existing expense rows, use the Insert > Rows command to insert a row for Advertising/Promotion expenses:

1. Position cursor on the Utilities row.
2. Use the Insert > Rows command. An "Inserted Row" now displays above the Utilities row and the Edit Row Label dialog opens.
3. Type Advertising/Promotion as the row label and click the OK button.

Your new expense row is now in place.

Delete an Expense Row

To delete the Insurance row:

1. Click anywhere in the row labeled Insurance.
2. Select the Edit > Delete > Rows command.
3. The software asks you to confirm that you want to delete the row (deleting a row cannot be undone).
4. Click the [Yes] button to delete that row.

TIPS

When to Delete an Expense Row

If you are not sure if you need a preset expense row, we recommend you keep it in the table. It shows a **$0** value and has no affect on your other table numbers.
It is easy to go back later and delete unused rows.

Input Expenses

Now that our expense rows are in place, we enter numbers:

1. Go to cell C23, the Building Lease for January. Type in 500. Press Enter.
2. Highlight the cells C23 through N23.
3. Use the Edit > Fill > Right command to copy the number in C23 to the selected cells.
4. Repeat these steps and enter the following expenses:
   Advertising/Promotion   =   100
   Utilities   =   50
   Other   =   50

Your Profit and Loss table should look like Figure 3-15 below.

Figure 3-15: Inputting Expenses in Profit & Loss Table

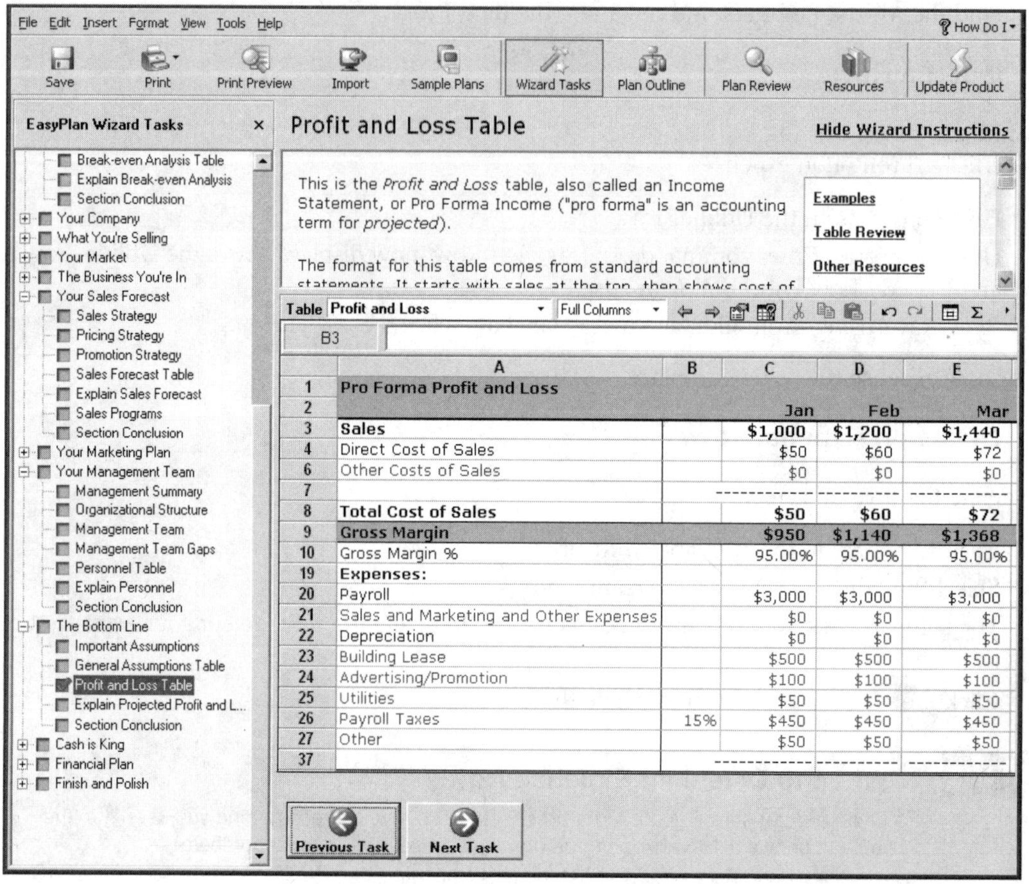

	A	B	C	D	E
1	**Pro Forma Profit and Loss**				
2			Jan	Feb	Mar
3	**Sales**		**$1,000**	**$1,200**	**$1,440**
4	Direct Cost of Sales		$50	$60	$72
6	Other Costs of Sales		$0	$0	$0
7			------------	------------	------------
8	**Total Cost of Sales**		**$50**	**$60**	**$72**
9	**Gross Margin**		**$950**	**$1,140**	**$1,368**
10	Gross Margin %		95.00%	95.00%	95.00%
19	**Expenses:**				
20	Payroll		$3,000	$3,000	$3,000
21	Sales and Marketing and Other Expenses		$0	$0	$0
22	Depreciation		$0	$0	$0
23	Building Lease		$500	$500	$500
24	Advertising/Promotion		$100	$100	$100
25	Utilities		$50	$50	$50
26	Payroll Taxes	15%	$450	$450	$450
27	Other		$50	$50	$50
37			------------	------------	------------

This view shows the expenses entered for the Profit and Loss. Note the Payroll Taxes row, as described in the previous Personnel table section tips.

Help For step-by-step procedures, click the dialog Help button or the Help menu.

Cash Flow

We now see how our numbers are affecting the Cash Flow. To start, take a look at our current Cash Flow chart.

1. Select the View > Charts menu.
2. From the pull-down menu, select Cash.

You should see a chart like the one in Figure 3-16. Notice how the projected cash balance shows a negative in all months, with July through September the worst.

FIGURE 3-16: INITIAL CASH FLOW CHART

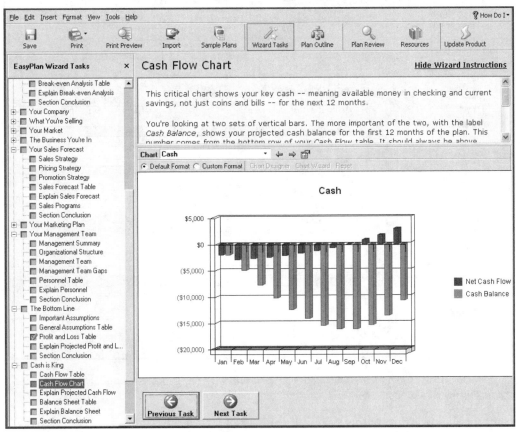

The chart shows a negative cash problem of more than $16,000.

A negative cash balance means we do not have the money to cover our expenses. In the real world that means bounced checks. This is our first chance to "test" our business idea. At this point, we need to take a closer look at the Cash Flow table and see where that negative balance is coming from.

To move from a chart to a table:

1. Locate the Cash chart in the EasyPlan Wizard Tasks (it is highlighted).
2. Click on the Cash Flow Table task above it.

You should see the Cash Flow table, shown in Figure 3-17.

FIGURE 3-17: INITIAL CASH FLOW TABLE

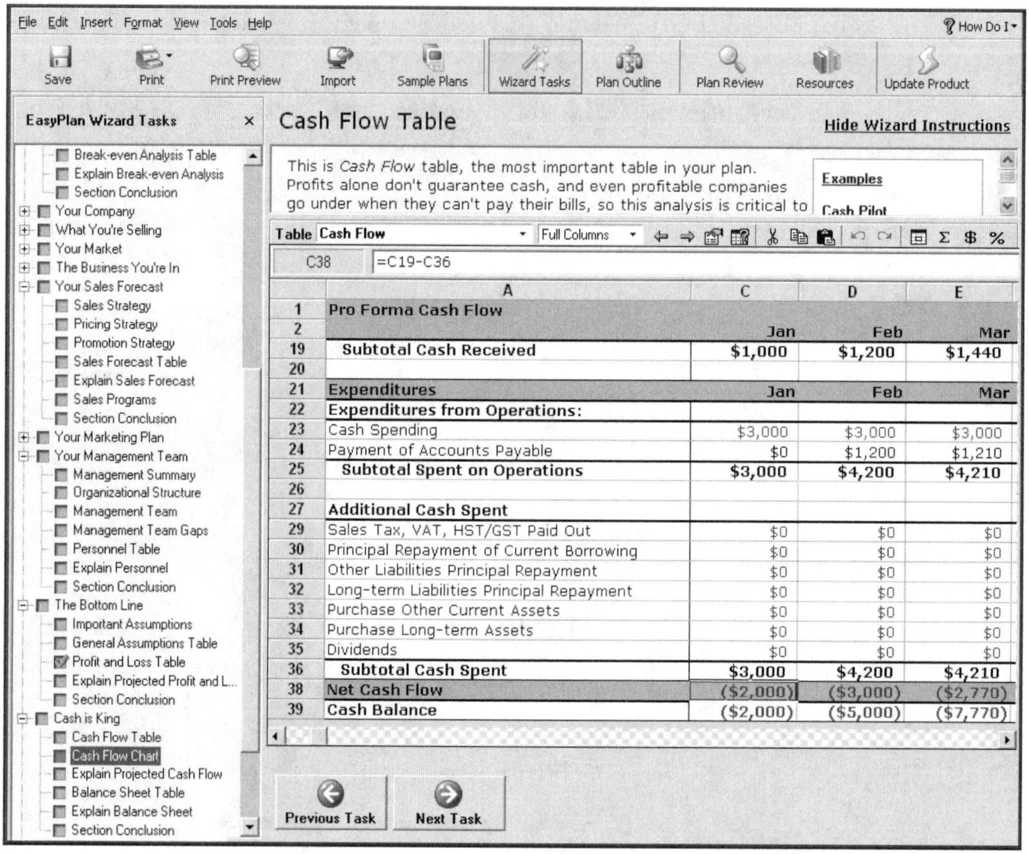

This is the initial Cash Flow table, after a first run through sales and expenses, before any adjustments.

What the cash flow shows at this point is the impact of your business assumptions. The table starts with profits, adds back depreciation, then accounts for balance sheet changes including expenses not paid (which show up as Accounts Payable instead of checks written) and sales amounts not received (which show up as Accounts Receivable instead of money in the bank account). For now, though, we continue the Tour.

Start-up Table

Take a look at the Start-up table. It is divided into two sections—Start-up Expenses and Assets, and Start-up Funding.

Start-up Expenses and Assets Needed

Start-up expenses are those expenses incurred before the business is running. Figure 3-18 shows the estimated start-up costs for this hypothetical business. To create this table as shown in the illustration, we use the default Start-up table, delete the expenses that are not going to be included, and add the assets shown (instructions are on the next page).

FIGURE 3-18: START-UP EXPENSES AND ASSETS

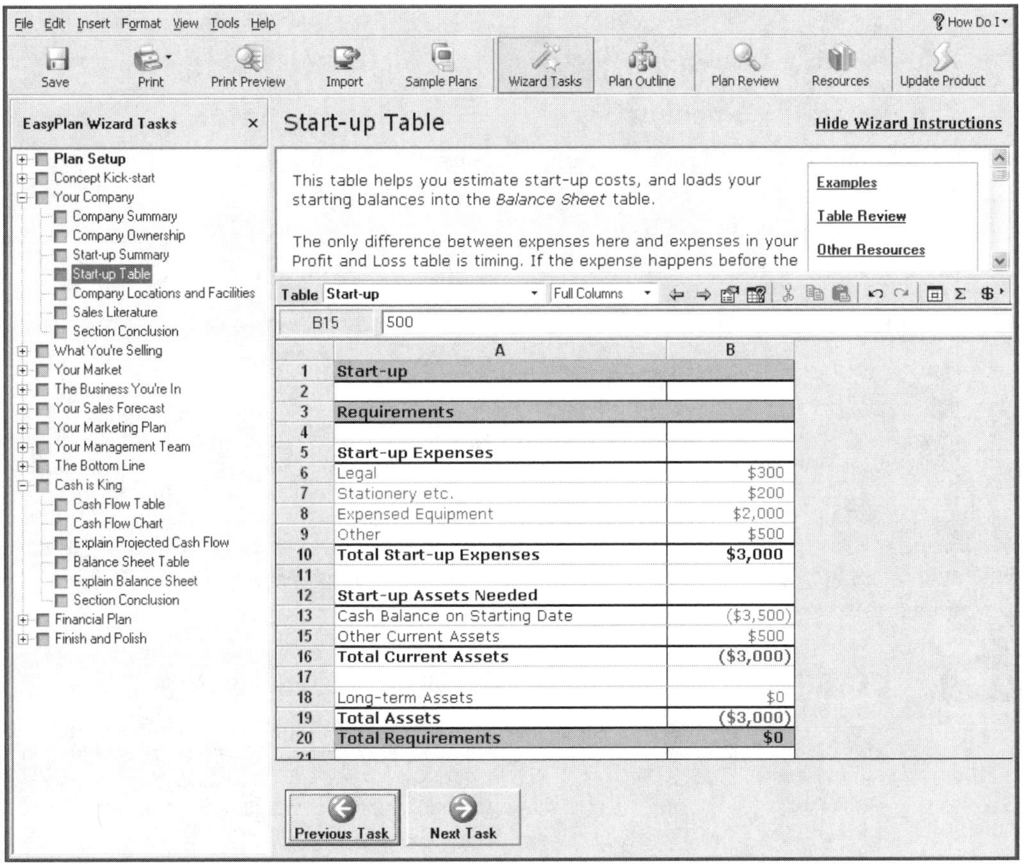

The start-up table shows the expenses and assets you need to start a business.

📌TIPS Starting Cash is Automatic

The Cash Balance on Starting Date is an important calculation: take the money you raise (investment or loans) in the bottom section of the table, and subtract the money you spend (expenses or assets) in the top section; the remainder is Cash Balance on Starting Date.

To create our Start-up table:

- Use the pull-down menu above the table display and choose "Start-up."

Now we delete unused expense rows and enter our start-up expenses and assets.

Delete Expense Rows

1. Click on the Brochures row.
2. Select the Edit > Delete > Rows command.
3. Answer Yes to confirm the delete.

Repeat the above steps to delete each of the following rows:

- Consultants
- Insurance
- Rent
- Research and Development

Input Start-up Expenses

1. Click on the cell in Column B for Legal expenses (B6).
2. Type 300. Press Enter.

Repeat for these additional expenses:

- Stationery etc.   =   200
- Expensed Equipment   =   2000
- Other   =   500

Input Start-up Assets Needed

- Other Current Assets   =   500

The first section of your Start-up table should now look like Figure 3-18 on the previous page.

How did we come up with these numbers? For the most part, they are educated guesses. For example, under Start-up Expenses, Expensed Equipment is intended to be a single computer. This would be a Start-up Asset except that the U.S. government allows businesses to deduct some computer expenses, and it is better as a tax deduction than as an asset.

TIPS

Expensed Equipment

In the U.S., the government lets you write off a certain amount of computer equipment (last time we looked it was $17,000, but tax laws change, so check with your accountant) as a deductible expense, instead of investment in assets. That is why we suggest expensed equipment as a start-up category; many companies need computer equipment when they are getting started.

Business Plan Pro generates the number for Cash Balance on Starting Date (shown in Figures 3-18 and 3-20) automatically by taking the estimated funding and subtracting expenses and purchased assets. So in this Guided Tour, we type in the Start-up Funding assumptions, as shown in Figure 3-19, which sets the cash balance.

FIGURE 3-19: START-UP FUNDING

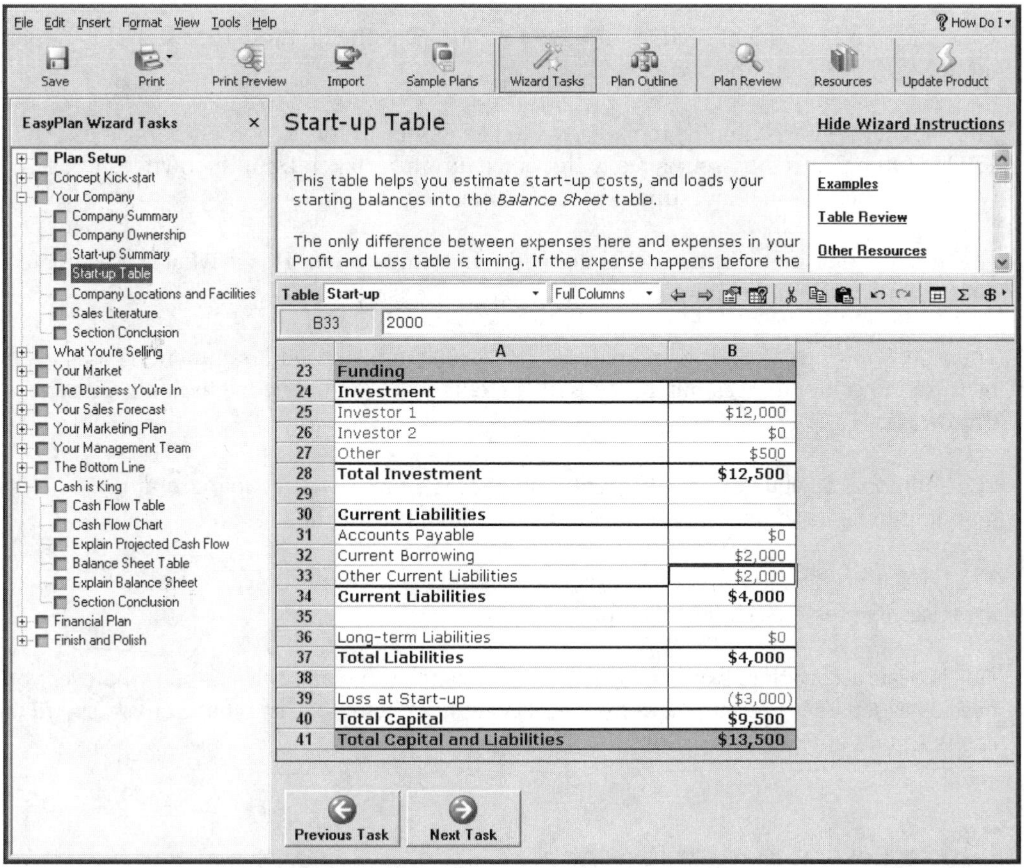

File Edit Insert Format View Tools Help   How Do I ▾

Save   Print   Print Preview   Import   Sample Plans   Wizard Tasks   Plan Outline   Plan Review   Resources   Update Product

EasyPlan Wizard Tasks   ✕   **Start-up Table**   **Hide Wizard Instructions**

- ☐ Plan Setup
- ☐ Concept Kick-start
- ☐ Your Company
  - ☐ Company Summary
  - ☐ Company Ownership
  - ☐ Start-up Summary
  - ☐ Start-up Table
  - ☐ Company Locations and Facilities
  - ☐ Sales Literature
  - ☐ Section Conclusion
- ☐ What You're Selling
- ☐ Your Market
- ☐ The Business You're In
- ☐ Your Sales Forecast
- ☐ Your Marketing Plan
- ☐ Your Management Team
- ☐ The Bottom Line
- ☐ Cash is King
  - ☐ Cash Flow Table
  - ☐ Cash Flow Chart
  - ☐ Explain Projected Cash Flow
  - ☐ Balance Sheet Table
  - ☐ Explain Balance Sheet
  - ☐ Section Conclusion
- ☐ Financial Plan
- ☐ Finish and Polish

This table helps you estimate start-up costs, and loads your
starting balances into the *Balance Sheet* table.

The only difference between expenses here and expenses in your
Profit and Loss table is timing. If the expense happens before the

Examples

Table Review

Other Resources

Table Start-up   ▾   Full Columns   ▾

B33   2000

	A	B
23	**Funding**	
24	**Investment**	
25	Investor 1	$12,000
26	Investor 2	$0
27	Other	$500
28	**Total Investment**	**$12,500**
29		
30	**Current Liabilities**	
31	Accounts Payable	$0
32	Current Borrowing	$2,000
33	Other Current Liabilities	$2,000
34	**Current Liabilities**	**$4,000**
35		
36	Long-term Liabilities	$0
37	**Total Liabilities**	**$4,000**
38		
39	Loss at Start-up	($3,000)
40	**Total Capital**	**$9,500**
41	**Total Capital and Liabilities**	**$13,500**

Previous Task   Next Task

*This figure shows the start-up funding portion of the Start-up table. Note that the sum of
capital and liabilities is $13,500, so it matches the sum of start-up assets. Also, the Loss at
Start-up is exactly $3,000, expressed as a negative number. The Start-up Expenses are exactly
$3,000 expressed as a positive number.*

To match this table in your own Guided Tour plan:

1. Scroll downward to the section on Funding.
2. Type in the amounts shown in the following list:
   - Investor 1   =   12000
   - Other   =   500
   - Current Borrowing   =   2000
   - Other Current Liabilities   =   2000

Unlike our "educated guess" approach for Start-up expenses, these numbers are not random:

1. We set up our Investment section into two rows because the first row (Investor 1) is actual money ($12,000) from the owner.

2. The $500 Other investment is money invested as Assets. In this hypothetical business, the $500 in Other Current Assets is really the office furniture, taken from the owner's house, which now becomes an investment in the business.

    The $12,500 in Total Investment, therefore, is owner investment. This is what our estimated guesses indicate is the required amount to start this business.

3. The $2,000 in Current Borrowing matches the $2,000 in Expensed Equipment. That is because the computer was purchased with a credit card. Purchases on credit are Current Borrowing.

4. The additional $2,000 in Other Current Liabilities is an interest-free loan from our grandmother. Grandmothers are like that. Entrepreneuring is like that too.

5. The Loss at Start-up (expressed as a negative number) is always exactly equal to Start-up Expenses (expressed as a positive number).

    This is basic accounting. Expenses are deductible, so without any sales as yet, whatever you have as expenses is the same as a loss. Assets are not deductible, so whatever you spend on assets should not show up as loss.

TIPS

Loss at Start-up is Normal

Almost all start-up companies have some expenses before they get revenues, which means they have a loss at start-up. It is normal.

Your Start-up table should now look like Figure 3-20.

FIGURE 3-20: COMPLETED START-UP TABLE

| Table | Start-up | ▾ | Full Columns | ▾ | ⇐ ⇒ 🗗 🖳 | ✂ |

| B41 | =startup_total_capital+startup_total_liabilities |

	A	B
5	**Start-up Expenses**	
6	Legal	$300
7	Stationery etc.	$200
8	Expensed Equipment	$2,000
9	Other	$500
10	**Total Start-up Expenses**	**$3,000**
12	**Start-up Assets Needed**	
13	Cash Balance on Starting Date	$13,000
15	Other Current Assets	$500
16	**Total Current Assets**	**$13,500**
18	Long-term Assets	$0
19	**Total Assets**	**$13,500**
20	**Total Requirements**	**$16,500**
22	**Funding**	
24	**Investment**	
25	Investor 1	$12,000
26	Investor 2	$0
27	Other	$500
28	**Total Investment**	**$12,500**
30	**Current Liabilities**	
31	Accounts Payable	$0
32	Current Borrowing	$2,000
33	Other Current Liabilities	$2,000
34	**Current Liabilities**	**$4,000**
36	Long-term Liabilities	$0
37	**Total Liabilities**	**$4,000**
39	Loss at Start-up	($3,000)
40	**Total Capital**	**$9,500**
41	**Total Capital and Liabilities**	**$13,500**

The completed Start-up table shows estimated expenses and assets as well as funding needed to start the business.

Review Cash Flow after Changes

With the Start-up table now complete, use the View > Charts menu to return to the Cash Flow chart. Figure 3-21 shows improved cash flow because the start-up financing provides the money necessary to support the deficit spending for the first few months. Unfortunately, the checkbook balance is now showing negative from June through November. We still need to correct a negative cash balance for these months.

FIGURE 3-21: CASH FLOW AFTER START-UP REVISIONS

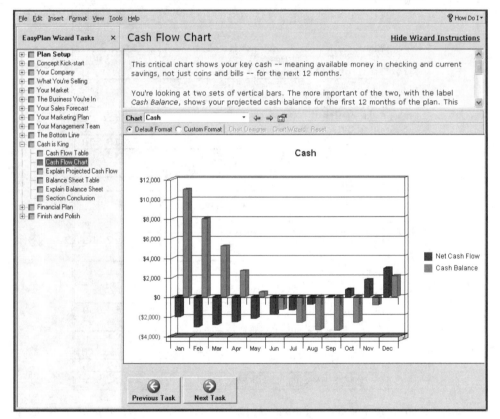

Cash flow has improved, but is still showing a negative cash balance.

You should now begin to see the power of working with linked tables. A change in one table is reflected in another. And the charts provide an overview of the results of your changes.

TIPS

How Much Cash do I Need?

Notice the answer for this question: it is a process, not a simple calculation. We projected sales, cost of sales, personnel, other expenses, and start-up expenses. Then we looked at cash flow and it looked bad. So after that, we went back to the start-up table and added more investment.

Balance Sheet

Use the View > Tables menu and choose the Balance Sheet table. This table (also known as the Pro Forma Balance Sheet), shows the business' capital position: assets, liabilities, and capital. Figure 3-22 shows the Balance Sheet as it now stands.

FIGURE 3-22: BALANCE SHEET TABLE

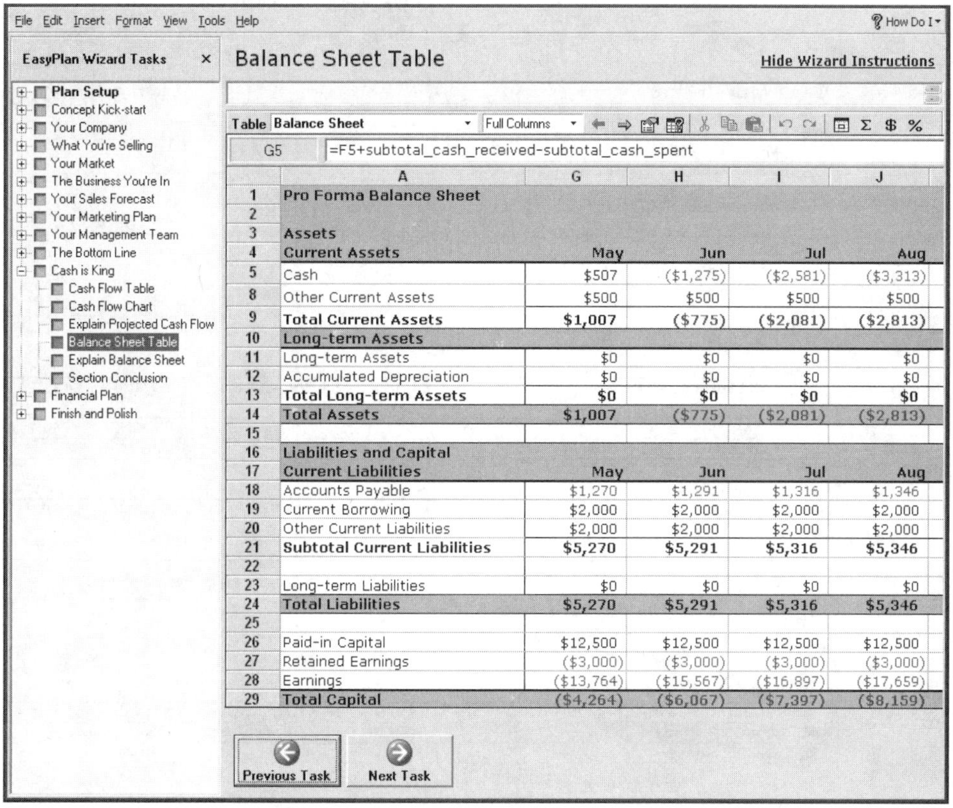

	A	G	H	I	J
1	Pro Forma Balance Sheet				
2					
3	Assets				
4	Current Assets	May	Jun	Jul	Aug
5	Cash	$507	($1,275)	($2,581)	($3,313)
8	Other Current Assets	$500	$500	$500	$500
9	Total Current Assets	$1,007	($775)	($2,081)	($2,813)
10	Long-term Assets				
11	Long-term Assets	$0	$0	$0	$0
12	Accumulated Depreciation	$0	$0	$0	$0
13	Total Long-term Assets	$0	$0	$0	$0
14	Total Assets	$1,007	($775)	($2,081)	($2,813)
15					
16	Liabilities and Capital				
17	Current Liabilities	May	Jun	Jul	Aug
18	Accounts Payable	$1,270	$1,291	$1,316	$1,346
19	Current Borrowing	$2,000	$2,000	$2,000	$2,000
20	Other Current Liabilities	$2,000	$2,000	$2,000	$2,000
21	Subtotal Current Liabilities	$5,270	$5,291	$5,316	$5,346
22					
23	Long-term Liabilities	$0	$0	$0	$0
24	Total Liabilities	$5,270	$5,291	$5,316	$5,346
25					
26	Paid-in Capital	$12,500	$12,500	$12,500	$12,500
27	Retained Earnings	($3,000)	($3,000)	($3,000)	($3,000)
28	Earnings	($13,764)	($15,567)	($16,897)	($17,659)
29	Total Capital	($4,264)	($6,067)	($7,397)	($8,159)

With the adjustments made in the Cash Flow table, the Balance Sheet recalculates automatically to show the results.

Scroll across the Cash row and see the negative cash balance starting in June. The next section shows different loan options that a business can pursue to help them deal with a temporary cash flow problem.

TIPS

Hide Row(s) and Column(s) in a table

It can be helpful to temporarily "hide" a row or column in order to see multiple areas in a table. This is not the same as deleting a row or column. A hidden column still exists.

To hide a row or column highlight a cell from the row or column to hide. Choose Format > Hide Row or Hide Column. To reverse this function, use Format > Show Row or Show Column.

More Cash Flow Revisions

Use the pull-down menu to return to the Cash Flow table. Figure 3-23 shows how we clear up the cash balance problem with loans, and then how we later pay back those loans, and the initial start-up loan from our grandmother. (**NOTE**: To focus attention to key areas in this table, several rows and columns have been "hidden".)

FIGURE 3-23: CASH FLOW REVISIONS

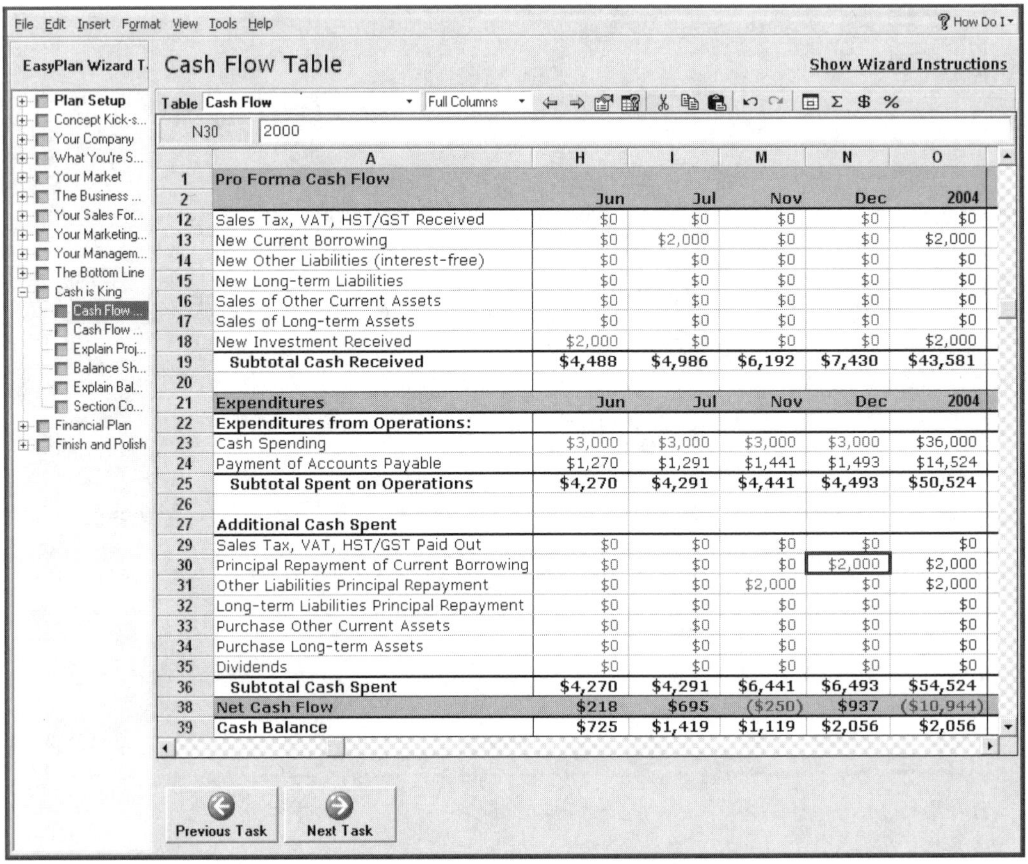

	A	H	I	M	N	O
1	**Pro Forma Cash Flow**					
2		Jun	Jul	Nov	Dec	2004
12	Sales Tax, VAT, HST/GST Received	$0	$0	$0	$0	$0
13	New Current Borrowing	$0	$2,000	$0	$0	$2,000
14	New Other Liabilities (interest-free)	$0	$0	$0	$0	$0
15	New Long-term Liabilities	$0	$0	$0	$0	$0
16	Sales of Other Current Assets	$0	$0	$0	$0	$0
17	Sales of Long-term Assets	$0	$0	$0	$0	$0
18	New Investment Received	$2,000	$0	$0	$0	$2,000
19	**Subtotal Cash Received**	**$4,488**	**$4,986**	**$6,192**	**$7,430**	**$43,581**
20						
21	**Expenditures**	Jun	Jul	Nov	Dec	2004
22	**Expenditures from Operations:**					
23	Cash Spending	$3,000	$3,000	$3,000	$3,000	$36,000
24	Payment of Accounts Payable	$1,270	$1,291	$1,441	$1,493	$14,524
25	**Subtotal Spent on Operations**	**$4,270**	**$4,291**	**$4,441**	**$4,493**	**$50,524**
26						
27	**Additional Cash Spent**					
29	Sales Tax, VAT, HST/GST Paid Out	$0	$0	$0	$0	$0
30	Principal Repayment of Current Borrowing	$0	$0	$0	$2,000	$2,000
31	Other Liabilities Principal Repayment	$0	$0	$2,000	$0	$2,000
32	Long-term Liabilities Principal Repayment	$0	$0	$0	$0	$0
33	Purchase Other Current Assets	$0	$0	$0	$0	$0
34	Purchase Long-term Assets	$0	$0	$0	$0	$0
35	Dividends	$0	$0	$0	$0	$0
36	**Subtotal Cash Spent**	**$4,270**	**$4,291**	**$6,441**	**$6,493**	**$54,524**
38	**Net Cash Flow**	**$218**	**$695**	**($250)**	**$937**	**($10,944)**
39	**Cash Balance**	**$725**	**$1,419**	**$1,119**	**$2,056**	**$2,056**

We used the Format > Row > Hide and > Column > Hide commands to show this view.

With the following changes, the cash balance stays (just barely) above zero. No more bounced checks. Now we have a plan. The Cash Flow adjustments show borrowing money in June and July and paying it back in November and December:

1. We are going to add Capital (New Investment Received row) in the amount of $2,000 for the month of June. This comes from our savings. We are investing in ourselves.

2. We also loan the company another $2,000 (New Current Borrowing row) in July. This is a loan, not an investment. We expect to pay it back. It is important to track this transaction as a loan for tax reasons and proper accounting.

Input New Investment for June

1. Locate New Investment Received row.

2. Click on the cell for June column (H18).

3. Type 2000 into the cell.

Input Loan for July

1. Locate the New Current Borrowing row.

2. Click on the cell for July (I13).

3. Type 2000 into the cell.

We plan to repay all the loans before the end of the year:

Input Loan Payment for November

1. Locate the Other Liabilities Principal Repayment row; we are paying Grandma back.

2. Click on the cell for November (M31).

3. Type 2000 into the cell.

Input Loan Payment for December

1. Locate the Principal Repayment of Current Borrowing row. This is repaying credit card debt. Interest is high and it is a good idea to pay this off as soon as possible.

2. Click on the cell for December (N30).

3. Type 2000 into the cell.

Now that these adjustments are made, let us see what the Cash Flow chart shows. Use the View > Charts > Cash command. Your chart should look like Figure 3-24.

FIGURE 3-24: ADJUSTED CASH FLOW CHART

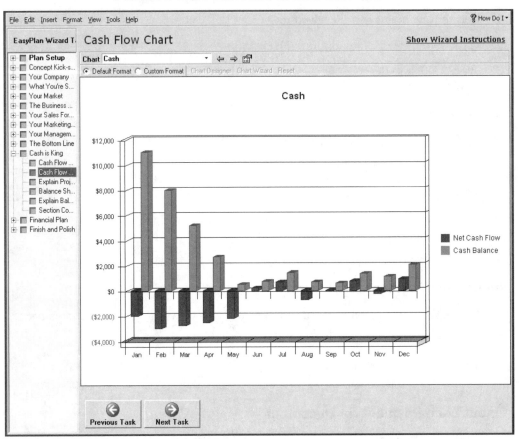

Our corrected cash flow now shows a positive cash balance throughout the year. We are no longer bouncing checks!

TIPS

Use the Charts

As we go through this guided Tour, we keep referring to the cash chart for a quick view of cash flow. That is one of the powerful advantages of the business charts; it gives us a quick view, at a single glance.

The Rest of the Tables

With your main table input completed, you can take a moment to visit the other tables.

1. Break-even Analysis shows what sales a company needs to equal its expenses and "break even" in a given month.

2. Market Analysis is where a company estimates its potential customer base and what percentage of growth they hope to achieve for their plan.

   Both of the above tables are still empty, but you can fill those in later. You have instructions for those in Chapter 6: Your Plan Tables.

3. Milestones is where you list the key tasks to accomplish in order to achieve your goals. Including a date of completion and estimated budget for each task helps you measure the success of your goals. The Milestones table is critical to business planning, but not hard to understand.

4. The Balance Sheet, your estimated assets and liabilities, is already done. So are the Business Ratios. You can read about those in detail in the Hurdle book and in Chapter 6 of this manual.

 Chapter 6 Covers All the Tables

For the complete details on all the tables included with Business Plan Pro, turn to Chapter 6: Your Plan Tables. For Advanced help on the spreadsheet programming facilities included, turn to Chapter 10: Advanced Tables.

Charts are Automatic

All of the charts in Business Plan Pro are automatically linked to tables. As you saw throughout our Tour, when you fill in your tables, your charts start to show data.

 Chapter 7 Covers All the Charts

For the complete details on key charts included with Business Plan Pro, turn to Chapter 7: Your Plan Charts.

Printing is Automatic

Business Plan Pro prints out a plan with an automatic format.

- It merges the topics, tables, and charts into a professional-looking format. This includes automatic indenting of paragraphs and formatting of topic titles. Bullet points and numbered lists can be added into your text through the formatting toolbar.
- It prints the annual tables with the topics and the monthly tables as Appendices.
- It creates a Table of Contents.
- It has a standard cover sheet that you can customize with a company logo and standard text formatting.
- An optional Legal page can be included. Basic text on confidentiality is provided with the template.
- A Print Preview option lets you see the plan document before you print.

For complete details on your Print options, please see Chapter 8: Print and Publish, in this manual.

TIPS

Chapter 8 Covers Printing Your Plan

For the complete details on all of the print options included with Business Plan Pro, turn to Chapter 8: Print and Publish.

Congratulations!

You have completed the Guided Tour. We hope you found the Tour helpful in understanding the process of creating a business plan.

The other chapters in this manual are written to give you background on working in Business Plan Pro and getting the most from its features. Be sure to see detailed instructions in your main Help file.

Starting a Plan

CHAPTER 4: STARTING A PLAN

This chapter describes the different options available for getting started on your business plan. These options include:

1. *EasyPlan Wizard®*

2. *Sample Plan Browser™*

EasyPlan Wizard

Business Plan Pro® was designed to develop any business plan from scratch, customizing the outline and structure for the type of business, and guiding you through the process. That is why we designed the EasyPlan Wizard. Let the EasyPlan Wizard guide you through the questions, set up your plan, and take you through the plan from beginning to end.

EasyPlan Wizard Introduction

When you start a new plan, the EasyPlan Wizard Plan Setup screen displays, as shown in Figure 4-1.

FIGURE 4-1: EASYPLAN WIZARD INTRODUCTION

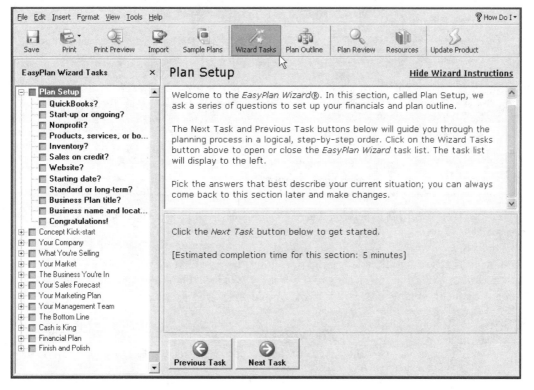

The Plan Setup section introduces you to the EasyPlan Wizard and how to get started.

- Click the **Previous Task** **Next Task** buttons to move through the Wizard screens.

As you continue with the EasyPlan Wizard, the Plan Setup section asks you a series of questions. Each question on the form includes details about how to answer it.

FIGURE 4-2: EASYPLAN WIZARD PLAN SETUP QUESTIONS

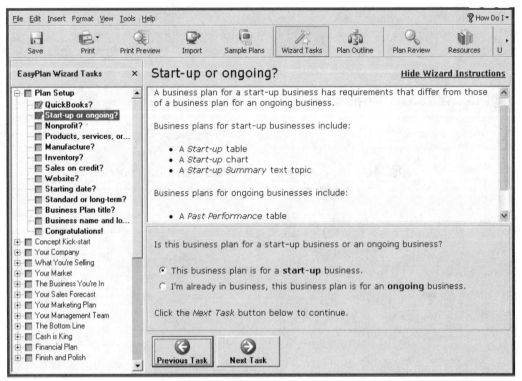

The EasyPlan Wizard Plan Setup section asks questions about your business to help set up your plan.

Based on your answers to the Plan Setup questions, the EasyPlan Wizard matches the Plan Outline to your type of business. The final question asks for a plan title. This can be your company name, the name of the project, etc. Figure 4-3 shows an example.

 TIPS

If you are not sure how to answer an EasyPlan Wizard question...

Each question provides a "default" answer. In many cases, the EasyPlan Wizard describes the default answer in its description.

If you are not sure how to answer a question, simply accept the default for now. You can always come back later and change it.

Nonprofit Plans

?

To Learn more about...	Search the Help Index for...
Nonprofit plans	nonprofit, sample plans

FIGURE 4-3: EASYPLAN WIZARD BUSINESS PLAN TITLE

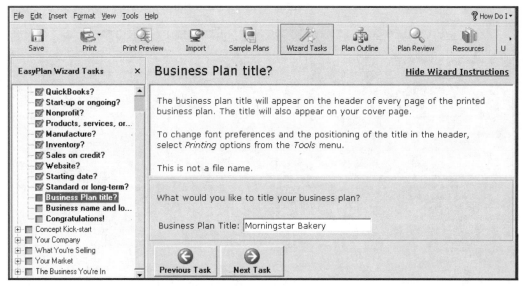

The plan title automatically prints at the top of every page of your business plan.

Once all questions are answered, the Congratulations screen displays, as shown in Figure 4-4.

FIGURE 4-4: EASYPLAN WIZARD CONGRATULATIONS SCREEN

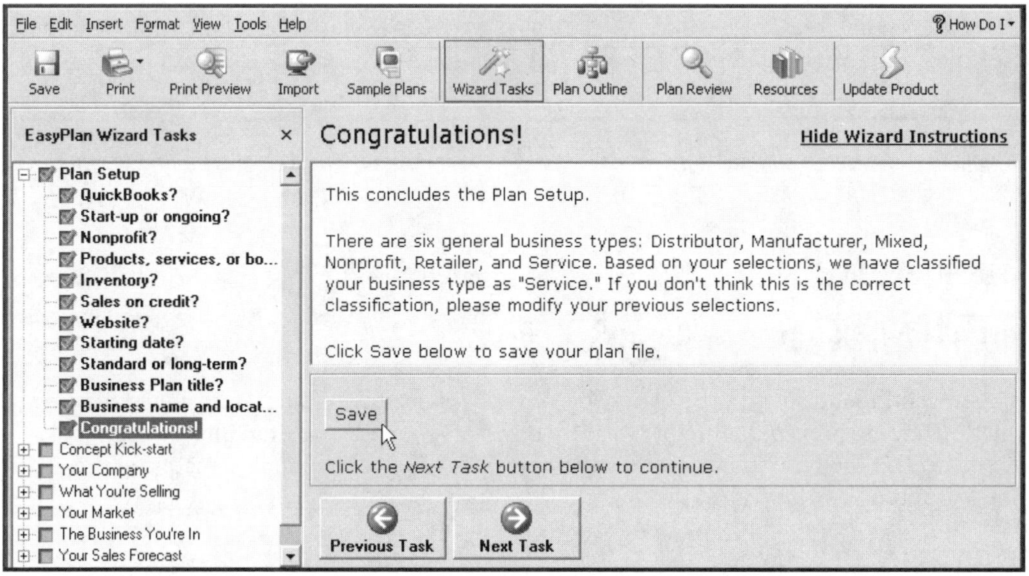

Click the Save button. The "default" filename is the plan title you entered earlier.

Once the Plan Setup section questions have been completed and the file has been saved, the next EasyPlan Wizard task is the Concept Kick-start, shown in Figure 4-5.

FIGURE 4-5: EASYPLAN WIZARD - CONCEPT KICK-START

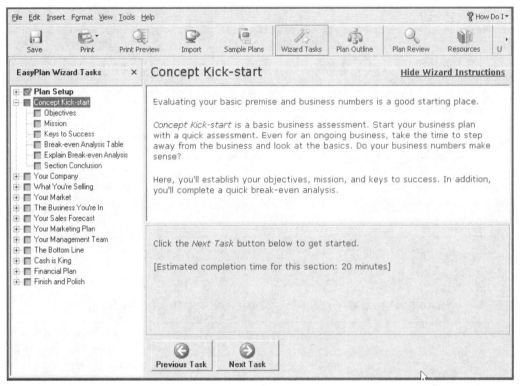

Now that the key assumptions have been set from the initial questions, you are ready to start working on your plan.

Help   For step-by-step procedures, click the dialog Help buttons or the Help menu.

Start a New Plan from a Sample Plan

Business Plan Pro includes a wide variety of sample business plans, and more are added regularly. They are provided primarily to give you ideas, show you what a finished plan looks like, and explain the process by example. We have created a tool to simplify accessing these plans for review and/or use. It is called the Sample Plan Browser.

Sample Plan Browser™

The Sample Plan Browser can be accessed by pressing the [Sample Plans] button in the toolbar at the top of your screen. The Browser opens in a separate window from the program. The primary benefit of the Sample Plan Browser is to make it easy to search our extensive sample plan library for plans that match your business needs. Figure 4-6 shows the Sample Plan Browser screen.

FIGURE 4-6: SAMPLE PLAN BROWSER

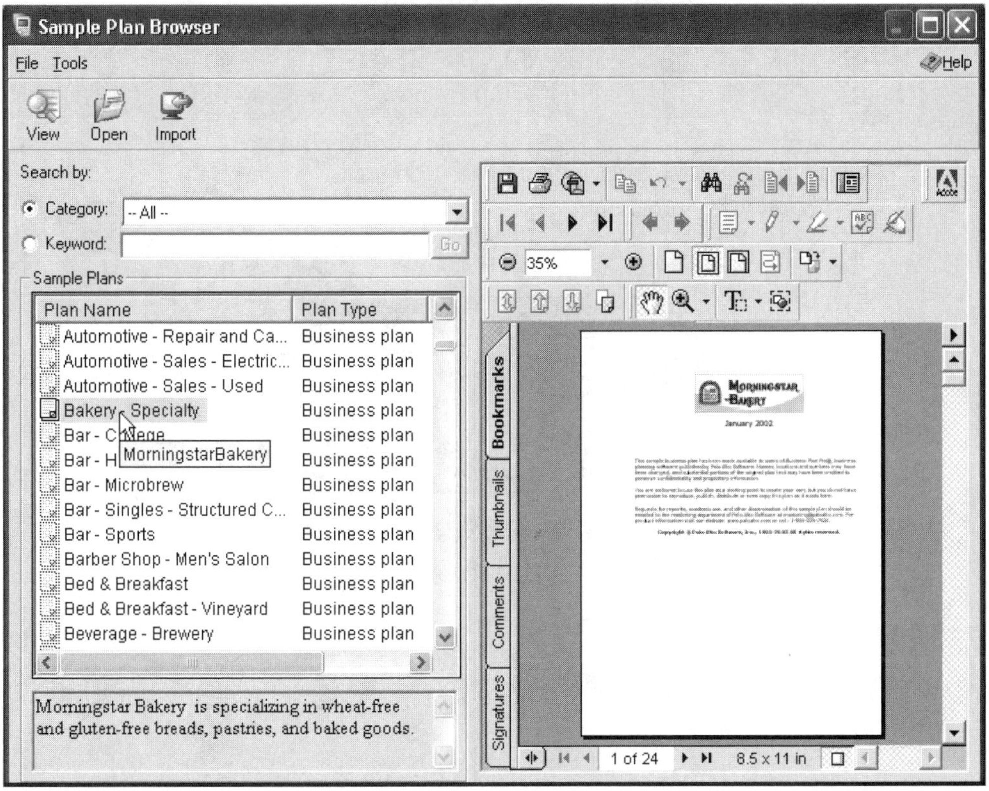

The Browser is divided into the Sample Plan List and the PDF Viewing screen.

The Sample Plan Browser lets you:

1. Sort sample plans by category.
2. Search for sample plans by keywords.
3. Read summaries of sample plans for a quick overview.
4. Print a sample plan to discuss and review with others.
5. Copy and paste text from the Browser screen into a new plan document.
6. Import components of a sample plan into an open plan file.
7. Open the complete sample plan as a starting point for your plan.

Sample Plan Location

The sample plans listed in the Sample Plan Browser are delivered over the Internet. This allows us to provide the most up-to-date content available, continually add to the sample plan library, and reduce the amount of hard-drive space required by the software.

If you do not have an Internet connection, please refer to the section titled "Install Sample Plans from CD-ROM."

Refresh the Sample Plan List

We are continually adding and updating our sample plans. To download the most current list from our website:

- From within the Browser, use the Tools > Refresh List command.
- Figure 4-7 shows this menu option.

FIGURE 4-7: REFRESH SAMPLE PLAN LIST

With an Internet connection, you can download the latest sample plan list.

View a Sample Plan

To view a sample plan, highlight the name in the plan list and click the View button in the Browser toolbar.

Open a Sample Plan

To open a working copy of a sample plan in Business Plan Pro, click the Open button in the Browser toolbar.

Import from a Sample Plan

The Import button lets you import selected topics/tables/charts into a business plan, instead of opening the entire sample plan.

Use Save-As to Create a New Plan

If you decide to open a sample plan as a starting point for your own plan, you need to save it under a new filename. The File > Save As dialog box lets you specify a new filename and choose a directory in which to save it.

FIGURE 4-8: SAVE AS DIALOG BOX

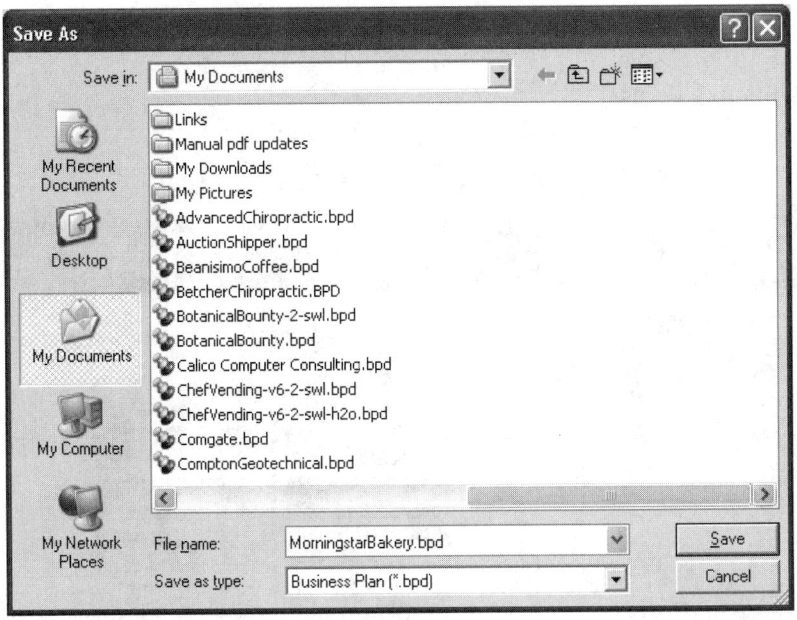

Avoid spaces and periods as part of the filename. An extension is automatically added (.bpd). We do not recommend saving to floppy disks because of file size and the potential for data loss.

Update Plan Setup in the EasyPlan Wizard

If you start with a sample plan, you need to go through the Plan Setup section in the EasyPlan Wizard to customize the plan for your particular business (start-up vs. ongoing, pay on credit, etc.), and in particular, to change the Plan Title (described earlier) which prints at the top of every page of your plan.

Install Sample Plans from CD-ROM

If you do not have an Internet connection (the recommended access to sample plans), you can install a sample plan library onto your hard drive from your installation CD-ROM (the CD library does not contain the most current list of sample plans).

- Insert the installation CD into your computer.
- The DemoShield displays its opening screen.
- Click **Contact Us**.
- Click **Support Tools**
- Click **Sample Plans**.
- Follow the screen prompts (this may take several minutes).

FIGURE 4-9: DEMOSHIELD OPENING MENU

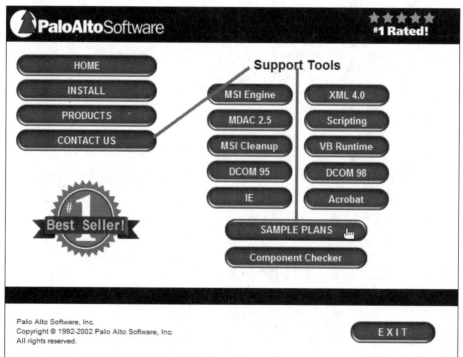

If you do not have an Internet connection, you can install a Sample Plan library onto your hard drive from your program CD-ROM.

Once the installation is finished, the Sample Plan Browser searchs for sample plans from your computer hard drive.

To access the most up-to-date library of sample plans, an Internet connection is required (see previous section on "Sample Plan Location").

Caution on Using Sample Plans

With this version of Business Plan Pro, we offer over 400 hundred different sample plans as part of the product. Most people like sample plans. We included two sample plans in 1995, 10 in 1997, 20 in 1998, and 150 in 2000. We try to offer a good mix of common types of businesses. However, there are potential benefits and cautions about sample plans:

Benefits:

- If a sample plan serves as an example, that is good. You do not need an exact match to see how a sample plan covered a market analysis or product/service list.
- If you use a sample plan as a starting point or head start, that can be good too, but develop your own plan, not somebody else's.
- Samples are also good for generating ideas. Look how somebody else segmented their market, and it may help you segment your own.

Cautions:

- Business Plan Pro is designed to create your business plan, not just copy an existing plan. You do not need a sample plan to start with.
- If you do not find a sample plan exactly like your business, do not worry. Just follow the EasyPlan Wizard, answer the questions, and you have a business plan. That is what Business Plan Pro is designed for.
- Every business is unique. No sample plan really works for copying without modification. Do not expect that to happen.
- Your mission, your objectives, your keys to success, your strategy, your management team, your financials, and your company description should be different from any sample. Your plan should represent YOU, YOUR idea, YOUR company, in YOUR city.

Make it Your Own

If you do decide to start with a sample plan, make sure you go over every word, and every number. Make it truly your own plan. That makes it a good compromise between the value of starting points and examples, and the importance of ending up with your own plan.

This page intentionally blank.

Your Plan Text

CHAPTER 5: YOUR PLAN TEXT

About Business Writing

Business writing should be clear, concise, and easy to read. Here are some suggestions when writing your plan:

1. Proofread and edit your work. Better still, have somebody else, who did not write it, read it. Check your spelling. Even if you do not care about spelling, others do. The built-in spell checker does not catch errors such as "there" instead of "their."
2. Be concise. Make your point and go on.
3. Do not use phrases such as "I feel," "I think," and "in my opinion." They weaken your effectiveness.
4. Avoid using unnecessary words, such as "really" and "very." They do not add value.
5. Avoid unexplained lists. Numbered lists are good when used with explanations.
6. Use bullet points within text, not in headlines or captions.

Keep it Simple

A business plan is about results. Use formatting that enhances its readability and keep it simple.

Standard Text Format

When people talk about a "professional" or "appropriate" format for a business plan, they mean a format that makes the content easy to read and follow. There is no true standard format for a business plan. You can use any text size, font, page size, and page layout that works.

Automatic Merge of Tables and Charts with Topics

Unlike Microsoft Word®, Business Plan Pro® automatically merges tables and charts with the topic outline and creates an excellent layout that is easy to read and thoroughly professional. It also prints cover pages, legal pages, table of contents, and table appendices.

Automatic Text Formatting

Business Plan Pro is designed to do the text formatting for you. However, in order to do all the page formatting automatically, Business Plan Pro is not as fully flexible and programmable as the more powerful word processing packages. If you work with it, not against it, you get better results.

- Avoid tabs for indenting (the program automatically indents paragraphs .5" from their topic title).

- Avoid carriage returns at the end of each line. This causes uneven flow of text when printing.

- Use the built-in text formatting toolbar when:

  - Creating bullet point lists and numbered lists wherever the content fits.

  - Increasing or decreasing the indent of text when you want to add emphasis.

TIPS

Automatic Text Formatting

Business Plan Pro is designed to do the formatting for you. Concentrate on content, do not try to arrange formatting beyond what is readily available in the program. Use the HTML formatting built in for bullet points, lists, and tables. Work with it, not against it, to get better results.

Sample Text Formatting Page

Figure 5-1 shows an example of a simple text page format (no table or chart) prepared using the automatic formatting built into Business Plan Pro.

FIGURE 5-1: BUSINESS PLAN PRO STANDARD TEXT FORMAT

AMT, Inc.

1.2 Mission

AMT is built on the assumption that the management of information technology for business is like legal advice, accounting, graphic arts, and other bodies of knowledge, in that it is not inherently a do-it-yourself prospect. Smart business people who aren't computer hobbyists need to find quality vendors of reliable hardware, software, service, and support. They need to use these quality vendors as they use their other professional service suppliers, as trusted allies.

AMT is such a vendor. It serves its clients as a trusted ally, providing them with the loyalty of a business partner and the economics of an outside vendor. We make sure that our clients have what they need to run their businesses as well as possible, with maximum efficiency and reliability. Many of our information applications are mission critical, so we give our clients the assurance that we will be there when they need us.

1.3 Keys to Success

1. Differentiate from box-pushing, price-oriented businesses by offering and delivering service and support -- and charging for it.
2. Increase gross margin to more than 25%.
3. Increase our non-hardware sales to 20% of the total sales by the third year.

2.0 Company Summary

AMT is a computer reseller based in the Uptown area. It was founded as a consulting-oriented VAR, became a reseller to fill the market need for personal computers, and is emphasizing service and support to differentiate itself from more price oriented national chains.

2.1 Company Ownership

AMT is a privately-held C corporation owned in majority by its founder and president, Ralph Jones. There are six part owners, including four investors and two past employees. The largest of these (in percent of ownership) are Frank Dudley, our attorney, and Paul Karots, our public relations consultant. Neither owns more than 15%, but both are active participants in management decisions.

Page 2

The standard text page has topics set apart and points in bullet and/or numbered lists. Writing is simple and clear, and the format makes it easy to access.

Sample Format - Including Tables and Charts with Topics

Business Plan Pro automatically puts tables and charts together on the page, merged into the topics with the text that refers to them. Figure 5-2 shows an example.

FIGURE 5-2: BUSINESS PLAN PRO PAGE WITH TABLE & CHART

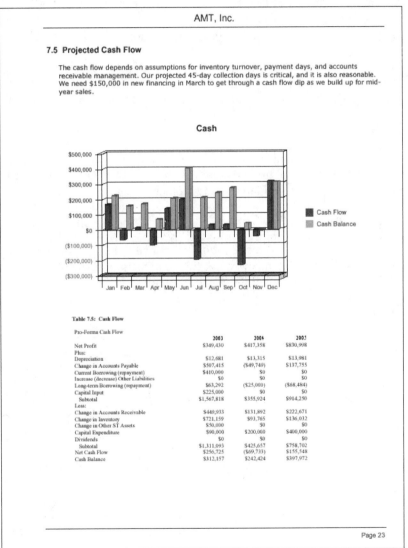

The ideal format merges table highlights and business charts on the same page with the text that refers to them.

Numbers and Charts are Essential

The numbers in a business plan are essential. Any normal plan shows sales forecast, cash flow, and profit and loss. Most plans include the full range of financial tables covering the complete business, from break-even to market analysis to milestones.

Your format should make these numbers easy to access and read, because they are an essential part of the plan. Generally a plan puts the main numbers into the text where the reader can find them easily as reference points. Putting the details into an appendix is acceptable.

Business graphics are an excellent way to display numbers. Most business plans include charts of the main financial projections, because charts are easier to read and interpret. Numbers are often attached in detail in appendices, while main concepts are included as business charts.

Insert Tables and Charts

The Insert icon from the Plan Outline toolbar lets you insert text topics, and attach tables and charts to topics as part of your final printed plan. See the Plan Outline section later in this chapter for more information on the Plan Outline toolbar.

Charts vs. Tables Linked to Text

Consider including only the charts in the text, and leaving all the numbers for the appendices. This is not the Business Plan Pro standard, but it can be a pleasant presentation. Use the Plan Outline to unlink tables from text topics, leaving only charts.

But before text formatting can begin, you must enter your text. And that is done from the Topic view screen.

Working in Topics

The Topic view is where you write text for each topic in the outline. Figure 5-3 shows an example of the Topic view.

FIGURE 5-3: TOPIC VIEW

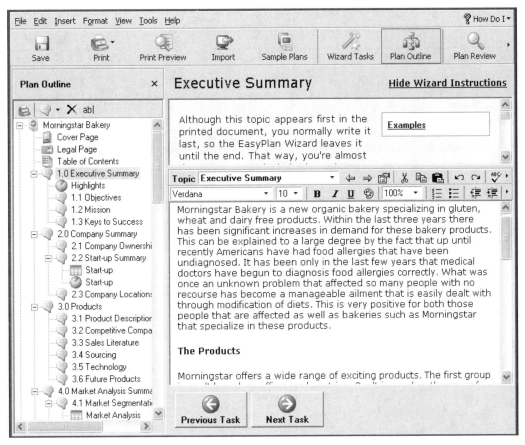

The Topic view provides a formatting toolbar for common text attributes, such as bold, underline, and italic, etc.

Formatting Toolbar

The formatting toolbar displays near the top of the text screen. It provides icons for commonly-used text formatting, text alignment, and numbered and bullet list generation.

Use the tools in the formatting toolbar to change the appearance of your text paragraphs.

Instructions and Examples

The EasyPlan Wizard provides instructions and examples for each topic in the outline. As you move from topic to topic, the instructions and examples change automatically. Click on the Show Wizard Instructions link to view the Instructions. Examples can be viewed by clicking the Examples link in the Instructions screen. Figure 5-4 shows how this looks on the screen.

FIGURE 5-4: TOPIC INSTRUCTIONS

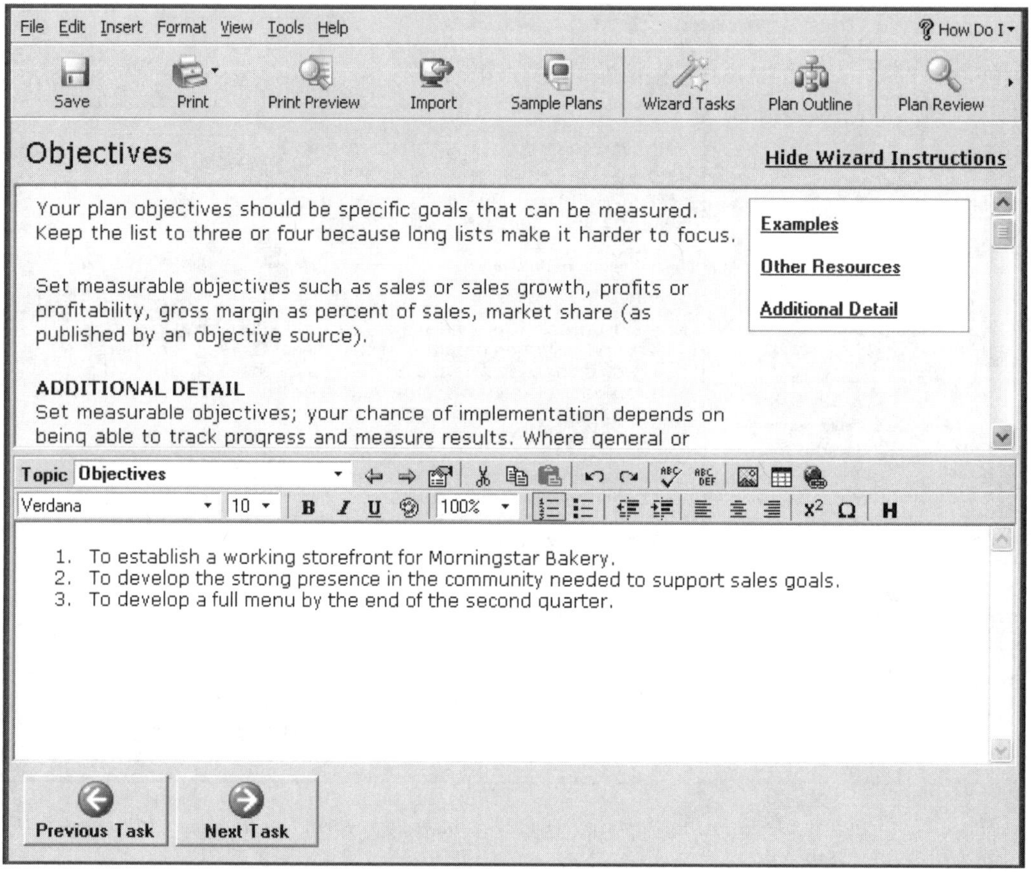

The Instructions describe what information is required for a topic.

TIPS

To View Examples:

Click on the Examples link in the upper right corner of the Instructions screen.

The Plan Outline

The standard Business Plan Pro outline includes up to eight chapters and approximately 50 separate topics, depending on your EasyPlan Wizard options. The EasyPlan Wizard creates this topic outline for you. Figure 5-5 shows the main chapters in the Plan Outline.

FIGURE 5-5: PLAN OUTLINE CHAPTERS

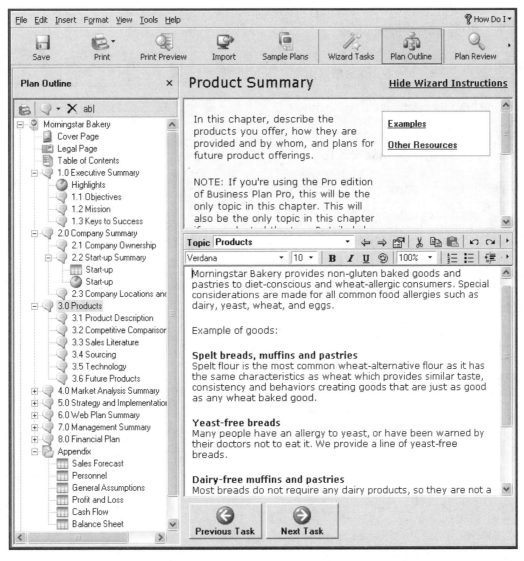

The Plan Outline includes toolbar buttons for adding new topics or deleting existing topics.

Changing the Plan Outline

You can change the outline. Use the Plan Outline toolbar, located at the top of the outline screen, to make the following changes.

The Plan Outline toolbar lets you print, insert topics/tables/charts, delete items which you do not want to include in the printed plan, and rename topic titles:

          =   Print a Topic

Click the Print tool to print the highlighted topic.

          =   Insert a Topic

Highlight a topic; click the Insert Topic tool. Type in the name of the new topic.

          =   Delete

Highlight the topic to delete and click the Delete tool.

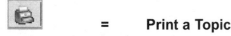   **=   Rename a Topic**

Highlight a topic; click the Rename tool; type the new name.

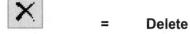 **Caution on Deleting a Topic from the Outline!**
Be careful. All sub-topics below a deleted topic are deleted as well. Once the topic is deleted, the outline automatically renumbers the remaining topics.

Working with HTML Formatting **H**

Business Plan Pro uses a simplified version of Hypertext Markup Language (HTML), the text formatting code used on the Internet. Business Plan Pro uses HTML tags for font name, font size, ordered lists, bullet lists, and basic table tags as well.

The HTML Editor screen can be displayed by clicking the **H** icon on the far right of the text toolbar. Figure 5-6 shows an example of the HTML Editor screen for a numbered list.

FIGURE 5-6: NUMBERED LIST IN HTML EDITOR

```
<FONT face=Verdana size=2>
<P>The primary expense to establish the Morningstar Bakery is the mortgage loan estimated at
$175,000 to purchase the vacant space on [Name omitted] street. The building was previously used as
a bakery and we plan to buy the used equipment along with the space. This cost is also calculated into
the loan estimate. Donna Sharp intends to invest $7,500 of her savings to cover the other cost of
start-up.</P>
<P>These costs include:
<OL>
<LI>Advertising brochures. </LI>
<LI>Bakery ingredients. </LI>
<LI>Insurance. </LI>
<LI>Bakery accessories, i.e. paper bags, cartons, etc.</LI></OL></FONT>
```

This is basic HTML code, the same as what is used to program Internet Web pages.

Figure 5-7 shows how the text above displays in the normal text screen.

FIGURE 5-7: NUMBERED LIST IN STANDARD TOPIC VIEW

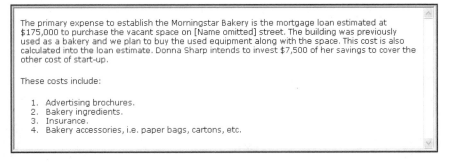

The primary expense to establish the Morningstar Bakery is the mortgage loan estimated at $175,000 to purchase the vacant space on [Name omitted] street. The building was previously used as a bakery and we plan to buy the used equipment along with the space. This cost is also calculated into the loan estimate. Donna Sharp intends to invest $7,500 of her savings to cover the other cost of start-up.

These costs include:

1. Advertising brochures.
2. Bakery ingredients.
3. Insurance.
4. Bakery accessories, i.e. paper bags, cartons, etc.

This is the screen you normally see when working on the topics in Business Plan Pro.

ᯤTIPS   Learn HTML Elsewhere

We do not believe extensive discussion of HTML is appropriate here, because Business Plan Pro assumes you stay in the standard Topic view while the background tools manage your numbered lists, bullet lists, and paragraph formats. If you want to learn more about HTML coding, there are HTML tutorials readily available from the Internet.

Import a File

You can import select topics and tables from other programs into your business plan file. If these programs are installed in your computer, the File > Import menu displays the program names in the Import Wizard, shown in Figure 5-8.

FIGURE 5-8: IMPORT WIZARD

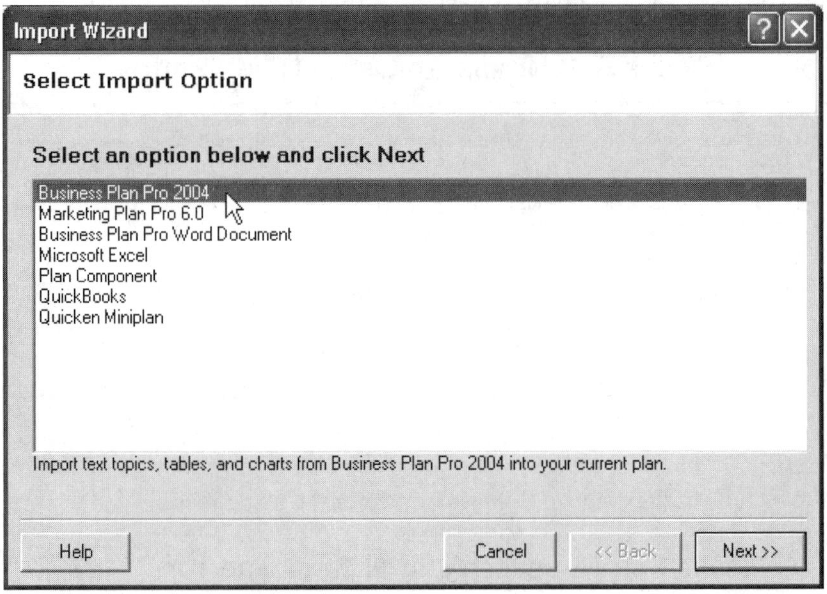

The program name lists vary depending on which programs you have installed.

| Help | For step-by-step procedures, click the dialog Help button or the Help menu.

Once you select a program, you can then select the file to import. A list of tables and topics lets you choose some or all to import. Figure 5-9 shows an example of importing from another Business Plan Pro file.

TIPS

Import from Microsoft Office, Quicken MiniPlan and QuickBooks

See also: Chapter 9: Working with Microsoft Office®, Chapter 11: Working with Quicken®, and Chapter 12: Working with QuickBooks®, for more information on how to export to and import from these programs.

FIGURE 5-9: IMPORT DIALOG BOX

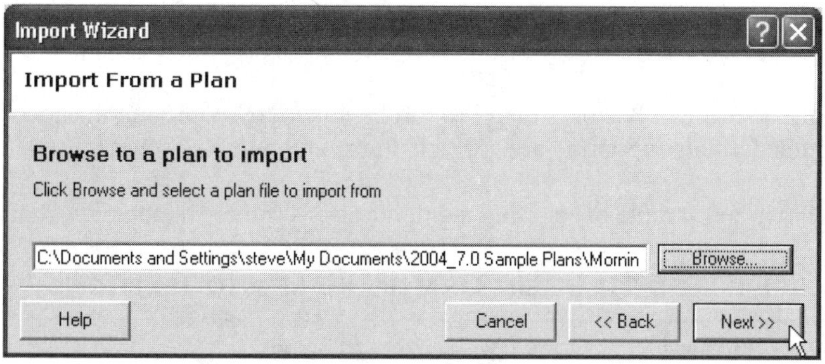

Use the Browse button to locate and select the file to import.

Once the file is selected, you can select the tables and/or topics from the file to be imported. Figure 5-10 shows an example.

FIGURE 5-10: SELECTING TABLES/TOPICS TO IMPORT

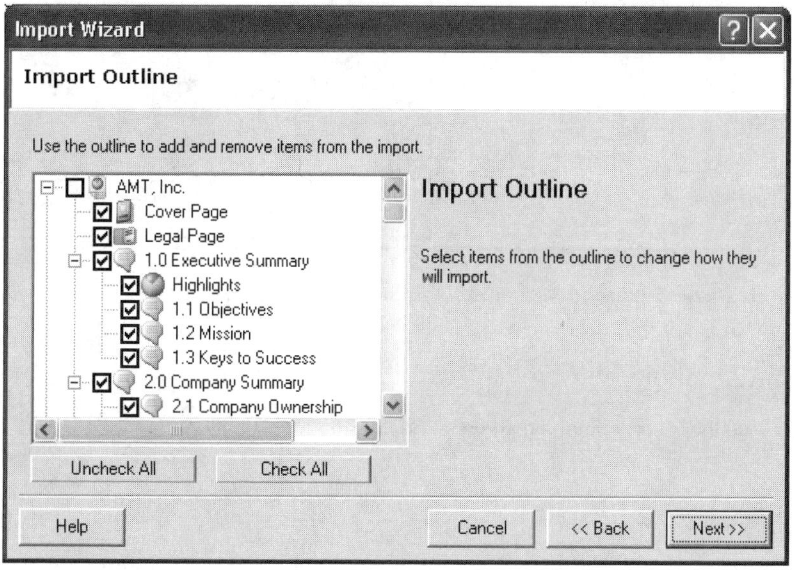

Use the list to select the tables and topics to import.

Follow the series of screen prompts as you are asked to confirm the topics, tables, and plan outline settings as you import.

Insert Tools

Graphic Image

Graphics created outside of Business Plan Pro can be linked to a topic and included with your plan. The graphic formats supported are .jpg, .gif, .bmp, and .wmf.

Figure 5-11 shows an example of selecting a graphic to insert into the topic, Marketing Strategy.

FIGURE 5-11: INSERT GRAPHIC IMAGE INTO TEXT TOPIC

Use the Insert Image feature to further enhance your text with graphics.

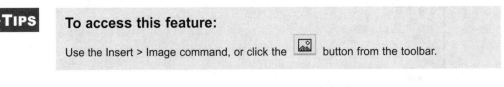

TIPS

To access this feature:

Use the Insert > Image command, or click the ▣ button from the toolbar.

Text Table

This feature is recommended to create a text column table format within a topic. It is a good alternative to using the Tab key to create a multiple-column text list because tabbed columns do not always align properly when printed. Typing your text into the table cells ensures that columns are aligned when printed. Figure 5-12 shows the dialog and an example of a 2-column, 5-row table.

FIGURE 5-12: INSERT TEXT TABLE - EXAMPLE

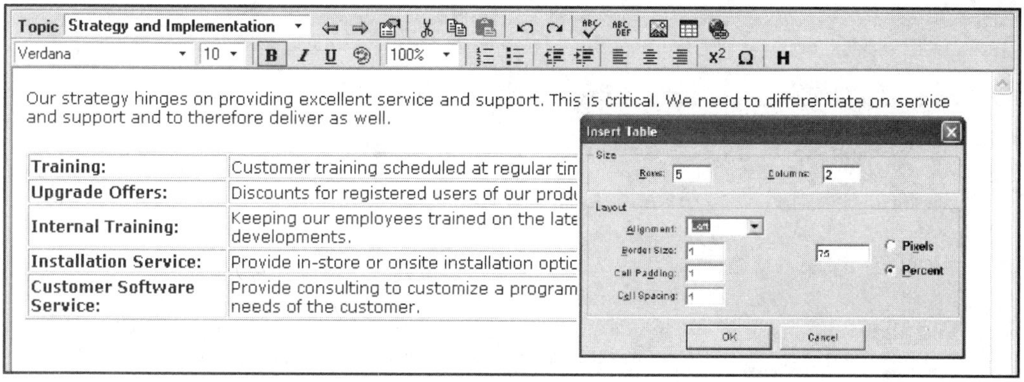

This example shows a 2-column, 5-row text table with left alignment within the cells.

TIPS

To Access this feature:

• Use the Insert > Table command, or use the [button] button from the toolbar.

Character Symbol

Business Plan Pro makes it easy to insert symbols into your text. Common symbols such as copyright, registered, and trademark are just a few examples of available symbols. Figure 5-13 shows an example using the copyright symbol.

FIGURE 5-13: INSERT A SYMBOL IN TEXT

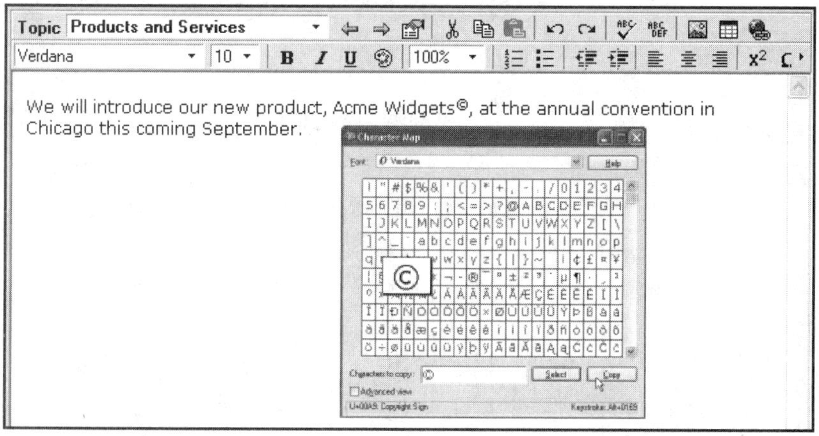

The Show Character Map button on the toolbar makes it easy to insert a symbol into your text.

TIPS

To see the Character Map screen:

• Click the Ω button from the toolbar, or choose the Insert > Symbol command.

To Superscript a symbol:

• Highlight the symbol; use the x^2 button from the toolbar.

Hyperlink

This feature allows you to include active Internet links in your topics when you export your plan to a .doc or .html document (see Chapter 8: Print and Publish). If your reader has Internet access, this function lets them click on the caption and the link connects and displays the website address.

Figure 5-14 shows an example of a website link within a topic. The Insert Hyperlink dialog box lets you type a website address. The caption is placed in the text topic at the cursor position. It displays in an underlined and colored highlight.

FIGURE 5-14: INSERT A LINK EXAMPLE

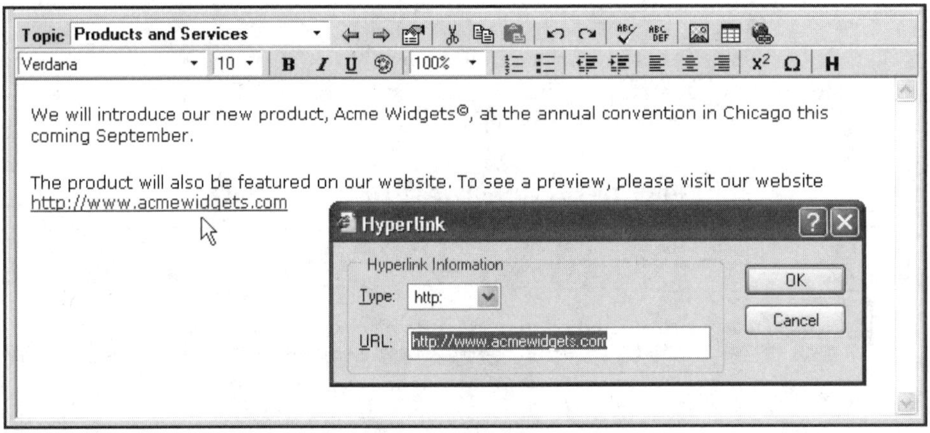

This dialog also lets you create links for email addresses, file transfer protocol (.ftp) and many other HTML codes.

TIPS

To access the Insert Hyperlink feature:

• Choose the Insert > Hyperlink command, or click the button from the toolbar.

Modify Plan Outline for Different Situations

Are you writing your business plan for investors? Are you a family-owned business looking to expand? Are you looking to sell your business? To buy a business? There are many reasons for writing a business plan and the topic outline and corresponding text, tables, and charts should target specifics to match the purpose. Here are examples of outline revisions to consider for different kinds of planning situations.

A Plan for Investors

If you are looking for outside investors, then you should add an Exit Strategy topic. This shows those investors how and when you expect to give them a return on their investment. The Exit Strategy topic would be added to your financial plan chapter.

Essentially, there are two possible exit strategies: public offering or acquisition.

The Exit Strategy topic should include references to the investment analysis, with Net Present Value (NPV) and Internal Rate of Returen (IRR), ending valuation, and assumptions for valuation.

You should also have at least one topic on valuation, covering valuation for the initial investment and valuation at the ending point of the exit strategy. You could have a topic related to valuation in the second chapter of the plan, about the company, and you should also have a topic in the last chapter, about the financial plan. The Investment Analysis table has some basic indicators on valuation, but sophisticated investors look for a detailed discussion of proposed valuations. Remember that credibility is very important.

Make sure you have strong discussions of competitive advantage and the management team. Add more subtopics as necessary.

A Plan to Buy or Sell a Business

Your first chapter should include at least one topic explaining the proposed deal, who is buying and who is selling, and why.

The second chapter, about the company, needs a topic to explain how the new owners intend to absorb the purchased company. Are the names changing? Are they purchasing both assets and liabilities, the whole business, or just a portion? How important is maintaining the branding and image of the existing business?

The financial chapter should include at least one topic detailing the proposed handling of the Balance Sheet, the possibility of the financial concept called Goodwill, and related subjects. Your CPA will be able to fill you in on this.

A Plan for a Family Business

The second chapter, about the company, should include a discussion of family ownership.

The sixth chapter, covering management, should include details of family members included in the management team, specifically, what their roles and responsibilities are.

If family owners and operators include more than a single generation, and outside investment is not moving the company toward an exit strategy, then there might be a need for a topic on succession planning.

An Operations Plan

The operations plan is an example of a specific business plan context that frequently involves deleting some topics included in the standard outline. For example:

- Many operations plans do not include the second chapter, about the company, because the plan is internal and there is no need for taking the extra time to describe the company to itself.
- Many operations plans either skip the chapter on management team, or include it only if the operations plan involves making changes to the team.

An Expansion Plan

The expansions plan is another example of a specific business plan context where deleting some topics included in the standard outline may produce a better plan. For example:

- On an expansion plan, you want to emphasize the new market, or new product or service. You still need an executive summary, but not need to summarize the company background. For the management team, focus on the expansion management instead of the whole management.

Adjust Your Own Plan

You can see from these examples that you want to adjust your plan to your exact context. Use the text formatting features to enhance the readability of your text, but do not skimp on solid content and well researched information.

Your Plan Tables

CHAPTER 6: YOUR PLAN TABLES

This is the business age of numbers. You cannot get a new company financed without a business plan built on believable numbers. You cannot get through your company's capital budgeting process (that is, you cannot get your company to invest in your idea) without a business plan.

Business Plan Pro® is intended to help you meet the numbers demands without getting bogged down in the mechanics.

Spreadsheet Overview

The linked financial tables in Business Plan Pro provide you with a very powerful tool for financial forecasting. Chapter 6 takes you through all of the standard tables included, and Figure 6-4 shows you how the main ones link together. These tables are all part of a built-in spreadsheet that can make all the financial calculations you need for your business plan. In the Business Plan Pro PREMIER version you can even add worksheets and use them as you would any other spreadsheet (Microsoft Excel, Lotus 1-2-3, or Works) to customize your plan.

Referring to Cells and Ranges

Spreadsheets are based on a matrix, the mathematical name for a layout that has rows and columns. Rows are always horizontal, columns vertical.

As we work with spreadsheet formulas in Business Plan Pro, we refer to cells the way most spreadsheet software does, with their row and column notation. The cell in the fourth column of the fifth row, for example, is cell D5. We refer to blocks of cells by showing the upper left first and the bottom right last, separated by a colon. So the range that goes from B5 to N10 is written as B5:N10.

 The Spreadsheet View: Row and Column Headings

Spreadsheet row numbers and column letters automatically show in your tables. However, because Business Plan Pro does not need them for standard default handling you can go to the Tools > Options > Tables menu to hide them, or set them to show as you prefer.

Data Cells vs. Locked Cells

Data Cells

With a few exceptions, green cells are unlocked. You can input data, formulas, or text.

Locked Cells

Business Plan Pro prevents accidental errors by locking important formula cells. All black cells are locked. They contain formulas, so you cannot type into them. When you try, an error message tells you that these cells cannot be changed.

This locking is done on purpose, and for your benefit. It preserves the links between tables, such as the Sales Forecast table to the Profit and Loss table. The same is true for certain row labels. For example, in the Profit and Loss table, the row named "Gross Margin" is defined as Sales less Cost of Sales. Since the formula cannot be changed, the label should not be changed either. Nobody would want Gross Margin to be accidentally renamed to Net Margin or Profit Margin or Contribution Margin or anything else.

For More Help on How to Use the Tables

This manual chapter is your main resource for understanding the financial and forecasting tables included in Business Plan Pro. It begins with important background information related to business planning and forecasting, and then goes through each of the tables one by one with more detail, explanations, tips, and examples. However, this manual is not the main resource for the program's general help and details which are available elsewhere in the program. The last pages of this chapter have more information on how to access this help.

Instructions and Examples

Table-specific instructions and examples are included in the EasyPlan Wizard® instructions.

FIGURE 6-1: WIZARD INSTRUCTIONS

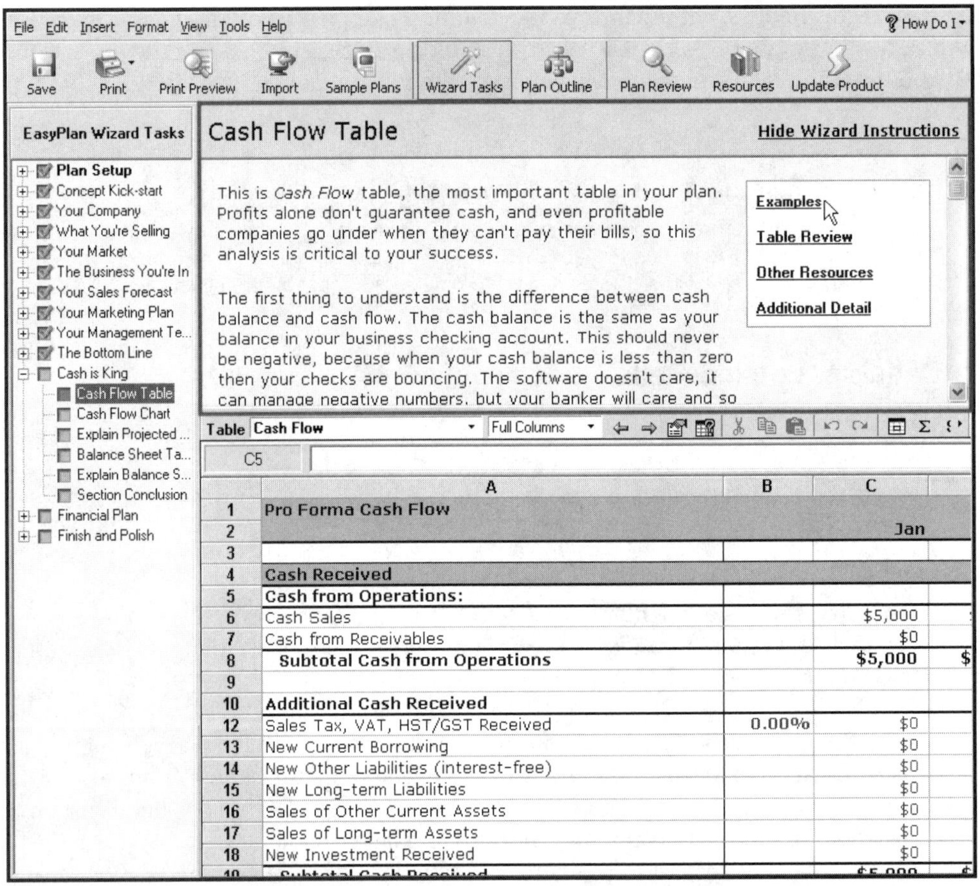

The EasyPlan Wizard includes instructions (highlighted in the illustration) and examples for every table. These are your initial sources for information about using the tables.

To Learn More About...	Search the Help Index for...
Viewing Table Instructions and Examples	Instructions

Detailed Row-by-Row Help

Row-by-row help includes detailed explanations for each row in the table. You can right-click the mouse in any row and select row-by-row help from the menu to open a detailed explanation.

FIGURE 6-2: ROW-BY-ROW HELP

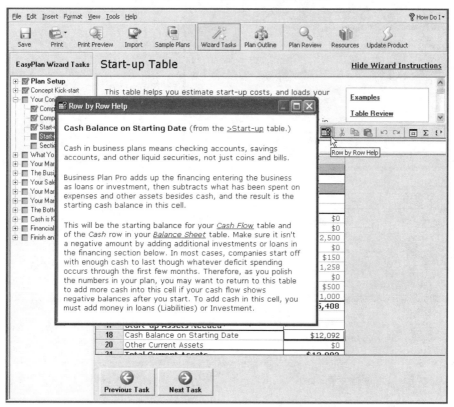

In Business Plan Pro row-by-row help gives you details for the row you have selected, throughout the tables. You can access row-by-row help by clicking on a cell and then clicking the *button on the toolbar.*

To Learn More About...	Search the Help Index for...
Table row explanations and usage	Row-by-row Definitions

Formula Backstep

The Formula Backstep feature helps you find the source information for table formulas. You can choose to switch tables to find the source information for a formula. For example, when you see a formula referring to the name "Sales," Formula Backstep lets you jump from any table to the table that contains the source range named "Sales." In Figure 6-3, the reference is to "subtotal_cash_spent" in the selected cell below. Right-click the mouse to show the Formula Backstep option.

FIGURE 6-3: FORMULA BACKSTEP

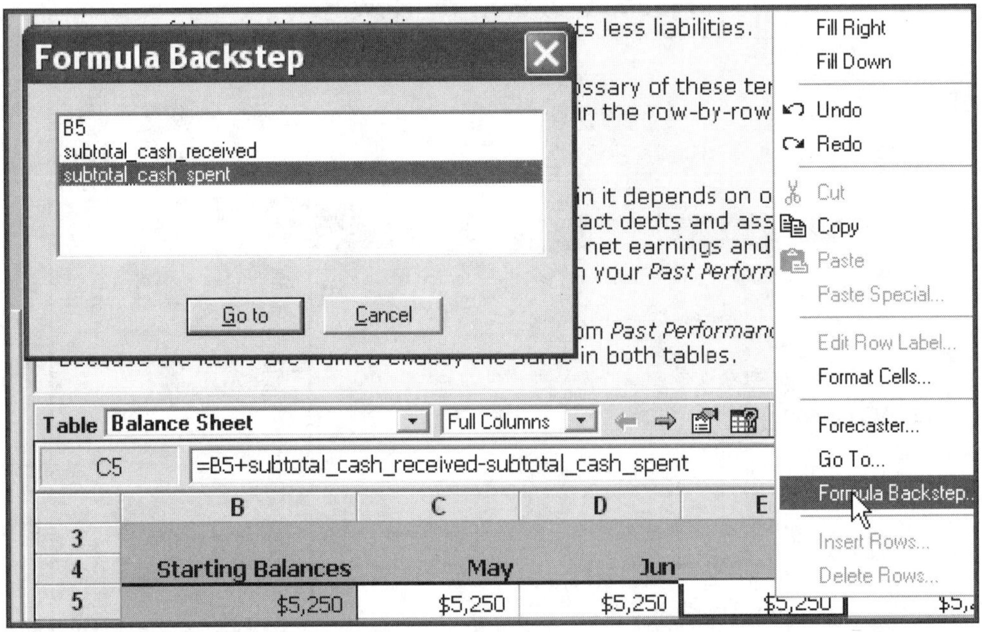

The Business Plan Pro Formula Backstep feature gives you the option of jumping to other ranges used in cell formulas. You can access this feature by right-clicking on a cell.

?	To Learn More About...	Search the Help Index for...
	Find source of table formula components	Formula Backstep
	Add or delete topics, tables, charts	Plan Outline

Help   For step-by-step procedures, click the dialog Help buttons or the Help menu.

One Year or Two (PREMIER version)

One year of monthly data is automatically included in all tables. However, over the years Business Plan Pro users have asked for a second year of monthly financial tables. PREMIER version offers this option which adds a second year of monthly data for key financial tables. (NOTE: a second year of monthly data is not required for a good business plan).

In the EasyPlan Wizard Setup question "2nd year of monthly data?" choose "**Yes,** include a 2nd year of monthly data to my financials."

FIGURE 6-4: 2ND YEAR OF MONTHLY FINANCIALS

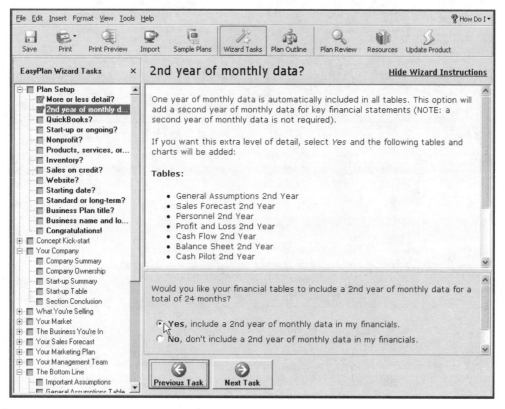

The EasyPlan Wizard Setup lets you add a second year of monthly data to your plan.

These tables are added to your plan:

- General Assumptions 2nd Year
- Sales Forecast 2nd Year
- Personnel 2nd Year

- Profit and Loss 2nd Year
- Cash Flow 2nd Year
- Balance Sheet 2nd Year
- Cash Pilot 2nd Year

FIGURE 6-5: 2ND YEAR PROFIT AND LOSS TABLE (PREMIER VERSION)

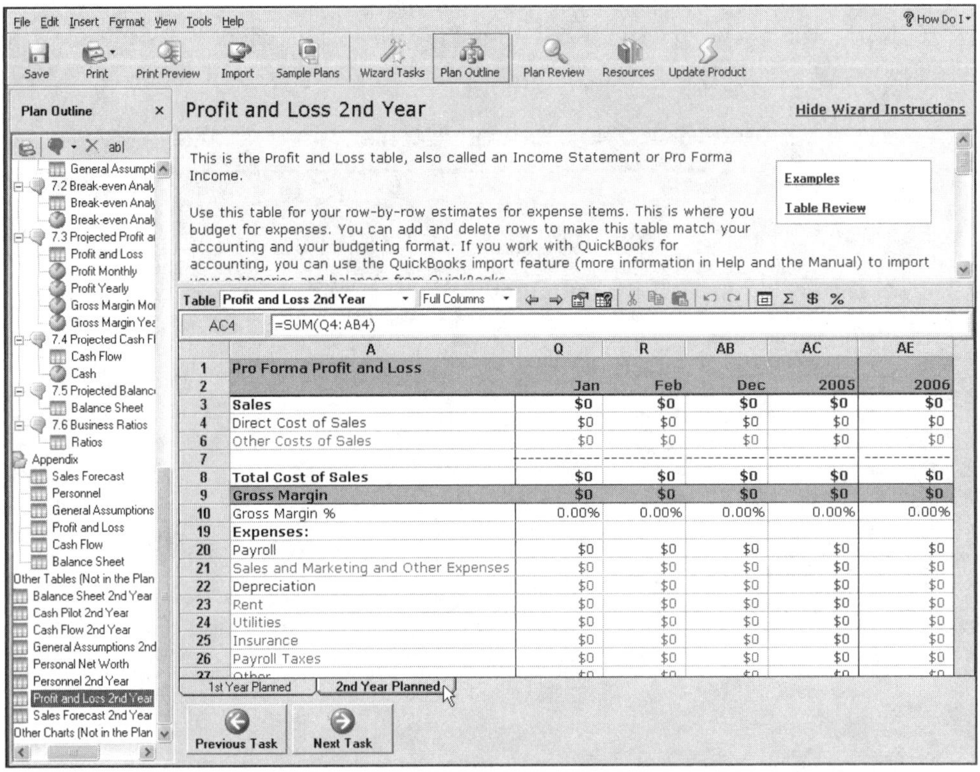

The 2nd year Profit and Loss table is shown; note the screen tabs and the Plan Outline.

Each table displays screen tabs for jumping between 1st year and 2nd year. You can also access the 2nd year tables from the Plan Outline. Initially they appear at the bottom of the outline, listed as Other Tables (Not in the Plan Outline) and do not print out as part of your finished business plan. If you wish to have your 2nd year tables print, you can link them to the monthly financials appendix.

The 2nd year annual column automatically displays and prints in your 1st year planning table.

You Need the Numbers

This financial tool has been developed and refined for more than 19 years now, has been used with hundreds of thousands of successful business plans, and it works. It is financially and mathematically correct.

The software helps you generate the business projections you need: linked financial statements, practical forecasts, and milestones with budgets. You can do the whole analysis, from start-up to business ratios, by taking the tables one at a time and working in your assumptions. All you do is type your assumptions in the green cells and avoid the black cells. You do not have to program anything. Sales, personnel, income, cash, balance, ratios, and other tables are linked together already, so a change in one flows logically to all the others.

However, like all business models, or any other projection of the future, it is at best a very good educated guess. It depends on assumptions. It is a general tool that can be applied to millions of specific cases. It can always be improved, tailored, and customized. The objective of this chapter is to give you an understanding of the underlying assumptions, the mathematics, and the mechanics of the Business Plan Pro projections. This manual helps you to use the specifics of the software effectively.

We want you to use Business Plan Pro for what it does well. It has a solid, tested, robust financial model at its core, linking all of the key financial views into a complete system. Change any one element and all the others change automatically. Use it to develop your business financials. Use its "what-if" facilities. Work with your business plan financials to understand the key assumptions and think about how they might change. What happens if you sell more or less than planned, and what if you spend more than planned? What if utilities double, or rent increases? You have to at least consider these possibilities, and use your business plan to anticipate the implications. That is a lot of what Business Plan Pro is about.

Remember, however, that the software is a tool. It is only as good as the assumptions you put into it. Furthermore, it depends on mathematical modeling to project critical elements— receivables, for example—into the future, based on assumptions. These projections are just that, projections, and the math behind them is complex and elegant, but still subject to some important assumptions.

This chapter points out key assumptions and shows you in detail how to work with them, and how to change them when you think you should.

Within this manual we look at these points and show you how to adjust and perfect your specific plan, using the knowledge of the programmability of Business Plan Pro.

Planning with Computers

Computers do not think, they just do the numbers. Computers are very dumb contraptions that can be downright dangerous when you expect them to think for you. They are absurdly literal, and, worse still, literal in their own very narrowly defined language. Program a computer to tell you that 2+2=5 and it will swear that 2+2=5.

Use your financial projections but do not believe them—especially when dealing with computers and software. Because there is something magical about neatly ordered rows and columns of numbers shining at you through a computer screen or marching from the printer, you may forget how separated from reality they really are.

So use the dumb machine for what it does well. You do the thinking, let the computer do the numbers, and the division of labor will work wonders. Remember the origins of the spreadsheet, back with the pencils and green lined paper, and think in those terms; you are still in that realm, but now you have got a tireless worker to change your numbers instantly. Now that is the computer's real power.

The best analyst uses human judgement to guide the number crunching. If you accept the great split between rational, analytic thinking and intuitive, creative thinking, then you probably realize the best work requires a little of both. Use your head to guide the analysis.

How do you get the right combination? The simplest way is by doing the numbers while running the financial analysis. Change factors repeatedly. Each new iteration of the plan is another go at understanding a problem, each is another possibility to be considered. The world is far too complex for simple answers. Solving problems is akin to recording stereo music: the artist sings multiple tracks into a single tape and magnifies and multiplies the voice and voice effects. The more angles considered, the better the understanding of the final product and its alternatives. Look at your business plan at many different volumes, at many different prices, at many different kinds and levels of expense, and the set of numbers you finally accept will be a better representation of the full range of possibility.

There is an irony here. The best market forecasters use a lot of computer models, but they do not believe them. Output from different models stimulates thinking about alternatives, causes and effects, and different outcomes, but output is not to be believed, just considered.

TIPS **Words and Numbers**

A complete business plan needs both words and numbers. You cannot tell the whole story with words alone, and you cannot tell it with just numbers either. Make sure the numbers match the words.

Planning vs. Accounting

There is a clear distinction between planning and accounting. Planning begins today and goes forward into the future. Accounting ends today and goes backward into the past. Planning is for making decisions, setting priorities, and management. Accounting is also for information and management, of course, but there are legal obligations related to taxes. Accounting must necessarily go very deep into detail. Planning requires a balance between detail and concept, because there are times when too much detail is not productive.

Many people fail to understand the distinction and put disproportionate attention, as they develop a plan, into accounting details. For example, tax reporting and proper accounting requires detailed lists of assets and depreciation, where for planning purposes a good estimate is more efficient.

To understand this difference, consider the relative proportion of uncertainty in a forward-looking estimate of depreciation vs. a sales forecast. The AMT computer store, one of our Business Plan Pro sample plans, projects depreciation of approximately $13,000 per year. It expects sales to rise from $5 million to $9 million in three years. AMT could develop a plan that lists future asset purchases and uses depreciation functions to depreciate each future asset according to accepted formulas. Doing that would probably reduce the uncertainty built into the depreciation estimate, but how much uncertainty would be reduced, for how much effort. A 50% variation in the projected depreciation, either way, comes to less than $10,000, while a 10% variation in the sales forecast in the last year is worth $900,000. A good business plan process maintains proportion between effort and value. Accounting needs detailed depreciation in this company, after the fact; but the business plan, looking three years ahead, does not.

TIPS

Make it Yours

Remember, nothing about Business Plan Pro is carved in stone…you change formulas, revise formulas, ignore the built-in tables, or even (with the PREMIER version) add your own Excel-compatible tables…it is your plan.

You can also unlink tables so they do not show. Use the Plan Outline view to add and delete topics, unlink tables, and—if you have the PREMIER version—add tables.

Basic Accounting Principles

Business Plan Pro respects the principles of accounting. It has to; without that, it cannot do the financial analysis people expect. If you are not familiar with basic bookkeeping, at least be aware of these basic accounting rules:

- **Assets are always equal to capital plus liabilities.** Business Plan Pro uses this fact to predict your cash balance in the Start-up table, Cash Flow, and Balance Sheet.

- **Cash Flow is different from Profit and Loss.** Your profits are an accounting concept, sales less costs and expenses. Cash flow includes Balance Sheet changes that are not covered in Profit and Loss. For example, sales on credit produce profits but no money until invoices are paid. Paying off loan principal does not affect Profit and Loss. Purchasing assets does not affect Profit and Loss.

- **Do not confuse expenses with assets.** Most businesses prefer expenses to assets, because money spent on expenses is deductible, but money spent on assets is not. Do not try to make research or software development money into assets, because you would end up with higher taxes, and assets on your books that cannot be sold. If development produces a new product, your business gets the benefits in future sales and profits, not in assets, on its books.

- **One of the most important principles of accounting is the principle of materiality.** This principle means that if it does not make much difference, you do not have to worry about it. It is because of this principle that we recommend not getting into infinite detail in depreciation, assets, and tax treatments. When you are working with a sales forecast and estimating uncertainty far into the future, you should not worry much about detailed depreciation three years from now. The difference in sales plan-vs.-actual is far more important than that in the details of depreciation.

TIPS

More on Accounting Principles In Hurdle: The Book on Business Planning

Make sure you read the *About Business Numbers* section of your Hurdle book, which explains this in greater detail. Use the Tools > Resources > Books > Hurdle link to read the book in PDF format.

Modular, Linked Tables

Business Plan Pro builds its financial analysis on logical modules, separate tables all linked together. Figure 6-6 offers a visual explanation. It shows how these relationships work in general.

FIGURE 6-6: MODULAR, LINKED TABLES

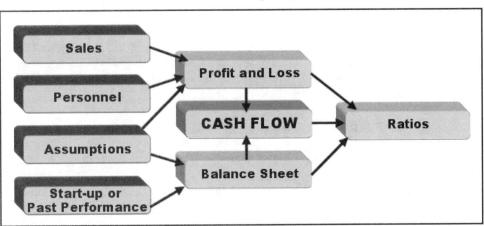

The business analysis tables are linked together for cleaner analysis.

The key is that changes in any one of these tables automatically reflects properly in all the others.

- Your Sales Forecast should show Sales and Cost of Sales. The same numbers in the Sales Forecast are the ones you use in the Profit and Loss.
- You have a separate Personnel table, and the numbers you input into that table are the same numbers that show up for Payroll Expenses in your Profit and Loss table.
- Your Profit and Loss table should show the same numbers as Sales and Personnel Plan tables in the proper areas. It should also show Interest Expenses as a logical reflection of interest rates and balances of debt.
- Your Cash Flow has to reflect your Profit and Loss, plus changes in Balance Sheet items and non-cash expenses such as depreciation, which are on the Profit and Loss. The changes in the Balance Sheet are critical. For example, when you borrow money, it does not affect the Profit or Loss (except for interest expenses later on), but it makes a huge difference to your checking account balance.
- The Balance Sheet has to reflect the Profit and Loss and the Cash Flow.
- Your Business Ratios should calculate automatically, based on the numbers in Sales, Profit and Loss, Personnel, Cash Flow, and Balance Sheet.

TIPS

Navigation Tip:

You can also use the Views menu to select any of the tables included in your plan. Once you have a table displayed, you can use the table dropdown in the tool bar to switch to any other table. Also, to display any topic, table, or chart, click on its name from the Plan Outline screen.

Working with Linked Tables

Figure 6-7 shows how the links work for the Profit and Loss table in a sample business plan. The view shows the top of the table, not the whole table. The actual links showing in the illustration are coming in from the Sales Forecast and the Personnel Plan.

FIGURE 6-7: WORKING WITH LINKED TABLES

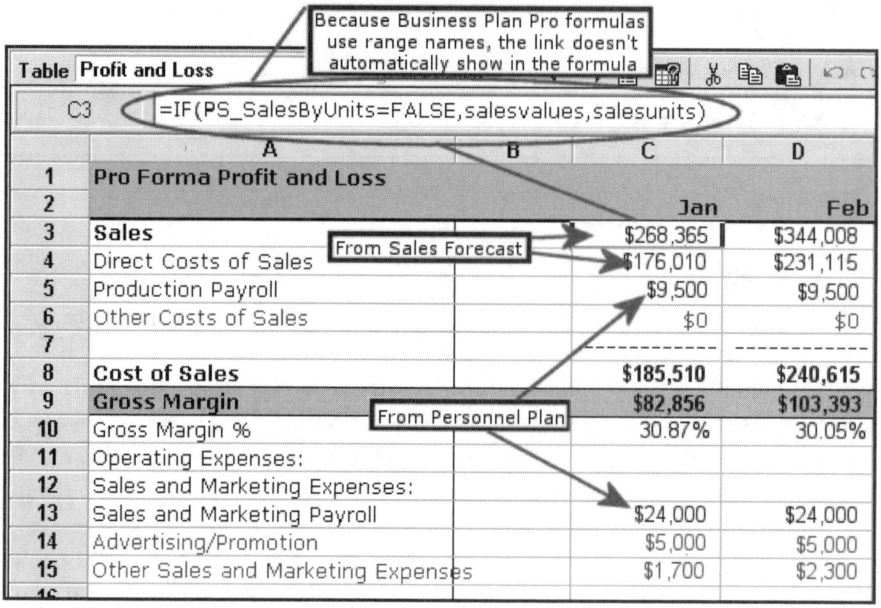

Simple spreadsheet formulas link the tables together.

- At the top of the table you see Sales and Direct Costs of Sales. These rows come from the summary rows in the Sales Forecast. The cells are locked on purpose; they cannot be changed.

- The rows containing the linked information are locked. Users cannot change them. Otherwise, users who do not understand linking could type over the linking formulas.

- The formulas in linked cells do not always easily show that they are linked cells. In the example in Figure 6-7, the formula for sales in cell C3, which shows in the edit bar, uses an

IF function and named ranges. It is not immediately obvious that the named ranges come from another worksheet, one named Sales. That is clear in the documentation and in the help files, but not in the formula itself.

- You can use the Formula Backstep feature to jump automatically to the source information when a cell formula refers to other worksheets or variable names.

To Learn More About...	**Search the Help Index for...**
Find source of table formula components	Formula Backstep

TIPS | **Tables Are not Strictly Sequential**

Do not expect to finish one table before starting another. Normally, you go back and forth among the tables, revising as you go. A plan is not really built one table at a time.

Developing Your Own Links

Because Business Plan Pro is built on its own Microsoft Excel® compatible spreadsheet, it includes the facility to use more than 100 spreadsheet functions compatible with Microsoft Excel. For example, you can easily link a row in the Personnel Plan or Profit and Loss to a specific row in the Sales Forecast, for calculating commission payments to employees or outside representatives.

Users of the PREMIER version can also link from the user-defined tables into the tables for sales, expenses, or cash flow. You can create specific worksheets for example, or three years in quarters, or for a 10-year plan. You can create worksheets to itemize capital expenses, or detail depreciation, or to break payroll burden into components.

Since the background is a complete spreadsheet, as programmable as the major spreadsheets, there is very little you cannot do. If you use an Excel function exactly as it would work in Excel, it probably works the same in Business Plan Pro.

The details are explained in Chapter 10: Advanced Tables, of this manual. There you can find detailed instructions, background information, and examples with illustrations. A complete list of range names is included in Appendix A.

Simplifying Assumptions

Business Plan Pro follows the general model of business planning, as opposed to accounting, when it comes time to make simplifying assumptions. We want to call your attention to several of the more important assumptions we make. We also explain why we make them, why they work in most cases, when they do not work, and what to do when they do not work.

The Government Does Not Pay for Losses

As the Business Plan Pro documentation explains in several places, taxes are based on simple mathematics. Your estimated tax in the Profit and Loss table is the product of multiplying pretax profits by the tax rate in your General Assumptions table.

However, Business Plan Pro looks at your annual profits and sets the tax rate to zero if you have a loss for the year. This avoids the awkward situation of overestimating your cash by assuming negative taxes in a loss year.

Furthermore, Business Plan Pro does not automatically calculate loss carried forward situations. The loss carried forward refers to losses in previous tax years that reduce taxes in a profitable year. That happens when a company finally makes a profit after initial losses, and those losses are deducted from current year taxes.

The simplifying assumption in this case is that taxes are figured using simple mathematics. When you have a profit for the end of the year, Business Plan Pro multiplies pretax profits by the tax rate percentage in your General Assumptions table, and that is its estimate for taxes. If you do not have a profit, Business Plan Pro sets your tax rate to zero.

This is rather simple. We could make it a lot more complex with lookup functions for graduated tax rates. We could do formulas to change tax treatment in different countries. We automatically change the treatment for loss situations, but only in a simple global way, setting the effective tax rate to zero when the entire year produces a loss. The tax rate forms specify pages of different rates. Furthermore, the real rates depend on specific deductions and specific situations.

Still, this is about planning, not accounting, and simple is good. The estimated tax rate is easy to understand and easy to apply. You get a lot more planning power from a simple and obvious estimated input than from a complex, hard-to-follow formula. There is a real danger of automating assumptions to the point at which users do not realize how much is involved, and how critical those assumptions are.

Depreciation as a Single Row of Simple Input

Business Plan Pro uses a single row of data input to contain your estimated depreciation. This simplifying assumption is much better than a complex set of depreciation formulas, for several good reasons:

- Government tax authorities set strict rules for when and how assets can be depreciated. These rules are not always logical.
- Different assets are allowed to be depreciated according to different formulas: there is straight-line depreciation, double declining balance, sum-of-the-years-digits, and several other formulas.

- The formulas cannot be applied to groups of assets; each asset generally has its own set of rules, according to which type of asset it is.
- If we decided to apply detailed formulas to future assets, we would have to estimate the purchase of those assets, and keep track of each significant asset separately. We would also have to keep track of each asset's depreciation formula. The detail required would produce an artificially difficult data problem without really reducing uncertainty in any practical way.

TIPS

Depreciation Tip

If you do have a business that depends on high-priced capital assets, so that depreciation and purchase of assets is very significant, you can get detailed instructions and even examples of depreciation functions from Chapter 10: Advanced Tables.

An educated guess is a better option. If you take a percent of assets value per year, based on past years' depreciation, that is a good option. If you do not have past data to use, then ask somebody who does. Ask your accountant. In the worst case, you can take 10% of assets value per year and not go too far wrong.

?

To Learn More About...	Search the Help Index for...
Spreadsheet/table features	Tables, Add Other (PREMIER version) Linking Insert, Tables Financial Functions

Interest Rates as Simple Mathematics

Business Plan Pro treats loan interest and principal payments according to standard accounting: interest, which is deductible against income as an expense, is in the Profit and Loss table. Principal repayment, which is not deductible, affects the Cash Flow and the Balance Sheet, but not the Profit and Loss.

Following the accounting standard, it calculates monthly Interest Expenses by multiplying the balance for any given month by the Interest Rate assumption in General Assumptions. It calculates Annual Interest by taking the average balance and multiplying that times the Interest Rate in the General Assumptions. Both of these calculations are logical and easy to understand.

However, as easily understood and as logical as these calculations are, they are not nearly as exact as you would want them for accounting purposes after the fact.

- One potential problem is that the bank likely calculates interest based on the beginning balance, while Business Plan Pro calculates based on the ending balance.
- Another problem is the timing of the loan: a loan taken out on January 28 produces the same interest estimate in Business Plan Pro as a loan taken out on January 3.

- Furthermore, Business Plan Pro takes a loan received at any time during the second, third, fourth, or fifth year of a plan and calculates its average balance as ending balance plus beginning balance divided by two. Since the beginning balance was zero, that calculation divides the loan amount by half, for planning purposes. That means that interest is figured as if the loan were taken out on June 30, the middle of the year, regardless of whether it was planned for the first month or the last month.

Most of these problems are not really problems in business plans. Good practical estimates, easy to explain, are more valuable than detailed exact calculations based on uncertain assumptions. Remember this is a plan, not tax accounting, and it needs to summarize and simplify. If the business plan estimate does not match to the penny, do not worry; an estimate is acceptable.

⚑TIPS   **Principal Payment Tip**

Business Plan Pro includes financial functions you can use to determine correct principal payments and interest payments on loans, according to standard financial formulas. These are explained in detail in Chapter 10: Advanced Tables.

However, if your business plan should require more detailed interest calculations, because of the significance of the amounts, you can adjust the estimated interest rates in the General Assumptions table to produce exactly the interest you want. Then all you need to do for your plan is explain the reason for the interest rate assumptions in the text that accompanies the General Assumptions table.

Forecaster

Sometimes it is easier to develop a forecast using graphics tools. When you are in a table working on developing a forecast, you can go to the Edit > Forecaster command to pop up this unique Business Plan Pro graphic forecasting tool. Figure 6-8 shows an example.

FIGURE 6-8: THE FORECASTER™

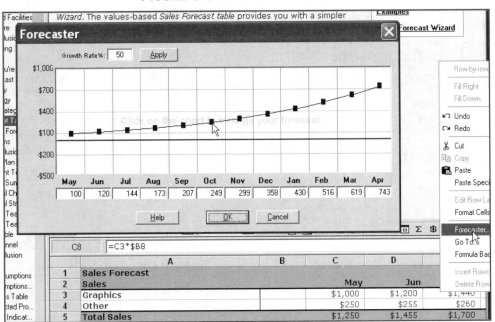

The Forecaster tool lets you develop your forecast by clicking the mouse and changing the line. It is quick and powerful, and built into the tables. Access it from the Edit menu or by right-clicking in a cell.

You can set growth rates by typing values in the Forecaster month cells, or by clicking the mouse in the graph to draw in a forecast.

Tables, One by One

Current = Short-term

In its financials tables, Business Plan Pro uses the term "**current**" rather than "short-term" for any liabilities, assets, interest, notes, borrowing, etc. with a time-frame of less than five years. Generally, anything with a time frame over five years is considered long-term.

Balance Sheet

TIPS

Balance Details

Do not be surprised to find the business plan Balance Sheet more summarized than the Balance Sheet in your accounting statements. This is normal. The accounting needs to build the Balance from detail, but in the business plan, your Balance Sheet needs a one-to-one correspondence with your Cash Flow estimate. You must have rows in Cash Flow to change the Balance Sheet items.

The three Balance Sheet input rows are three of the most important in your business plan: Accounts Receivable, Accounts Payable, and Inventory. Your plan settings determine whether you see Accounts Receivable and Inventory. Accounts Receivable appears only if you are set for sales on credit, and Inventory only if you are set for inventory, in plan settings.

?	To Learn More About...	Search the Help Index for...
	Matching your plan tables to your business	Plan Setup

Business Plan Pro calculates all the rest of the Balance Sheet automatically, from your assumptions in other tables.

- Either the Start-up table or Past Performance sets your Starting Balances. Each plan has one or the other, depending on answers to EasyPlan Wizard questions.
- Cash, assets other than receivables and inventory, liabilities other than payables, and capital all depend on inputs in either your Start-up, your Past Performance, or your Cash Flow table.

More Detail on Three Key Estimates

Figure 6-9 shows the balance sheet from a start-up pizza restaurant plan. In this example, because of plan settings, all three of the key input rows in the Balance Sheet are showing:

- Accounts Receivable starts at zero because there are no sales for the first two months. Beginning in the third month, amounts start to show.
- Inventory shows only the starting inventory balance in the first two months, but begins to have larger balances as sales begin in the third month.
- Accounts Payable begins in the first month, because expenses are incurred.

FIGURE 6-9: BALANCE SHEET TABLE

C18	=new_accounts_payable				
	A	B	C	D	E
1	Pro Forma Balance Sheet				
2					
3	Assets				
4	Current Assets	Starting Balances	Jan	Feb	Mar
5	Cash	$61,900	$48,642	$31,297	$20,801
6	Accounts Receivable	$0	$0	$0	$1,049
7	Inventory	$500	$500	$500	$5,195
8	Other Current Assets	$2,500	$2,500	$2,500	$2,500
9	Total Current Assets	$64,900	$51,642	$34,297	$29,545
10	Long-term Assets				
11	Long-term Assets	$20,000	$20,000	$20,000	$20,000
12	Accumulated Depreciation	$0	$1,250	$2,500	$3,750
13	Total Long-term Assets	$20,000	$18,750	$17,500	$16,250
14	Total Assets	$84,900	$70,392	$51,797	$45,795
15					
16	Liabilities and Capital				
17			Jan	Feb	Mar
18	Accounts Payable	$0	$2,965	$3,205	$12,973
19	Current Borrowing	$0	$0	$0	$0
20	Other Current Liabilities	$0	$0	$0	$0
21	Subtotal Current Liabilities	$0	$2,965	$3,205	$12,973
22					
23	Long-term Liabilities	$20,000	$19,742	$19,481	$19,219
24	Total Liabilities	$20,000	$22,706	$22,687	$32,192
25					
26	Paid-in Capital	$70,000	$70,000	$70,000	$70,000
27	Retained Earnings	($5,100)	($5,100)	($5,100)	($5,100)
28	Earnings	$0	($17,215)	($35,790)	($51,296)
29	Total Capital	$64,900	$47,685	$29,110	$13,604
30	Total Liabilities and Capital	$84,900	$70,392	$51,797	$45,795
31	Net Worth	$64,900	$47,685	$29,110	$13,604

The Balance Sheet lets you estimate balances for the three key items—Accounts Receivable, Inventory, and Accounts Payable—and gets the rest of its numbers from links to other tables.

 TIPS

The Cash Pilot Alternative

In the PREMIER version, you have the option of using the Cash Pilot to estimate these same three items: receivables, inventory, and payables.

?

To Learn More About...	Search the Help Index for...
Easy estimates for receivables, payables, inventory	Cash Pilot Table (*PREMIER version*)

Estimating Accounts Receivable

You can look in the edit bar in Figure 6-10 to see the default formula for Accounts Receivable in the third month, which is cell E6, the cell selected. The formula for that cell is:

$$=sales\_on\_credit+Assumptions!D11$$

You can use the Formula Backstep facility to see what the phrase "Assumptions!D11" stands for. It is a reference to cell D11 in the General Assumptions table, which is the sales on credit for the previous month. Therefore, the relatively simple Accounts Receivable estimate assumes the company has the last two months of sales on credit in its receivables at any time. This is equivalent to waiting two months to get paid, a conservative assumption.

And, of course, you can also use Formula Backstep to check the meaning of "sales_on_credit." That important number is in your General Assumptions table, where it is the result of multiplying your sales times your assumption for percent sales on credit.

The formula for the very first month is irrelevant in this example, but for the record, in the first month the default formula has to change because it does not have data for previous sales on credit by month. In a start-up company this rarely matters; for an ongoing company the default formula takes half of the starting receivables in the first month, and the remainder in the second month.

To calculate annual receivables, the default formula establishes the mathematical relationship between total sales on credit in the first year and the ending balance of receivables, and applies that relationship to the next year's sales on credit.

Remember, this is just an educated guess. You do not harm your business plan in any way by replacing this with your own guess, if you believe your own data is more accurate. All the cash flow assumptions and the rest of the financials still work correctly, whether or not you keep the original receivables formula.

For example, one change you might decide to make would replace the formula in E6 with the more simple one-month receivables formula, which is simply:

$$=sales\_on\_credit$$

A company that gets paid exactly one month after delivering its invoices always has its current month sales on credit as the ending balance for that month. This simple change improves your estimated cash flow, by reducing the amount of receivables to finance.

You can follow this logic to make your estimated receivables roughly equivalent to whatever you want them to be. For another example, make the formula for E6:

$$=sales\_on\_credit+(.5*Assumptions!D11)$$

... and with that you have approximately 45 days of sales on credit in receivables. If you follow that logic, you can imagine how to adjust this formula however you want. Furthermore, there is no need to follow that logic either; you can also just type your direct estimates into the balance sheet row.

Of course whatever adjustments you make, you need to copy into multiple columns using the Copy and Paste commands in the Table Edit menu.

However, is it accurate? Does your company really get paid in one month? That is the critical question, and it is not related to mathematical formulas. If you are an ongoing company, you have real results to analyze, and your Past Performance table helps. If you are a start-up, you have to make an educated guess. If you know your industry well or you can talk to people now in the same business, they may be able to help you make a good estimate.

FIGURE 6-10: RECEIVABLES ESTIMATOR FORMULA

E6	=sales_on_credit+Assumptions!D11				
	A	**B**	**C**	**D**	**E**
4	Current Assets	Starting Balances	Jan	Feb	Mar
5	Cash	$61,900	$48,642	$31,297	$20,801
6	Accounts Receivable	$0	$0	$0	$1,049

The formula for March Accounts Receivables shows in the edit bar in this illustration.

TIPS   Educated Guesses on Three Critical Rows

Default formulas assume that your company pays its bills in a month, but gets paid for invoices in two months, and has about 10% more inventory than cost of goods sold. These are just educated guesses. Those formulas are unprotected so that you can change them. Type your own estimates directly, or use your own formulas. This is not math or financial dogma, it is just a good guess.

Estimating Inventory

The default formula for inventory is quite simple, and one that you may well want to override with your own estimate. Figure 6-11 shows the standard formula in cell F7 in the example. The formula is:

$$=IF(E7-cost\_of\_unit\_sales>0,E7-cost\_of\_unit\_sales,1.1*cost\_of\_unit\_sales)$$

FIGURE 6-11: INVENTORY ESTIMATOR FORMULA

F7	=IF(E7-cost_of_unit_sales>0,E7-cost_of_unit_sales,1.1*cost_of_unit_sales)				
	A	C	D	E	F
4	Current Assets	Jan	Feb	Mar	Apr
5	Cash	$48,642	$31,297	$20,801	$6,604
6	Accounts Receivable	$0	$0	$1,049	$2,885
7	Inventory	$500	$500	$5,195	$9,086

The standard inventory estimator formula is an educated guess. You can replace it with your own estimate or your own formula.

We can look at this formula in detail:

- The phrase "cost_of_unit_sales" comes from your sales forecast. It represents the inventory included in cost of goods sold, or cost of sales.
- The =IF Function is a good example of built-in Excel-compatible spreadsheet functions. For more detail, search your Help Index for "=IF Function" or refer to the advanced programming instructions in Chapter 10: Advanced Tables of this manual. The function checks whether or not the previous inventory balance (in cell E7) was greater than the current month's cost of sales. This is an Excel-compatible, standard spreadsheet function. The first portion, before the first comma, is called a logical test. If that test is true (meaning that the amount in E7 less inventory usage is greater than 0), then the formula processes the second portion, between the first comma and the second. If the test is not true, then the formula processes the final portion, after the second comma.
- Therefore, if the previous period's ending inventory is greater than inventory in cost of sales, the formula simply subtracts that amount from inventory. In other words, if the previous inventory was enough for this month's sales, the formula just subtracts that amount from inventory.
- Also, if the previous inventory was not more than this period's inventory use, then the formula makes the ending balance the same as this month's use plus an additional 10% (**1.1** in the example). This is not high finance or complex mathematics, it is just a way to estimate ending inventory.

To calculate annual inventory, the default formula establishes the mathematical relationship between direct cost of sales in the first year and the ending balance of inventory, and applies that relationship to the next year's projected direct cost of sales.

Remember, this is just an educated guess. You cannot harm your business plan in any way by replacing this with your own guess, if you believe your own data or estimates are more accurate. All the cash flow assumptions and the rest of the financials still work correctly whether or not you keep the original receivables formula.

For example, one change you might decide to make would replace the 10% in the formula in F7, Figure 6-11, with 20% (1.2), 50% (1.5), or 0. Or, for another example, you could set a minimum inventory level. Of course, whatever adjustments you make, you want to copy into multiple columns using the Copy and Paste commands in the Table Edit menu.

Estimating Accounts Payable

In Figure 6-9, the edit bar shows the formula for Accounts Payable in cell C18. The formula is simply:

$$=New\_Accounts\_Payable$$

You can use the Formula Backstep to jump to the range named "New_Accounts_Payable," or just go to the General Assumptions table to see the row named New Accounts Payable, as shown also in Figure 6-17.

What the formula ends up doing is assuming that you pay all your bills in one month, so that at the end of each month your ending balance of Accounts Payable is the same as all the new entries to Accounts Payable in that same month. The logic for this row is very much like the logic for Accounts Receivables, so you could, for example, assume payments in two months by changing the formula for D18 to:

$$=New\_Accounts\_Payable+Assumptions!C12$$

... or you could imitate payments in 45 days by making the formula:

$$=New\_Accounts\_Payable+(.5*Assumptions!C12)$$

To calculate annual Accounts Payable balances, the default formula establishes the mathematical relationship between sales in the first year and the ending balance of Accounts Payable, and applies that relationship to next year's projected sales.

Remember, this is just an educated guess. You cannot harm your business plan in any way by replacing this with your own guess, if you believe your own data or estimates are more accurate. All the cash flow assumptions and the rest of the financials still work correctly whether or not you keep the original receivables formula.

Many Balance Items Depend on Inputs in Cash Flow

Many Balance Sheet items depend completely on inputs in the Cash Flow table. For example, compare the entries in Other Current Assets in the Balance Sheet to the entries in rows related to Current Assets in the Cash Flow, which is the row named "Sales of Other Current Assets" in the upper section and "Purchase of Other Current Assets" in the lower section. What you input in Cash Flow changes the Balance Sheet. That is also true with all three of the Liability rows, and Long-term Assets as well. Amounts typed into Capital Input in Cash Flow directly affect Paid-in Capital in the Balance Sheet. Dividends in the Cash Flow subtract from Retained Earnings.

Understanding Earnings and Retained Earnings

Figure 6-12 shows how Business Plan Pro handles Retained Earnings, following standard accounting convention. The amounts in current-period earnings are moved into Retained Earnings once a year, at the end of the year.

FIGURE 6-12: RETAINED EARNINGS

Table	Balance Sheet		Full Columns					
P27	=O27+O28-dividends							
	A	B	C	N	O	P		
1	Pro Forma Balance Sheet							
2								
15								
16	Liabilities and Capital							
17	Current Liabilities		Jan	Dec	2004	2005		
18	Accounts Payable	$0	$14,464	$12,603	$12,603	$16,223		
19	Current Borrowing	$0	($1,000)	($12,000)	($12,000)	($12,000)		
20	Other Current Liabilities	$12,000	$12,000	$12,000	$12,000	$12,000		
21	Subtotal Current Liabilities	$12,000	$25,464	$12,603	$12,603	$16,223		
22								
23	Long-term Liabilities	$173,000	$172,646	$168,752	$168,752	$168,398		
24	Total Liabilities	$185,000	$198,110	$181,355	$181,355	$184,621		
25								
26	Paid-in Capital	$7,500	$7,500	$7,500	$7,500	$7,500		
27	Retained Earnings	($5,408)	($5,408)	($5,408)	($5,408)	($10,602)		
28	Earnings	$0	($8,195)	$806	$806	$22,472		
29	Total Capital	$2,092	($6,103)	$2,898	$2,898	$19,370		
30	Total Liabilities and Capital	$187,092	$192,007	$184,253	$184,253	$203,992		
31	Net Worth	$2,092	($6,103)	$2,898	$2,898	$19,370		

Some columns are hidden in order to show the starting balance, two monthly columns, and two annual balances.

In the January column, the formula adds earnings from the Starting Balance into Retained Earnings. It also subtracts any Dividends from the Cash Flow table (although in the example there are none). The formula in cell C27 is =**B27+B28-dividends** .

C27	=B27+B28-dividends					
	A	B	C	N	O	P
1	Pro Forma Balance Sheet					
2			Jan	Dec	2004	2005
27	Retained Earnings	($5,408)	($5,408)	($5,408)	($5,408)	($10,602)
28	Earnings	$0	($8,195)	$806	$806	$22,472

Retained Earnings remain unchanged throughout the rest of the year. The Earnings row accumulates earnings for the year, rather than showing the earnings of each month. That means that the Earnings shown for December include cumulative earnings from January through December. The formula for cell N28 is **=Net_profit+M28**

C27	=B27+B28-dividends				
	A	B	C	N	O	P
1	Pro Forma Balance Sheet					
2			Jan	Dec	2004	2005
27	Retained Earnings	($5,408)	($5,408)	($5,408)	($5,408)	($10,602)
28	Earnings	$0	($8,195)	$806	$806	$22,472

The result of this treatment is that the Earnings shown for the year 2004 in column O, cell 28, are the total earnings for the full year. This matches normal accounting conventions for an end-of-year Balance Sheet, displaying Earnings for the full year. This is why we do not move Earnings to Retained Earnings monthly, but only at the end of the year—so your annual Balance Sheet column, which is what prints in the text of the plan, shows the full year's earnings.

The next year's Retained Earnings follows the pattern, adding previous Earnings and subtracting Dividends. The formula for cell P27, 2005 Retained Earnings, shows in the Figure 6-12 edit bar. It adds previous Earnings to Retained Earnings and subtracts Dividends.

TIPS

Retained Earnings

If you have trouble with the flow of retained earnings, remember that earnings and retained earnings are essentially the same thing...we like to see the earnings show just the last period's earnings, but the sum of the two is what's really important. And you can watch how retained earnings closes the loop on the Balance Sheet, so that Capital plus Liabilities equals Assets.

Break-even Analysis

This table lets you determine what you need to sell, monthly or annually, to cover your costs of doing business—your break-even point. Figure 6-13 shows the break-even analysis included with Business Plan Pro.

TIPS

Do the Break-even Table Twice

Do the break-even table twice: first, with educated guesses for assumptions, as part of the initial assessment, and later on, using your detailed Sales Forecast and Profit and Loss numbers. Both are valid uses.

FIGURE 6-13: BREAK-EVEN ANALYSIS

O8	=total_operating_expenses/12	
	A	**O**
1	**Break-even Analysis:**	
2	Monthly Units Break-even	38,644
3	Monthly Sales Break-even	$38,644
4		
5	**Assumptions:**	
6	Average Per-Unit Revenue	$1.00
7	Average Per-Unit Variable Cost	$0.45
8	Estimated Monthly Fixed Cost	$21,254

The Break-even table gets data from Sales Forecast and Profit and Loss; you can override formulas and type your own assumptions.

Some Built-in Problems

The break-even analysis is not our favorite analysis because:

- It is frequently mistaken for the payback period, the time it takes to recover an investment. There are variations on break-even that make some people think we have it wrong. The one we use is the most common, the most universally accepted, but not the only one possible.
- It depends on the concept of fixed costs, a hard idea to swallow. Technically, a break-even analysis defines fixed costs as those costs that would continue even if you went broke. Instead, you may want to use your regular running fixed costs, also called "burn rate", which includes payroll and normal expenses. This gives you a better insight on financial realities.
- It depends on averaging your per-unit variable cost and per-unit revenue over the whole business.

However, whether we like it or not, this table is a mainstay of financial analysis. You may choose to leave it out of your own business plan, but Business Plan Pro would not be complete without it. Although there are some other ways to do a Break-even Analysis, this is the most standard.

Developing Break-even Assumptions

The Break-even Analysis depends on three key assumptions:

- **Average per-unit sales price (per-unit revenue):** This is the price that you receive per unit of sales. Business Plan Pro gets this value from your Sales Forecast, but leaves the cell unlocked so you can change it, and type in your own assumption if you choose. For non-unit based businesses (PREMIER version only), Business Plan Pro makes the per-unit revenue $1 and puts your costs as a percent of a dollar.

  The most common question about this input relates to averaging. "How can I produce a single estimate for this when I have so many different products?" The answer to this question is that the analysis requires a single number, and if you fill in your Sales Forecast first, then Business Plan Pro calculates it for you automatically. If it makes you feel better, remember that you are not alone in this. The vast majority of businesses sell more than one item and have to average for their Break-even Analysis.

- **Average per-unit variable cost:** This is the incremental cost, or variable cost, of each unit of sales. If you manufacture goods, this is the cost of materials and production per unit. If you buy goods for resale, this is what you paid, on average, for the goods you sell. If you sell a service, this is what it costs you, per dollar of revenue or unit of service delivered, to deliver that service. Business Plan Pro gets this assumption from your Sales Forecast, but leaves the cell unlocked so you can override if you want.

  As with the previous assumption, this one also generates questions related to having to average across the whole business. Fill in your Sales Forecast and Business Plan Pro does this for you automatically.

- **Estimated Monthly Fixed Cost:** Technically, a Break-even Analysis defines fixed costs as costs that would continue even if you went broke. Instead, we recommend that you use your regular running fixed costs, including payroll and normal expenses (total monthly Operating Expenses). This gives you better insight on financial realities. For this input, if averaging and estimating is difficult, just fill in your Profit and Loss table and Business Plan Pro calculates a working fixed cost estimate automatically—it is a rough estimate, not necessarily to the exact detail level some financial analysts would want, but it provides a useful input for a conservative Break-even Analysis.

Break-even and Units-Based Forecasts (PREMIER version)

If you have a units-based forecast, the automatic formula in break-even picks up the unit assumptions from your sales forecast. Instead of setting the sales unit as 1 and picking up the percent of variable cost, it calculates the average per-unit price by dividing total sales by total units, from your sales forecast. It also calculates the average per-unit variable cost from the sales forecast, dividing total cost of sales by total units. Figure 6-14 shows an example.

FIGURE 6-14: UNITS-BASED BREAK-EVEN CALCULATIONS

O6	=IF(PS_SalesByUnits=FALSE,1,IF(total_unit_sa

	A	O
1	**Break-even Analysis:**	
2	Monthly Units Break-even	3,308
3	Monthly Sales Break-even	$38,644
4		
5	**Assumptions:**	
6	Average Per-Unit Revenue	$11.68
7	Average Per-Unit Variable Cost	$5.26
8	Estimated Monthly Fixed Cost	$21,254

The example here shows units-based break-even that Business Plan Pro PREMIER *calculates automatically, from the units-based sales forecast.*

TIPS

Formula Unlocked

This formula feature is unlocked in Business Plan Pro, so you can change it. If you want to do a simple break-even analysis as part of an initial assessment, for example, you can just type in your numbers.

Business Ratios

Figure 6-15 shows the Business Ratios table. It includes dozens of standard business ratios used and expected by bankers, financial analysis, and investors. It also includes statistical indicators for thousands of specific types of business. This information is classified and categorized by Standard Industrial Classification (SIC) codes. The data involved comes from the databases of Integra Information Systems and Bizminer, two leading providers of industry-specific economic information. This information loads automatically into the final column of the table as you set your type of industry using the Industry Profile Wizard, located on the right side of the table Instructions/Examples frame.

FIGURE 6-15: STANDARD RATIOS

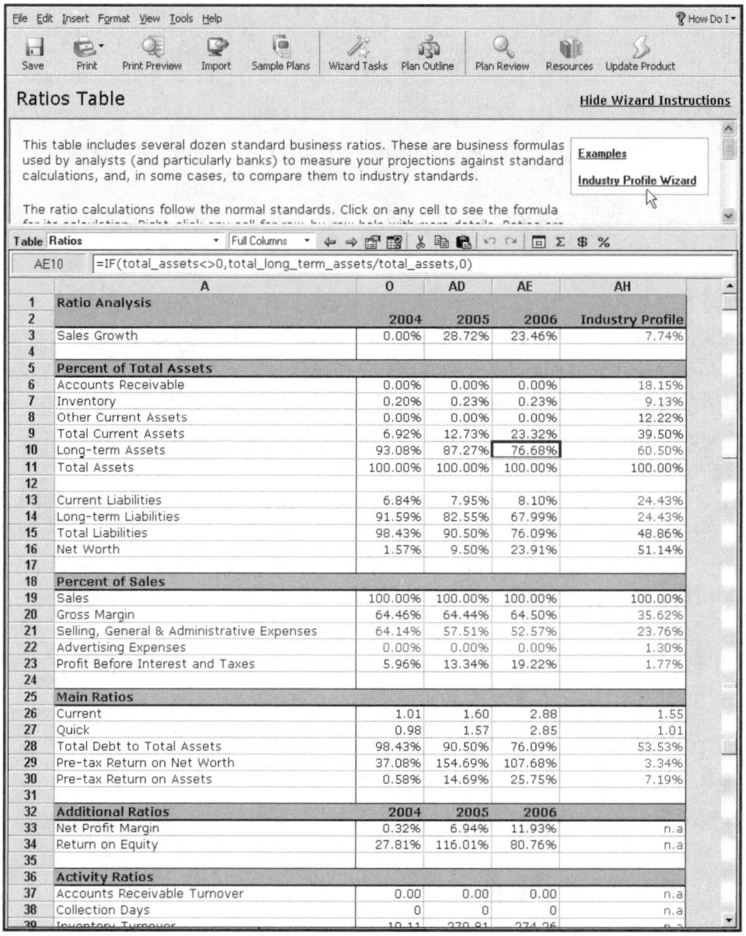

	A	O	AD	AE	AH
1	Ratio Analysis				
2		2004	2005	2006	Industry Profile
3	Sales Growth	0.00%	28.72%	23.46%	7.74%
4					
5	Percent of Total Assets				
6	Accounts Receivable	0.00%	0.00%	0.00%	18.15%
7	Inventory	0.20%	0.23%	0.23%	9.13%
8	Other Current Assets	0.00%	0.00%	0.00%	12.22%
9	Total Current Assets	6.92%	12.73%	23.32%	39.50%
10	Long-term Assets	93.08%	87.27%	76.68%	60.50%
11	Total Assets	100.00%	100.00%	100.00%	100.00%
12					
13	Current Liabilities	6.84%	7.95%	8.10%	24.43%
14	Long-term Liabilities	91.59%	82.55%	67.99%	24.43%
15	Total Liabilities	98.43%	90.50%	76.09%	48.86%
16	Net Worth	1.57%	9.50%	23.91%	51.14%
17					
18	Percent of Sales				
19	Sales	100.00%	100.00%	100.00%	100.00%
20	Gross Margin	64.46%	64.44%	64.50%	35.62%
21	Selling, General & Administrative Expenses	64.14%	57.51%	52.57%	23.76%
22	Advertising Expenses	0.00%	0.00%	0.00%	1.30%
23	Profit Before Interest and Taxes	5.96%	13.34%	19.22%	1.77%
24					
25	Main Ratios				
26	Current	1.01	1.60	2.88	1.55
27	Quick	0.98	1.57	2.85	1.01
28	Total Debt to Total Assets	98.43%	90.50%	76.09%	53.53%
29	Pre-tax Return on Net Worth	37.08%	154.69%	107.68%	3.34%
30	Pre-tax Return on Assets	0.58%	14.69%	25.75%	7.19%
31					
32	Additional Ratios	2004	2005	2006	
33	Net Profit Margin	0.32%	6.94%	11.93%	n.a
34	Return on Equity	27.81%	116.01%	80.76%	n.a
35					
36	Activity Ratios				
37	Accounts Receivable Turnover	0.00	0.00	0.00	n.a
38	Collection Days	0	0	0	n.a

Business Plan Pro *includes standard industry data for thousands of business types. The Industry Profile Wizard, located in the Instructions frame, guides you in locating your Standard Industrial Classification (SIC) code and importing your industry ratios.*

Main Ratios

- **Current**. Measures company's ability to meet financial obligations. Expressed as the number of times current assets exceed current liabilities. A high ratio indicates that a company can pay its creditors. A number less than one indicates potential cash flow problems.
- **Quick**. This ratio is very similar to the Acid Test (see below), and measures a company's ability to meet its current obligations using its most liquid assets. It shows Total Current Assets excluding Inventory divided by Total Current Liabilities.
- **Total Debt to Total Assets**. Percentage of Total Assets financed with debt.
- **Pre-Tax Return on Net Worth**. Indicates shareholders' earnings before taxes for each dollar invested. This ratio is not applicable if the subject company's net worth for the period being analyzed has a negative value.
- **Pre-Tax Return on Assets**. Indicates profit as a percentage of Total Assets before taxes. Measures a company's ability to manage and allocate resources.

Additional Ratios

- **Net Profit Margin**. This ratio is calculated by dividing Sales into the Net Profit, expressed as a percentage.
- **Return on Equity**. This ratio is calculated by dividing Net Profit by Net Worth, expressed as a percentage.

Activity Ratios

- **Accounts Receivable Turnover**. This ratio is calculated by dividing Sales on Credit by Accounts Receivable. This is a measure of how well your business collects its debts.
- **Collection Days**. This ratio is calculated by multiplying Accounts Receivable by 360, which is then divided by annual Sales on Credit. Generally, 30 days is exceptionally good, 60 days is bothersome, and 90 days or more is a real problem.
- **Inventory Turnover**. This ratio is calculated by dividing the Cost of Sales by the average Inventory balance.
- **Accounts Payable Turnover**. This ratio is a measure of how quickly the business pays its bills. It divides the total new Accounts Payable for the year by the average Accounts Payable balance.
- **Payment Days**. This ratio is calculated by multiplying average Accounts Payable by 360, which is then divided by new Accounts Payable.
- **Total Asset Turnover**. This ratio is calculated by dividing Sales by Total Assets.

Debt Ratios

- **Debt to Net Worth**. This ratio is calculated by dividing Total Liabilities by total Net Worth.
- **Current Liab. to Liab**. This ratio is calculated by dividing Current Liabilities by Total Liabilities.

Liquidity Ratios

- **Net Working Capital.** This ratio is calculated by subtracting Current Liabilities from Current Assets. This is another measure of cash position.
- **Interest Coverage.** This ratio is calculated by dividing Profits Before Interest and Taxes by total Interest Expense.

Additional Ratios

- **Assets to Sales.** This ratio is calculated by dividing Assets by Sales.
- **Current Debt/Total Assets.** This ratio is calculated by dividing Total Assets by Current Liabilities.
- **Acid Test.** This ratio is calculated by dividing Current Liabilities by Current Assets (excluding Inventory and Accounts Receivable).
- **Sales/Net Worth.** This ratio is calculated by dividing Total Sales by Net Worth.
- **Dividend Payout.** This ratio is calculated by dividing Dividends by Net Profit.

TIPS

Ratios

In the real world, financial profile information involves some compromise. Very few organizations fit any one profile exactly. Variations, such as doing several types of business under one roof, are quite common. If you cannot find a classification that fits your business exactly, use the closest one and explain in your text how and why your business is different from the standard.

Remember, if you do not want to include the ratios, go to the Plan Outline screen and delete that table. It is still in your plan, but not in the printed output. You can also use the Format > Row command to hide any row, so that the specific row does not show in the print.

Cash Flow

Cash Flow is simply not intuitive. Business Plan Pro is built around a powerful cash flow model that deserves detailed explanation. To understand this logic, we look at the Cash Flow table in detail, as shown in Figure 6-16. You can see how this process of adjusting income and balance works out.

FIGURE 6-16: CASH FLOW TABLE

G31	=PPMT(long_term_interest_rate/12,plan_month,60,20000)*-1			
	A	F	G	H	I
1	Pro Forma Cash Flow	Apr	May	Jun	Jul
2					
3	**Cash Received**				
4	Cash from Operations:				
5	Cash Sales	$16,520	$19,170	$22,517	$24,385
6	Cash from Receivables	$0	$1,049	$1,836	$2,130
7	Subtotal Cash from Operations	$16,520	$20,220	$24,352	$26,515
8					
9	Additional Cash Received				
10	Non Operating (Other) Income	$0	$0	$0	$0
11	Sales Tax, VAT, HST/GST Received	$0	$0	$0	$0
12	New Current Borrowing	$0	$10,000	$0	$0
13	New Other Liabilities (interest-free)	$0	$0	$0	$0
14	New Long-term Liabilities	$0	$0	$0	$0
15	Sales of Other Current Assets	$0	$0	$0	$0
16	Sales of Long-term Assets	$0	$0	$0	$0
17	New Investment Received	$0	$0	$25,000	$0
18	Subtotal Cash Received	$16,520	$30,220	$49,352	$26,515
20	**Expenditures**	Apr	May	Jun	Jul
21	Expenditures from Operations:				
22	Cash Spending	$17,480	$17,480	$17,480	$17,480
23	Payment of Accounts Payable	$12,973	$15,857	$14,861	$16,905
24	Subtotal Spent on Operations	$30,453	$33,337	$32,341	$34,385
25					
26	Additional Cash Spent				
27	Non Operating (Other) Expense	$0	$0	$0	$0
28	Sales Tax, VAT, HST/GST Paid Out	$0	$0	$0	$0
29	Principal Repayment of Current Borrowing	$0	$778	$787	$797
30	Other Liabilities Principal Repayment	$0	$0	$0	$0
31	Long-term Liabilities Principal Repayment	$265	$267	$269	$271
32	Purchase Other Current Assets	$0	$0	$0	$0
33	Purchase Long-term Assets	$0	$0	$0	$0
34	Dividends	$0	$0	$0	$0
35	Subtotal Cash Spent	$30,718	$34,381	$33,397	$35,453
36					
37	**Net Cash Flow**	($14,197)	($4,161)	$15,955	($8,938)
38	Cash Balance	$6,604	$2,443	$18,398	$9,460

The Cash Flow table focuses on money flowing in and out of the business, regardless of profits or losses.

Cash Flow Logic

The logic of the cash flow follows its format. It starts with items that generate cash, first from regular operations, then from balance-related items such as new loans and new investment. Then it plans items that cost cash, including normal payments in cash and payments of accounts payable, loan repayment, and investing in new assets. Cash in less cash out equals cash flow, and last month's balance plus this month's cash flow equals this month's ending balance.

The math is simple, and the logic is simple, but the concepts are not. Cash Flow is not intuitive. We strongly recommend reading **Hurdle: the Book on Business Planning** (included with Business Plan Pro) Chapters 13-16, a summary of basic business numbers, and the critical importance of cash and cash flow.

> **TIPS**
>
> ### More on Cash Flow in Hurdle: The Book on Business Planning
> Make sure you read the *About Business Numbers* and *Cash Is King* sections of your Hurdle book, which explains this in greater detail. Click the Resources button on the toolbar, then Books > Hurdle to read the book in PDF format.

Profits vs. Cash

Several of the most important elements of the Business Plan Pro cash model are explained in greater detail in the *Cash is King* chapter of the Hurdle book. This chapter provides a few key points that are important to understand:

- "Cash" in a business plan is not bills and coins; it is checking account balance. It includes liquid securities. It is the most vital resource in your business.
- Changes in balance items can have a huge impact on your cash flow. Companies can and do go broke while making profits. If all your cash is in inventory and accounts receivable, for example, you can be broke and profitable at the same time.

Critical Factors

Here are concrete steps involved in developing your cash flow projection. First, finish up initial drafts of Sales Forecast, Personnel Plan, and Profit and Loss—you may well change those again later, but you need to have good initial estimates before going to cash. Then continue with the following steps:

1. Estimate Cash Spending. This happens in the row named "Cash Spending." Most businesses pay for relatively few things in cash, putting most of their purchases into Accounts Payable (money owed and waiting to be paid) where they wait for a month or so before payment. As you reach the Cash Flow table, you first estimate payments in cash in the row named "Cash Spending." The default formula assumes payroll is always paid immediately, instead of waiting in Accounts Payable. That formula is:

=payroll_expenses

You can use Formula Backstep to find where Payroll Expenses are, or simply go to your General Assumptions table to see the row in that table.

?	To Learn More About...	Search the Help Index for...
	Find source of table formula components	Formula Backstep

Many companies pay additional amounts in cash beyond payroll, but that is up to you. You can make an educated guess or, if you have business history, look at past results. For example, if you suspect you will pay payroll plus an additional $1,000 per month as cash spending, then the formula for that might be:

$$=payroll\_expenses+1000$$

2. Review payments of Accounts Payable. The line below "Cash Spending" calculates your payments of Accounts Payable based on the estimated balance of Accounts Payable (in the Balance Sheet) plus the calculated "New Accounts Payable" (in your General Assumptions table), calculated automatically from assumptions elsewhere.

TIPS

Important: Payments of Accounts Payable Should Never be Negative

If Payments of Accounts Payable is negative, then either your estimated Cash Spending or your estimated Accounts Payable balance is too high. You must revise one or both of these assumptions to correct the negative payments assumption, which is illogical. You can use the Edit > Formula Reset command to correct erroneous assumptions, and restore the original formulas.

3. Review Cash Sales. Business Plan Pro calculates the row named "Cash Sales" by subtracting "Sales on Credit" from Sales. Sales on Credit is one of the information items in your General Assumptions table, the result of multiplying sales times the sales on credit percentage in that same table. Cash sales go straight to your cash flow.

4. If your plan settings include sales on credit, review Cash from Receivables. Most businesses that sell to other businesses sell on credit, meaning that they deliver goods and services to their business customers along with an invoice to be paid. Business customers are supposed to pay those invoices in 30 days (in most cases), and some do, but many pay in 45 days, 60 days, or more. The amounts of money waiting to be paid by customers are called Accounts Receivable, or, in this case, "Receivables." The average wait time is called collection days. These are important concepts, because your sales have been made, profits are calculated for Profit and Loss, but the money is not in the bank. Business Plan Pro calculates Cash from Receivables based on your Sales on Credit and your estimated balance of Accounts Receivable in the Balance Sheet.

> **TIPS** **Important: Cash From Receivables Should Never be Negative**
>
> If Cash from Receivables is negative, then your estimated Accounts Receivable balance in the Balance Sheet is too high for the amount of sales on credit. Go back to the Balance Sheet and reduce the estimated Receivables. A negative balance is illogical. You can use the Edit > Formula Reset command to correct erroneous assumptions restore the original formulas.

5. If your plan settings include inventory, review Inventory. Although Inventory does not show up directly in Cash Flow, unrealistic inventory estimates affect cash flow through the payables estimates. Check the Inventory balance in the Balance Sheet to make sure that it is always a positive number. Then check the purchase of new Inventory in the General Assumptions, which Business Plan Pro calculates using your direct cost of goods sold and your estimated inventory balance. It should never be a negative number.

> **TIPS** **Important: Inventory Purchase Should Never be Negative**
>
> If inventory purchase is negative, your estimated inventory balance is too low. You must revise this assumption to correct the negative purchase, which is illogical. You can use the Edit > Formula Reset command to correct erroneous assumptions restore the original formulas.

6. Is your cash balance negative? Then you have to generate more cash by borrowing money or bringing in new investment, or even selling assets—in the upper middle section of the Cash Flow. If you are a start-up company, and cash flow is negative, you can also revise your Start-up table to estimate higher initial loans or investment, to raise your starting cash.

    In the example shown in Figure 6-16, the pizza restaurant needed to borrow $10,000 in May and add $25,000 in new investment in June to keep its checking account balance (which is what we call Cash) above zero. As the plan was developed, initial investment did not fully cover cash needs, so the plan had to stipulate new loans and new investment to make the cash plan viable. They might also have increased the amount of initial investment, or borrowed more money initially.

Cash vs. Profits

Although the following rules do not make sense in every case, with the way the numbers work, accept these rules:

*   Every dollar of increase in your accounts receivable means one dollar less of cash. If you do not believe that, pull a dollar out of your wallet and loan it to a friend.
*   Every dollar of increase in accounts payable means an additional dollar of cash. If you do not believe that, pay a dollar less of your bills than you otherwise would have. You have an extra dollar each in payables, and in cash.
*   Every dollar of increase in inventory means a dollar less of cash. Sure, that can be cancelled by a dollar of increase in accounts payable, but you get the point.

How can this be? Simple logic. The cash flow table starts with net income. The income statement assumes that you paid for all your costs and expenses, and you received all of your sales, because it ignores balance sheet items such as accounts receivable or accounts payable. Therefore, the changes in balance items mean changes in cash.

Timing Distinguishes Cash Flow vs. Start-up

Most of the items in the Cash Flow table, including loans and assets, are the same concepts as in start-up assets and start-up financing in the Start-up table. The difference is timing. If the new loan or asset purchase happens during or after the first month of the plan, it belongs in the Cash Flow. If it happens before the first month, it belongs in the Start-up table.

Handling of Loans, Interest, and Repayment

Business Plan Pro handles loans, interest, and repayment following standard accounting convention.

- New loans go into the Cash Flow table in the upper section as sources of cash.
- Interest, which is an expense deductible against income, goes into the Profit and Loss statement. Business Plan Pro calculates interest automatically.
- Principal repayments go into the Cash Flow table in the lower section, as uses of cash.

Some people are confused by the concept of separating the payment into interest and principal. A common example, at least in the United States, is if you have a mortgage to pay.

Most lending institutions clearly separate payments into interest and principal components. Even if you write a single check each month to repay the mortgage loan, the payment is divided into interest and principal.

TIPS

Repayment Schedule

If you do not have documentation on repayments, your local bank, a standard financial worksheet, or even a financial calculator can give you the detailed repayment schedule to use with Business Plan Pro.

If you understand how to program spreadsheet formulas, you can also use the built-in Principal Payments function (PPMT). An example is provided in the **Expanded Principal Payments Formula** section.

Expanded Principal Payments Formula

Business Plan Pro also has built-in financial functions you can use to calculate loan payments. Here again, the normal expectation is that because this is planning, not accounting, you do not need to do that in this much detail. However, you can use this function if you want, and it can make sense when the numbers are very large.

This formula uses the Principal Payments (PPMT) function, which calculates monthly principal payments for a loan. The PPMT function syntax specifies:

=PPMT(interest rate, payment #, total payments, loan amount)

Figure 6-16 shows this function in use for the calculation of principal repayments of long-term debt. In that illustration, the edit bar shows the PPMT function as applied to cell G31, the selected cell. That formula is:

=PPMT(long_term_interest_rate/12,Plan_Month,60,20000)*-1

- Long_term_interest_rate/12 sets the interest rate. The range "long_term_interest_rate" contains the annual interest rate, and the formula divides it by 12. The source of this information is in your General Assumptions table.
- Plan Month establishes that this is the second payment of 60 total payments.
- 60 is the number of payments. This is specific information for your loan, your business situation. In this example, the loan involved is for five-year terms.
- 20000 is the amount of the loan principal. You can see that number started with the Start-up table.
- *-1 is because you need to make the result a positive number. It is normally negative because it is a cash flow function indicating money out, not in; but in the cash flow table, a payment shows up as a positive number.

> **TIPS**
>
> ### The Sources and Uses of Cash Statement
>
> The Business Plan Pro Cash Flow table includes all the information you need to produce what accountants call the "Sources and Uses of Cash" statement. It does not produce that statement, however, because it does not know ahead of time which items are sources, and which are uses.
>
> Accounts Payable, for example, is a source of cash if the balance increases over the year, and a use of cash if the balance decreases.

Cash-Sensitive Assumptions

The cash projections of a normal business depend especially on three key factors:

- **Accounts Receivable**, which you estimate directly in your Balance Sheet, and depends on that estimate plus sales on credit assumptions. If you do not set your plan for sales on credit, then Accounts Receivable are set to 0 and do not show. If you do have sales on credit, Accounts Receivable is in your Balance Sheet with a default estimation formula you can change if you need to. If Cash from Receivables turns negative, you must revise the balance estimate.
- **Inventory**, which you estimate directly in your Balance Sheet. If you do not have your plan set for inventory, in the plan settings, then Business Plan Pro hides the inventory and sets

the balance to 0. If you do have inventory, then Inventory is in your Balance Sheet with a default estimation formula you can change if you need to. If new inventory purchase (in General Assumptions) turns negative, you must revise the inventory balance estimate.

- **Payables**, which you estimate directly in your Balance Sheet. If Payments of Payables in Cash Flow is negative, you must revise the Payables estimate in the Balance Sheet.

Although your cash flow normally includes many other rows and assumptions, these three lines in the Balance Sheet drive your projected cash flow up or down more than most other elements. Recognizing how these balances influence the cash flow, the Business Plan Pro cash methodology uses the balance predictors to calculate the cash flow as a result of the balances.

TIPS

Cash Balance as Summary instead of Detail

Because a business plan needs to summarize instead of exploding into detail, Business Plan Pro ignores the subtle differences between cash, checking, and liquid securities.

However, you can show interest income in the Extraordinary Items row at the bottom of the Profit and Loss.

General Assumptions

The General Assumptions table, Figure 6-17, keeps track of important assumptions that affect the rest of your financials. These assumptions affect your profit and loss, balance sheet, personnel costs, cash flow, business ratios, and benchmarks chart. You can use this table to revise your assumptions whenever you have to.

This table also includes a row labeled "Other," which you can use for any other assumption you want to add to your own business plan. You can select that row and use the Insert Row command in the Edit menu to add additional rows, for additional assumptions. For example, some business plans include monthly or annual growth rates for sales and expenses, such as the "power variables" explained in detail in Chapter 10.

This table also has a set of calculated totals included, not to print out as part of your plan document, but rather, for your information because they are used in other formulas in other tables. Payroll expense, for example, is included in the default formula for Cash Spending in your Cash Flow table. None of these calculated totals print automatically, as part of the General Assumptions table, when you produce the plan document. You can print them directly from the table printing mode if you want.

FIGURE 6-17: GENERAL ASSUMPTIONS

M5	=L5					
	A	L	M	N	O	P	Q
1	General Assumptions						
2		Oct	Nov	Dec	2004	2005	2006
3	Plan Month	10	11	12	1	2	3
4	Current Interest Rate	10.00%	10.00%	10.00%	10.00%	10.00%	10.00%
5	Long-term Interest Rate	10.00%	10.00%	10.00%	10.00%	10.00%	10.00%
6	Tax Rate	30.00%	30.00%	30.00%	30.00%	5.00%	5.00%
7	Sales on Credit %	10.00%	10.00%	10.00%	10.00%	10.00%	10.00%
8	Other	0.00%	0.00%	0.00%	0.00%	0.00%	0.00%
9	Calculated Totals						
10	Payroll Expense	$16,480	$16,480	$16,480	$188,912	$241,680	$250,164
11	Sales on Credit	$3,617	$3,988	$3,992	$27,942	$70,730	$77,061
12	New Accounts Payable	$22,754	$24,427	$4,639	$181,153	$389,750	$420,490
13	Inventory Purchase	$18,115	$19,789	$0	$127,016	$321,010	$347,176

The General Assumptions table sets assumptions that affect several other tables.

Current vs. Long-term Interest Rates

Standard accounting makes an arbitrary division between current (also called short-term) assets and liabilities and long-term assets and liabilities. Long-term assets are also called capital assets, fixed assets, and plant and equipment. The idea behind this division is establishing a difference on how long such assets and liabilities last. The division between long-term and current liabilities might be three, five, or ten years. Each company makes its own decision, usually in agreement with financial management and accountants. You can make that decision yourself or ask an accountant. If you are just starting a new business, and have no idea, then make the division five years: assets or liabilities that last longer than five years are long term.

TIPS

An Unprotected Formula?

Figure 6-17 shows the spreadsheet formula for Long-term Interest Rate programming of the formula in cell M5, which is showing in the edit bar. This is a good example of how Business Plan Pro sometimes gives you program formulas that are not protected, and can be changed. It is a green cell, unlocked, and changeable. Our formula simplifies data entry for you by making all the cells refer to the cell to the left, so when you change the assumption for the starting month, you change all the others. This can be modified by your own programming of some other formula, or by simply typing in data.

You do not have to include the table in the printed document. The financials need these numbers, but your readers might not. Although interest rate and tax rate assumptions are standard, not every reader relates to them in detail, and Plan Month is obscure. Some choose to unlink this table so they do not have to explain it. You can also simply hide a row so it does not show in the printed document.

?

To Learn More About...	Search the Help Index for...
Removing a table from a topic	Plan, Outline
Masking a table row from view	Row, Format

Help For step-by-step procedures, click the dialog Help button or the Help menu.

Industry Profile

To include your industry's financial profile in your business plan:

• Go to the Ratios table Instructions/Examples frame and click on the Industry Profile Wizard link. Use the keyword search as shown in Figure 6-18.

FIGURE 6-18: INDUSTRY PROFILES - EXAMPLE

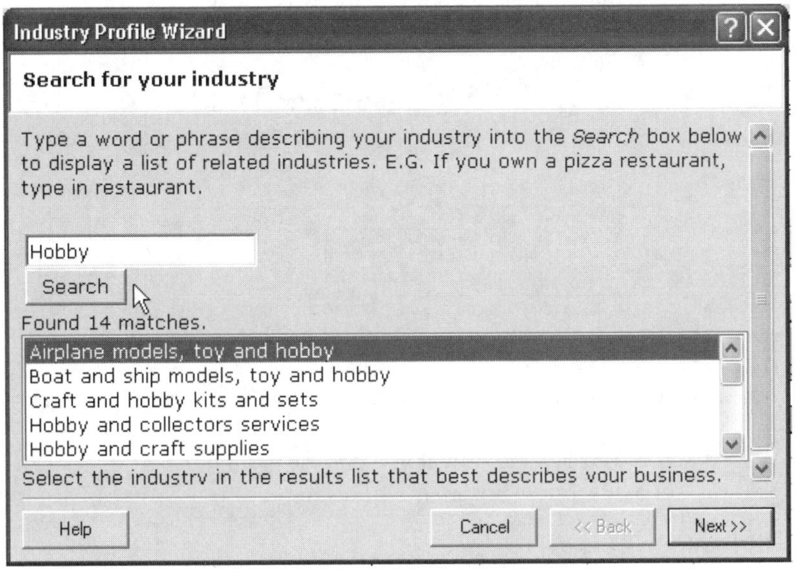

Your industry profile starts with a search for the right industry code.

FIGURE 6-19: INDUSTRY PROFILES - RESULTS

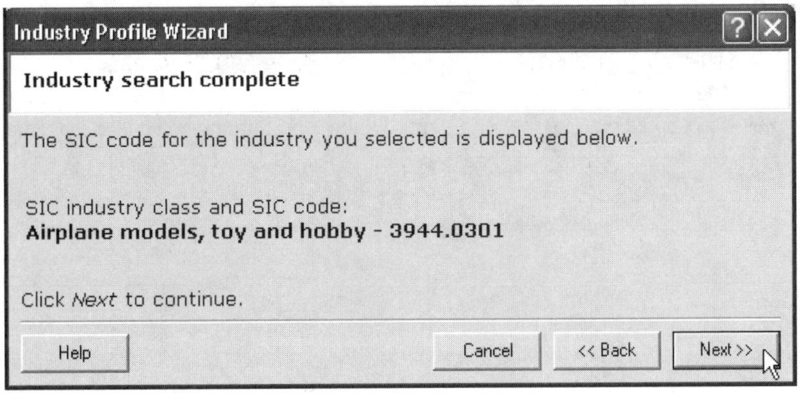

The Industry Profile Wizard gives you a SIC code and classification, and places data into your Ratios table.

Long-term

The Long-term table brings up some potential confusion about the time frames in business planning, according to Business Plan Pro. We recommend planning for the longer term. However, we do not recommend projecting detailed financials—separate Sales Forecast, Personnel Plan, Cash Flow, Balance Sheets—beyond three years. However, Business Plan Pro does allow for these detailed financials through five years, because users have asked for that. Furthermore, it also offers a macro-view plan for as many as 10 years, in the Long-term table shown in Figure 6-20.

FIGURE 6-20: LONG-TERM TABLE

Long-term	2004	2005	2006	2007	2008	2009	2010	2011	2012	2013
Sales	$6,468,631	$7,478,240	$9,182,745	$11,230,819	$14,184,120	$15,310,000	$16,140,000	$16,670,000	$16,970,000	$17,140,000
Cost of Sales	$4,847,513	$5,517,550	$6,425,184	$7,323,806	$8,777,099	$9,780,000	$10,360,000	$10,940,000	$11,390,000	$11,640,000
Gross Margin	$1,621,118	$1,960,690	$2,757,561	$3,907,012	$5,407,022	$5,530,000	$5,780,000	$5,730,000	$5,580,000	$5,500,000
Gross Margin %	25.06%	26.22%	30.03%	34.79%	38.12%	36.12%	35.81%	34.37%	32.88%	32.09%
Operating Expenses	$1,146,502	$1,370,462	$1,654,255	$2,023,212	$2,555,244	$2,758,069	$2,907,592	$3,003,071	$3,057,115	$3,087,740
Operating Income	$474,616	$590,228	$1,103,306	$1,883,800	$2,851,778	$2,771,931	$2,872,408	$2,726,929	$2,522,885	$2,412,260
Net Income	$348,450	$426,318	$839,958	$1,130,280	$1,711,067	$1,663,159	$1,723,445	$1,636,158	$1,513,731	$1,447,356
Current Assets	$2,389,696	$2,642,345	$3,198,015	$3,911,285	$4,939,812	$5,331,915	$5,620,974	$5,805,554	$5,910,033	$5,969,238
Long-term Assets	$377,093	$563,778	$949,797	$1,161,635	$1,467,103	$1,583,556	$1,669,405	$1,724,225	$1,755,255	$1,772,838
Current Liabilities	$1,257,528	$1,295,544	$1,465,759	$1,792,675	$2,264,084	$2,443,798	$2,576,283	$2,660,882	$2,708,769	$2,735,904
Long-term Liabilities	$348,154	$323,154	$254,670	$311,470	$393,376	$424,600	$447,619	$462,318	$470,638	$475,353
Equity	$1,161,107	$1,587,425	$2,427,383	$2,968,775	$3,749,456	$4,047,073	$4,266,477	$4,406,578	$4,485,881	$4,530,819

With the Long-term plan you can extend your financial assumptions out to 10 years.

The EasyPlan Wizard activates this table only if you choose certain expert options. If you choose to use it, then you can set assumptions for main financial indicators—you can see them in the illustration—for up to 10 years.

- The black cells in the Long-term table automatically pick up information for the first five years, if you have that in your plan. Years 6-10 are green (unlocked) so you can add your data.

TIPS

Do You Really Need This?

The fact that a table like this is included with Business Plan Pro does not mean that you need it. It is available for the special cases; most business plans do not need to go into this much detail for 10 years.

Yes, you should plan for the long term, but the long-term planning is more conceptual and less detailed.

Market Analysis

In Business Plan Pro, Market Analysis looks at the total potential market, usually divided into segments. Normally this is total potential market, not total actual customers. This is a market forecast and not a sales forecast, so it should focus not on customers you already sell to, and not on the portion of the total market you expect to sell to, but rather on the whole market.

For example, in the sample market analysis shown in Figure 6-21, the total market is 67,000 possible customers in 2004. The sample comes from a pizza restaurant, and the total potential market in this case is the total population of a local community. As you can see in the illustration, that includes several thousand college students, single individuals, and families. Normally the accompanying text in the plan has to explain the segmentation scheme, why and how the potential market groups are divided.

FIGURE 6-21: MARKET ANALYSIS

H4	$=(G4/C4)^{\wedge}(1/4)-1$							
	A	B	C	D	E	F	G	H
1	Market Analysis							
2	Potential Customers	Growth	2004	2005	2006	2007	2008	CAGR
3	University students	2.00%	17,000	17,340	17,687	18,041	18,402	2.00%
4	Single adults	5.00%	22,000	23,100	24,255	25,468	26,741	5.00%
5	Families	3.50%	28,000	28,980	29,994	31,044	32,131	3.50%
6	Total	3.63%	67,000	69,420	71,936	74,553	77,274	3.63%

The Market Analysis table estimates potential customers, not actual customers.

TIPS

No Fewer Than Two Rows

In the Market Forecast table, you cannot have fewer than two rows. The logic involves **SUM** formulas that need to have a top row and a bottom row.

If you need to delete a row, delete the middle row of the three starting rows.

Potential Customers, not Actual Customers

The Market Analysis normally shows potential customers, not actual customers. It indicates the size of the whole market, not your share of it. In the example here, the pizza restaurant's potential market is the whole adult population, including students, singles, and families. It is not just the subset of the population that goes to this restaurant, or that likes pizza. It is not the actual customers, or the served market, it is the potential market.

Growth Rates

You can change the market analysis if you want, because formulas are not protected, but normally it works by setting a starting population for the present year (the first year of the plan) in the third column, and a growth rate in the second column. The growth rate automatically applies to the second through the fifth year, using automatic formulas, unless you type over those formulas and replace them with either your own estimates, or a different formula. Type the starting market number as a number, and the growth rate as a percent value.

Compound Average Growth Rate (CAGR)

The CAGR is a standard formula which counts only the first and final values, without regard to the intervening values. The Market Analysis table uses the compound average growth rate (CAGR) formulas to determine the average growth rate. The formula is:

$$CAGR = (last/first)^{(1/years)}-1$$

In the example in Figure 6-21, there are four years of growth. In this forecast the growth years are 2005, 2006, 2007, and 2008. So in cell H4 for example, the CAGR portion of the formula in that cell is =(G4/C4)^(1/4)-1 .

TIPS

Market Research and Market Forecasting in Hurdle: The Book on Business Planning

Make sure you read the *Gathering Information and Forecasting* sections of your Hurdle book, which explain this in greater detail. Use the Tools > Resources > Books > Hurdle link to read the book in PDF format.

Inserting and Deleting Rows

Rows can be inserted within the middle section of the Market Analysis table. Use the Edit > Insert Row option. You cannot delete the top or bottom rows of this table because of the underlying SUM formulas. You can, however, transfer data from any middle row to the top or bottom, then delete that middle row.

?

To Learn More About...	Search the Help Index for...
Adding rows to a table	Table, Insert Rows
Removing rows from a table	Delete, Data Entry Rows

Unprotected Formulas

Figure 6-22 shows the formula for column D. It calculates this second-year value using simple math from the first-year value and the growth rate assumption in column B. In this table, the unprotected formula calculates an estimation for the second through the fifth year if you type in values for the first year and the growth rate.

This is an excellent example of an unprotected formula. It is there for your convenience, but not required. If you type in data and assumptions on your own, you can overwrite the formulas to create a different growth pattern.

TIPS

Watch for Unprotected Formulas

The Market Analysis table is full of formulas that are not protected, which means that you can use them if you want, but it is not required. Instead of accepting a steady growth rate, you can just type year-by-year assumptions.

In Figure 6-22, the row labeled "Straight" is built using the programmed growth formulas. Each column represents 78 percent growth from the previous year. In the row labeled "Natural," in contrast, although the growth to 2008 is the same, none of the intervening columns follows the "Straight" row. All of the values were typed into the cells as estimates, changing the formula.

FIGURE 6-22: STRAIGHT LINE VS. ESTIMATED MARKET GROWTH

D3	=ROUND(C3*(1+$B3),0)							
	A	B	C	D	E	F	G	H
1	Market Analysis							
2	Potential Customers	Growth	2004	2005	2006	2007	2008	CAGR
3	Straight	78%	1,000	1,780	3,168	5,639	10,000	77.83%
4	Natural	78%	1,000	5,400	7,700	9,300	10,000	77.83%
5	Total	77.83%	2,000	7,180	10,868	14,939	20,000	77.83%

Both examples have the same final growth rate, but the numbers are very different.

In this case, it is important to treat the growth rate in column B, cell B4, as we did for the example. By making its growth rate equal to the growth in the last column, we avoid a logical contradiction. The overall growth rate is what's shown in column H, the CAGR column.

In Figure 6-23 you can see how different the two forecasts are. The "Straight" forecast line curves up with a steady increase. The "Natural" forecast line is growing faster at first and then slower later on. Notice that both forecasts get to the same endpoint, and they both have the same growth rate for the full period.

FIGURE 6-23: THE MARKET CONTRAST

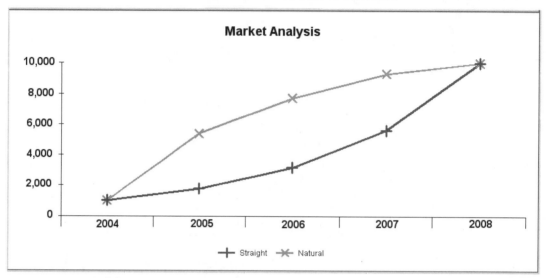

Both lines have the same 5-year growth rate, but very different numbers.

Milestones

The Milestones table is one of the most important in your business plan. It sets the plan into practical, concrete terms, with real budgets, deadlines, and management responsibilities. Please be sure to read the Planning for Implementation chapter of the Hurdle book. That chapter focuses on the Milestones table and plan-vs.-actual management as keys to making a business plan real.

The table provides you with a list of activities. Each activity is assigned a starting date, ending date, manager responsible, department responsible, and a budget. As you build your business and implement the plan, you can use the Milestones list to guide your management. Figure 6-24 shows the opening screen of the Milestones table, before entry.

FIGURE 6-24: MILESTONES TABLE

	A	B	C	D	E	F
1	Milestones					
2	Milestone	Start Date	End Date	Budget	Manager	Department
3	Name me	1/1/2003	1/15/2003	$0	ABC	Marketing
4	Name me	1/1/2003	1/15/2003	$0	ABC	Marketing
5	Name me	1/1/2003	1/15/2003	$0	ABC	Web
6	Name me	1/1/2003	1/15/2003	$0	ABC	Web
7	Name me	1/1/2003	1/15/2003	$0	ABC	Department
8	Name me	1/1/2003	1/15/2003	$0	ABC	Department
9	Name me	1/1/2003	1/15/2003	$0	ABC	Department
10	Name me	1/1/2003	1/15/2003	$0	ABC	Department
11	Name me	1/1/2003	1/15/2003	$0	ABC	Department
12	Name me	1/1/2003	1/15/2003	$0	ABC	Department
13	Totals			$0		

Table: Milestones — Full Columns — C5: 1/15/2003

Use the Edit > Row Label to give each milestone a unique name. Include starting and ending dates to track whether your goals were met during the set time frame.

Sort the Milestones

The Milestones table is the only table that sorts items. You can go to the Edit menu while on the Milestones, and the Sort command is enabled. You can sort the Milestones on Start Date, End Date, Budget, Manager, or Department. This sorting facility is intended to facilitate real management.

For example, before a meeting with all managers, sort the Milestones table by date to get all the relevant milestones for that time period. Are you on budget? On time? Do you need to make any corrections?

Sort the Milestones on Manager to highlight the activities of each manager. Figure 6-25 shows the sorting facility.

FIGURE 6-25: SORTING THE MILESTONES TABLE

Table	Milestones	▾	Full Columns	▾	⇐ ⇒							
E3	Ireneskya R											

	A	B	C	D	E	F
1	**Milestones**					
2	**Milestone**	**Start Date**	**End Date**	**Budget**	**Manager**	**Department**
3	Upgrade Mailer	3/1/2004	4/15/2004	$5,000	Ireneskya R	Sales
4	Presentations	5/1/2004	5/15/2004	$0	Ireneskya R	Sales
5	Business Plan Review	3/1/2004	4/1/2004	$0	Renaldo J	GM
6	Advertising	3/15/2004	3/30/2004	$115,000	Renaldo J	GM
7	New Accounts (3)	3/1/2004	5/10/2004	$2,500	Sally D	President
8	Service Revamp	3/1/2004	5/1/2004	$2,500	Silas G	Service
9	Direct Mail	4/15/2004	4/20/2004	$3,500	Tombaugh B	Marketing
10	Tech Expo 2004	5/10/2004	5/15/2004	$15,000	Tombaugh B	Marketing
11	Other	1/1/2004	1/1/2004	$0	Zenda P	Admin
12	**Totals**			$143,500		

The Milestones table can be sorted by any column, allowing you to analyze current performance. This illustration was sorted by Manager.

Past Performance

The EasyPlan Wizard sets each business plan as either a start-up or an ongoing company. Ongoing companies have Past Performance instead of Start-up. Either one of these tables establishes the starting balances in column B of the Balance Sheet table.

The Past Performance table is almost entirely data entry, with no important calculations. Business Plan Pro uses it for just a few objectives:

- **To set starting balances for ongoing companies.** The final column of the Past Performance table links directly into column B of the Balance Sheet.
- **For values used in the Benchmarks chart (PREMIER version) for ongoing companies.** For ongoing companies, the Benchmarks chart compares six years of business numbers, three from the past and three in the future.
- **Collection Days and Inventory Turnover Ratios offer insight into your business' critical cash flow.** We use estimators based on these ratios to project future cash. The Past Performance table gives you actual results on these indicators, from your past results. That can help you project the future. Figure 6-26 shows a sample.

Collection Days

The Collection Days indicator in Past Performance is unlocked for the first year because it does not have a previous year ending balance, so the formula is slightly off. If you have access to these numbers, you can type the correct number into the table and replace the formula. If not, then the formula is still a good estimate.

Inventory Turnover

The Inventory Turnover indicator is unlocked for all three years because the calculation is based on Cost of Sales, instead of Direct Cost of Sales. This makes it slightly incorrect, although still valuable for estimation. If you have access to the correct number from past financials, type it in.

FIGURE 6-26: PAST PERFORMANCE TABLE

	A	B	C	D
1	Past Performance			
2		2001	2002	2003
3	Sales	$3,773,889	$4,661,902	$5,301,059
4	Gross Margin	$1,189,495	$1,269,261	$1,127,568
5	Gross Margin %	31.52%	27.23%	21.27%
6	Operating Expenses	$752,083	$902,500	$1,052,917
7	Collection Period (days)	48	35	41
8	Inventory Turnover	6.88	7.97	7.41
9				
10	Balance Sheet			
11	Current Assets	2001	2002	2003
12	Cash	$23,341	$44,090	$55,432
13	Accounts Receivable	$302,738	$273,694	$395,107
14	Inventory	$375,605	$475,689	$651,012
15	Other Current Assets	$19,904	$18,956	$25,091
16	Total Current Assets	$721,588	$812,429	$1,126,642
17	Long-term Assets			
18	Capital Assets	$255,098	$289,887	$351,435
19	Accumulated Depreciation	$35,988	$42,890	$51,661
20	Total Long-term Assets	$219,110	$246,997	$299,774
21	Total Assets	$940,698	$1,059,426	$1,426,416
22				
23	Capital and Liabilities			
24		2001	2002	2003
25	Accounts Payable	$189,566	$191,854	$223,897
26	Current Borrowing	$120,000	$11,000	$90,000
27	Other Current Liabilities	$9,870	$69,659	$15,000
28	Subtotal Current Liabilities	$319,436	$272,513	$328,897
28	Subtotal Current Liabilities	$319,436	$272,513	$328,897
29				
30	Long-term Liabilities	$0	$0	$284,862
31	Total Liabilities	$319,436	$272,513	$613,759
32	Paid-in Capital	$400,000	$548,908	$500,000
33	Retained Earnings	$168,116	$221,262	$238,005
34	Earnings	$53,146	$16,743	$74,652
35	Total Capital	$621,262	$786,913	$812,657
36	Total Capital and Liabilities	$940,698	$1,059,426	$1,426,416
37				
38	Other Inputs	2001	2002	2003
39	Payment Days	21	16	16
40	Sales on Credit	$2,302,072	$2,983,617	$2,987,128
41	Receivables Turnover	7.60	10.90	7.56

The Past Performance table calculates Gross Margin and gives you an estimation of Collection Days and Inventory Turnover.

Additional Information - Past Performance

Using Your Own Statements Instead

You may have many good reasons to include your own financial statements in a business plan, instead of using the Business Plan Pro Past Performance table. You can include your financials as an appendix to your business plan. If you do that, you may choose not to print the Business Plan Pro Past Performance table as part of your plan.

The Past Performance table is linked to the Company Summary topic. If you do not want this table to print as part of your plan, you can "unlink" it from its topic. The table still exists, but it does not print.

You must fill in the final column of the Past Performance table because this provides your Balance Sheet starting balances. These items include Cash, Accounts Receivable, Inventory, Other Current Assets, Long-term Assets, Accumulated Depreciation, Accounts Payable, Current Notes, Other Current Liabilities, Long-term Liabilities, Paid-in Capital, Retained Earnings, and Earnings.

Estimating Interim Ending Balances

Owners and managers of ongoing companies frequently have to estimate ending balances for the current year, as they plan the next year. This problem comes with the process of business planning. For example, if you are in the summer of 2003, developing a plan starting in January of 2004, then you need to estimate what your final 2003 balances. Ideally you can pick up those balances from your previous year's plan.

Does this influence the values in the next year? It does, but this kind of estimation is unavoidable. This is planning, not accounting. Estimates and educated guesses are part of the process.

Personal Financial Statement

The Personal Net Worth table is not really part of a business plan. Business Plan Pro offers this table as a convenience to business owners whose business plans might be related to application for commercial bank loans. Figure 6-27 shows an example of this table.

FIGURE 6-27: PERSONAL FINANCIAL STATEMENT (NET WORTH)

Assets		
Current Assets	**Notes:**	**Balance**
Checking	Local bank account # 0000-00000	$574.03
Savings	Local bank account # 0000-00000	$2,350.00
Investment	Brokerage account # 0000-00000	$12,050.00
Household goods	Estimated	$25,000.00
Auto	2001 Chevrolet Impala	$32,000.00
Auto	1995 Ford Escort	$6,000.00
All other		$0.00
Total Current Assets		$77,974
Long-term Assets		
Main Residence	121 Elm St. Mytown, Mystate, 00000	$225,000
Improvements	Estimated	$15,000
Account		$0
All other		$0
Total Long-term Assets		$240,000
Total Assets		$240,000
Liabilities		
Current Borrowing		**Balance**
Credit card	Visa bank account # 0000-00000	$578
Credit card	Amex account # 0000-00000	$220
Credit card	Discover account # 0000-00000	$740
Auto Loan	Local bank auto loan # 0000-00000	$14,500
Other current debt		$0
Other current debt		$0
All other		$0
Subtotal Current Borrowing		$16,038
Long-term Borrowing		
Mortgage	Mortgage account # 0000-00000	$145,000
Other long-term loans		$0
All other		$0
Subtotal Long-term Borrowing		$145,000
Total Liabilities		$161,038
Net Worth		$78,962

The Personal Net Worth table shows the financial position of an individual. It is included here for business owners applying for commercial credit.

Personnel Plan

The standard Personnel Plan is a simple list with a sum at the bottom, as shown in Figure 6-28. You can list your personnel by name, as individuals, or in groups such as sales, marketing, etc.

FIGURE 6-28: STANDARD PERSONNEL PLAN

F7	=E7						
	A	C	D	E	F	G	H
5	Personnel Plan						
6		Jan	Feb	Mar	Apr	May	Jun
7	Kevin	$3,000	$3,000	$3,000	$3,000	$3,000	$3,000
8	Erika	$3,000	$3,000	$3,000	$3,000	$3,000	$3,000
9	Daryl	$6,000	$6,000	$6,000	$6,000	$6,000	$6,000
10	Other	$0	$1,120	$3,472	$4,480	$4,480	$4,480
11							
12	Total People	3	7	7	7	7	7
13	Total Payroll	$12,000	$13,120	$15,472	$16,480	$16,480	$16,480

This simple example shows a personnel plan for a start-up pizza restaurant. The total flows automatically into the Profit and Loss table as Payroll.

The example shows three people identified by their name, and four other people grouped together as "Other." You can also have groups such as "Sales staff," "Marketing team," "Retail clerks," etc. You do not need a single row for every person.

Employee Count is Simple Data Input

Total People stands for total number of employees. Business Plan Pro includes this row because many analysts consider it important, and it also contributes to the sales per employee calculation in the Ratios table. In the standard Personnel Plan and the Personnel by categories option in the PREMIER version, this row is a data entry. Business Plan Pro does not calculate employee count automatically because there is no way to know how many people are included.

In the PREMIER version Personnel by People option, because you set number of people in each of the categories, Business Plan Pro calculates the employee count for you.

More Expanded Options (PREMIER version)

In the PREMIER version, you have the choice of two more detailed Personnel Plan models:

1. **Expanded Categories.** In the PREMIER version if you choose to break your expenses into categories, you get a four-part Personnel Plan. The EasyPlan Wizard screens let you set the category names (e.g. production, marketing, administration, etc.). Figure 6-29 shows how the breakdown into categories works for the same sample pizza restaurant whose standard personnel are in Figure 6-28.

FIGURE 6-29: PERSONNEL BY CATEGORY

F38	=Payroll3P+Payroll3SM+Payroll3GA+Payroll3OTH						
	A	C	D	E	F	G	H
15	Personnel Plan						
16	Pizza Chefs Person	Jan	Feb	Mar	Apr	May	Jun
17	Head Chef	$0	$0	$2,000	$2,000	$2,000	$2,000
18	Other	$0	$0	$0	$0	$0	$0
19	Subtotal	$0	$0	$2,000	$2,000	$2,000	$2,000
20							
21	Sales and Marketing Personnel						
22	Erika	$3,000	$3,000	$3,000	$3,000	$3,000	$3,000
23	Other	$0	$0	$0	$0	$0	$0
24	Subtotal	$3,000	$3,000	$3,000	$3,000	$3,000	$3,000
25							
26	General and Administrative Personnel						
27	Daryl	$6,000	$6,000	$6,000	$6,000	$6,000	$6,000
28	Kevin	$3,000	$3,000	$3,000	$3,000	$3,000	$3,000
29	Other	$0	$0	$0	$0	$0	$0
30	Subtotal	$9,000	$9,000	$9,000	$9,000	$9,000	$9,000
31							
32	Kitchen Personnel						
33	TBD	$0	$1,120	$1,472	$2,480	$2,480	$2,480
34	Other	$0	$0	$0	$0	$0	$0
35	Subtotal	$0	$1,120	$1,472	$2,480	$2,480	$2,480
36							
37	Total People	3	7	7	7	7	7
38	Total Payroll	$12,000	$13,120	$15,472	$16,480	$16,480	$16,480

This illustration shows the Personnel by Category option (PREMIER version), which breaks personnel into four categories. The first category is automatically included in costs of sales.

Your Personnel numbers appear in different areas in your Profit and Loss statement. The first category, regardless of its name, goes into the Cost of Goods or Cost of Sales section. The other three categories of Personnel go into the Operating Expenses. Figure 6-30 shows how the first Personnel category ("Pizza Chefs" in this example) automatically appears in Profit and Loss, as "Pizza Chefs Payroll."

FIGURE 6-30: PERSONNEL AS COST OF SALES IN P&L

G5	=IF(PS_ExpenseCategories=TRUE,IF(PS_PersonnelbyPeople=TRUE,Payroll4P,Payroll3			
	A	**E**	**F**	**G**	**H**
1	Pro Forma Profit and Loss				
2		Mar	Apr	May	Jun
3	Sales	$10,494	$18,356	$21,300	$25,018
4	Direct Costs of Goods	$4,722	$8,260	$9,585	$11,258
5	Pizza Chefs Payroll	$2,000	$2,000	$2,000	$2,000
6	Other Costs of Goods	$100	$100	$100	$100
7		------------	------------	------------	------------
8	Cost of Goods Sold	$6,822	$10,360	$11,685	$13,358
9	Gross Margin	$3,672	$7,996	$9,615	$11,660
10	Gross Margin %	34.99%	43.56%	45.14%	46.61%
11	Operating Expenses:				
12	Sales and Marketing Expenses:				
13	Sales and Marketing Payroll	$3,000	$3,000	$3,000	$3,000
14	Advertising/Promotion	$100	$100	$100	$100
15	Other Sales and Marketing Expens	$25	$25	$25	$25
16		------------	------------	------------	------------
17	Total Sales and Marketing Expen:	$3,125	$3,125	$3,125	$3,125
18	Sales and Marketing %	29.78%	17.02%	14.67%	12.49%

If you choose to break expenses into categories, then the first Personnel option is included in Costs of Sales.

2. **Number of People/Department.** The people-based personnel plan, as shown in Figure 6-31, available only in the PREMIER version, lets you forecast numbers of people and average compensation per person. This is a matter of preference and how you choose to forecast your personnel.

FIGURE 6-31: PERSONNEL BY PEOPLE

	E62	=Payroll4P+Payroll4GA+Payroll4SM+Payroll4OTH					
	A	**C**	**D**	**E**	**F**	**G**	**H**
40	**Personnel Plan**						
41	**Pizza Chefs Person**	Jan	Feb	Mar	Apr	May	Jun
42	People	0	0	1	1	1	1
43	Average per Person	$2,000	$2,000	$2,000	$2,000	$2,000	$2,000
44	Subtotal	$0	$0	$2,000	$2,000	$2,000	$2,000
45							
46	**Sales and Marketing Personnel**						
47	People	1	1	1	1	1	1
48	Average per Person	$3,000	$3,000	$3,000	$3,000	$3,000	$3,000
49	Subtotal	$3,000	$3,000	$3,000	$3,000	$3,000	$3,000
50							
51	**General and Administrative Personnel**						
52	People	2	2	2	2	2	2
53	Average per Person	$4,500	$4,500	$4,500	$4,500	$4,500	$4,500
54	Subtotal	$9,000	$9,000	$9,000	$9,000	$9,000	$9,000
55							
56	**Kitchen Personnel**						
57	People	0	4	3	3	3	3
58	Average per Person	$0	$280	$491	$827	$827	$827
59	Subtotal	$0	$1,120	$1,472	$2,480	$2,480	$2,480
60							
61	**Total People**	3	7	7	7	7	7
62	**Total Payroll Exper**	$12,000	$13,120	$15,472	$16,480	$16,480	$16,480

In this Personnel option, you estimate people and average compensation per person. Total People is an automatic calculation.

QuickBooks® Option and Personnel

If your plan is set for the QuickBooks option, you can choose to ignore the Personnel Plan to enhance QuickBooks compatibility. QuickBooks lumps personnel costs into the operating expenses.

To Learn More About...	Search the Help Index for...
Leaving the Personnel Plan table out of your plan	Plan, Outline

Profit and Loss

The Profit and Loss in Business Plan Pro follows standard conventions, the format that most bankers, investors, and accountants are used to, by putting Sales at the top, followed by Cost of Sales or Cost of Goods Sold, to show Gross Margin, which is Sales less Cost of Sales. After that comes operating expenses, and, at the bottom, Profit as the bottom line. Figure 6-32 shows an example.

FIGURE 6-32: STANDARD PROFIT AND LOSS

N51	=profit_before_interest_and_taxes+net_other_income-interest_expense-taxes_incurred					
	A	L	M	N	O	P	Q
1	**Pro Forma Profit and Loss**						
2		Oct	Nov	Dec	2004	2005	2006
3	**Sales**	$36,167	$39,885	$39,920	$279,415	$707,301	$770,608
4	**Direct Costs of Goods**	$16,275	$17,948	$17,964	$125,737	$318,286	$346,773
6	Other Costs of Goods	$100	$100	$100	$1,200	$1,320	$1,452
7		------------	------------	------------	------------	------------	------------
8	**Cost of Goods Sold**	$16,375	$18,048	$18,064	$126,937	$319,606	$348,225
9	**Gross Margin**	$19,792	$21,837	$21,856	$152,478	$387,696	$422,382
10	**Gross Margin %**	54.72%	54.75%	54.75%	54.57%	54.81%	54.81%
11	**Operating Expenses:**						
20	**Payroll**	$16,480	$16,480	$16,480	$188,912	$241,680	$250,164
21	**Depreciation**	$1,250	$1,250	$1,250	$15,000	$35,000	$35,000
22	Advertising	$100	$100	$100	$1,200	$1,200	$1,200
23	Rent	$1,500	$1,500	$1,500	$18,000	$36,000	$36,000
24	Insurance	$200	$200	$200	$2,400	$3,600	$3,600
25	Payroll taxes	$2,472	$2,472	$2,472	$28,337	$36,252	$37,525
26	Other	$175	$175	$175	$2,025	$2,228	$2,450
27		------------	------------	------------	------------	------------	------------
37	**Total Operating Expenses**	$22,177	$22,177	$22,177	$255,874	$355,960	$365,939
38	**Profit Before Interest and Taxes**	($2,385)	($340)	($321)	($103,395)	$31,736	$56,443
39	**Interest Expense**	$167	$167	$167	$2,000	$2,000	$2,000
40	**Taxes Incurred**	$0	$0	$0	$0	$1,487	$2,722
51	**Net Profit**	($2,552)	($507)	($488)	($105,395)	$28,249	$51,721
52	**Net Profit/Sales**	-7.06%	-1.27%	-1.22%	-37.72%	3.99%	6.71%
53	**Include Negative Taxes**				FALSE	TRUE	TRUE

The standard Profit and Loss table is arranged the way bankers and accountants expect to see it.

If you are working with a QuickBooks compatible plan, the Business Plan Pro Profit and Loss appears slightly different. The format closely matches what you see in a QuickBooks summary Income Statement.

Expanded Profit and Loss (PREMIER version)

One important PREMIER option allows you to show non-operating income and non-operating expenses, on the Profit and Loss, below the gross profit. You can set this option in the Plan Setup in the EasyPlan Wizard Tasks view. Look for the setting for "Other Income and Expenses." Figure 6-33 shows you how this option expands the table to allow for these additional items.

FIGURE 6-33: PROFIT AND LOSS SHOWING OTHER INCOME

O42	=SUM(C42:N42)						
	A	L	M	N	O	P	Q
1	Pro Forma Profit and Loss						
2		Oct	Nov	Dec	2004	2005	2006
3	Sales	$36,167	$39,885	$39,920	$279,415	$707,301	$770,608
4	Direct Costs of Goods	$16,275	$17,948	$17,964	$125,737	$318,286	$346,773
6	Other Costs of Goods	$100	$100	$100	$1,200	$1,320	$1,452
7		------------	------------	------------	------------	------------	------------
8	Cost of Goods Sold	$16,375	$18,048	$18,064	$126,937	$319,606	$348,225
9	Gross Margin	$19,792	$21,837	$21,856	$152,478	$387,696	$422,382
10	Gross Margin %	54.72%	54.75%	54.75%	54.57%	54.81%	54.81%
11	Operating Expenses:						
20	Payroll	$16,480	$16,480	$16,480	$188,912	$241,680	$250,164
21	Depreciation	$1,250	$1,250	$1,250	$15,000	$35,000	$35,000
22	Advertising	$100	$100	$100	$1,200	$1,200	$1,200
23	Rent	$1,500	$1,500	$1,500	$18,000	$36,000	$36,000
24	Insurance	$200	$200	$200	$2,400	$3,600	$3,600
25	Payroll taxes	$2,472	$2,472	$2,472	$28,337	$36,252	$37,525
26	Other	$175	$175	$175	$2,025	$2,228	$2,450
27		------------	------------	------------	------------	------------	------------
37	Total Operating Expenses	$22,177	$22,177	$22,177	$255,874	$355,960	$365,939
38	Profit Before Interest and Taxes	($2,385)	($340)	($321)	($103,395)	$31,736	$56,443
39	Interest Expense	$167	$167	$167	$2,000	$2,000	$2,000
40	Taxes Incurred	$0	$0	$0	$0	$1,487	$2,722
41	Other Income						
42	Interest Income	$100	$100	$100	$1,200	$0	$0
43	Other Income Account Name	$0	$0	$0	$0	$0	$0
44	Total Other Income	$100	$100	$100	$1,200	$0	$0
45							
46	Other Expense						
47	Account Name	$0	$0	$0	$0	$0	$0
48	Other Expense Account Name	$0	$0	$0	$0	$0	$0
49	Total Other Expense	$0	$0	$0	$0	$0	$0
50	Net Other Income	$100	$100	$100	$1,200	$0	$0
51	Net Profit	($2,452)	($407)	($388)	($104,195)	$28,249	$51,721
52	Net Profit/Sales	-6.78%	-1.02%	-0.97%	-37.29%	3.99%	6.71%
53	Include Negative Taxes				FALSE	TRUE	TRUE

In the PREMIER version, use your EasyPlan Wizard Tasks, the Plan Setup area, to set the plan to show Other Income and Other Expenses.

Figure 6-34 shows an example of the detailed Profit and Loss table, which is available in the PREMIER version. You can get this detail by choosing to break expenses into categories, in the Plan Setup portion of the EasyPlan Wizard Tasks. You can experiment with this difference by going to the EasyPlan Wizard and switching between breaking expenses into categories or in the Plan Setup. When you break into categories, you see more rows in Profit and Loss. When you do not, you see fewer rows, but they are some of the same rows.

FIGURE 6-34: EXPANDED PROFIT AND LOSS TABLE

M5	=IF(PS_ExpenseCategories=TRUE,IF(PS_PersonnelbyPeople=TRUE,Payroll4P,Payroll3

	A	L	M	N	O	P
1	Pro Forma Profit and Loss					
2		Oct	Nov	Dec	2004	2005
3	Sales	$36,167	$39,885	$39,920	$279,415	$707,301
4	Direct Costs of Goods	$16,275	$17,948	$17,964	$125,737	$318,286
5	Pizza Chefs Payroll	$2,000	$2,000	$2,000	$20,000	$28,000
6	Other Costs of Goods	$100	$100	$100	$1,200	$1,320
7		------------	------------	------------	------------	------------
8	Cost of Goods Sold	$18,375	$20,048	$20,064	$146,937	$347,606
9	Gross Margin	$17,792	$19,837	$19,856	$132,478	$359,696
10	Gross Margin %	49.19%	49.73%	49.74%	47.41%	50.85%
11	Operating Expenses:					
12	Sales and Marketing Expenses:					
13	Sales and Marketing Payroll	$3,000	$3,000	$3,000	$36,000	$51,240
14	Advertising/Promotion	$100	$100	$100	$1,200	$12,000
15	Other Sales and Marketing Expens	$25	$25	$25	$300	$0
16		------------	------------	------------	------------	------------
17	Total Sales and Marketing Expens	$3,125	$3,125	$3,125	$37,500	$63,240
18	Sales and Marketing %	8.64%	7.84%	7.83%	13.42%	8.94%
19	General and Administrative Expe					
20	General and Administrative Payr	$9,000	$9,000	$9,000	$108,000	$123,240
21	Depreciation	$1,250	$1,250	$1,250	$15,000	$35,000
22	Rent	$1,500	$1,500	$1,500	$18,000	$36,000
23	Insurance	$200	$200	$200	$2,400	$3,600
24	Payroll taxes	$2,472	$2,472	$2,472	$28,337	$36,252
25	Other General and Administrative E	$100	$100	$100	$1,125	$1,238
26		------------	------------	------------	------------	------------
27	Total General and Administrative	$14,522	$14,522	$14,522	$172,862	$235,330
28	General and Administrative %	40.15%	36.41%	36.38%	61.87%	33.27%
29	Kitchen Expenses:					
30	Kitchen Payroll	$2,480	$2,480	$2,480	$24,912	$39,200
31	Other Kitchen Expenses	$50	$50	$50	$600	$0
32		------------	------------	------------	------------	------------
33	Total Kitchen Expenses	$2,530	$2,530	$2,530	$25,512	$39,200
34	Kitchen %	7.00%	6.34%	6.34%	9.13%	5.54%
35		------------	------------	------------	------------	------------
36	Total Operating Expenses	$20,177	$20,177	$20,177	$235,874	$337,770
37	Profit Before Interest and Taxes	($2,385)	($340)	($321)	($103,395)	$21,926
38	Interest Expense	$167	$167	$167	$2,000	$2,000
39	Taxes Incurred	$0	$0	$0	$0	$996
50	Net Profit	($2,552)	($507)	($488)	($105,395)	$18,930
51	Net Profit/Sales	-7.06%	-1.27%	-1.22%	-37.72%	2.68%
52	Include Negative Taxes				FALSE	TRUE

The detailed Profit and Loss table in the PREMIER version divides expenses into categories.

Help   For step-by-step procedures, click dialog Help buttons or the Help menu.

Additional Background - Profit and Loss

Links from Other Tables

One of the most common errors with Profit and Loss is the failure to realize the extent to which it gets data from other tables. Sales and Costs of Sales come from the Sales Forecast. Payroll comes from the Personnel Plan. Interest Expenses are calculated automatically, from the Balance of Liabilities in the Balance Sheet and the Interest Rates in General Assumptions. Interest expenses generate more than their share of questions, so those are discussed in detail next.

Interest Expenses

Interest expenses depend on simplifying assumptions and simple mathematics. Business Plan Pro multiplies your liabilities by your assumed interest rate to calculate interest expenses.

Interest expenses do not include principal repayment, just interest. Principal payments go into the Cash Flow table as data inputs, while interest expenses appear in Profit and Loss.

Some people are confused by the separation of loan payments into interest and principal. Their confusion makes sense; you write a single check to the bank, why divide payments into two? The reason for this potential confusion is that this treatment matches what happens with standard accounting.

- Interest expense is deductible against income to reduce taxable income and the tax burden. Interest expenses reduce profits (or increase losses).
- Principal payments are not deductible against income, and are not allowed as expenses. They reduce cash, not profits.

One problem that comes up with the interest expense is timing. Technically, a loan taken out on the first of the month should cause more interest expense than one taken out at the end of the month. Interest compounded daily is greater than interest taken once a month. In both of these cases, Business Plan Pro settles for planning, not accounting; the difference in detail is far less than the uncertainty involved in your Sales Forecast, while the complexity involved in fine-tuning these details would hurt the overall planning process. It is a matter of relative uncertainty.

In the annual columns, this timing of interest is handled by simple averages. Since your outstanding balance normally changes from the beginning of the year to the end, Business Plan Pro simply takes the mathematical average of beginning of year and end of year balances, and applies interest to that average. If you pay off the loan at any time during the year, Business Plan Pro averages your starting balance and zero, so it estimates half a year's worth of interest. This again is a simplifying assumption, useful, and powerful, and worth noting.

You can work around these simplifying assumptions by adjusting your assumed interest rates. If you had a 10% loan to be paid off in the first month of the second year, change the effective interest to .833% (slightly less than one percent, 1/12 of 10%) and explain this change in the text associated with General Assumptions. You can also unlink the General Assumptions or hide the row, if you do not want to explain.

QuickBooks Option and Interest

If you choose the QuickBooks compatibility option, in the Plan Settings, then interest expenses are not automatic. Because QuickBooks lumps interest into the operating expenses, Business Plan Pro does not calculate interest automatically, and leaves that up to you, so it remains compatible with your QuickBooks expenses.

Taxes

Business Plan Pro handles taxes as simple mathematics, multiplying your assumed tax rate times the pre-tax profit without regard for graduated rates. If there's a loss for the year then it sets the effective tax rate at zero.

The pizza restaurant sample plan offers a useful example. First, take a look at this company's projected profitability, shown in Figure 6-34. This business plan projects losses during the first year of the plan, and profits in the second year. Business Plan Pro sets the effective tax rate to zero during the loss year, then calculates taxes by multiplying the tax rate in General Assumptions times pretax profits.

You can check the General Assumptions for this same plan by checking back to Figure 6-17, which contains the general assumptions table. Notice in that table that the tax rate for the first year is 30%, but taxes for the second and third year are 5%. This is the correct handling for taxes in a loss situation.

Because of the loss, Business Plan Pro ignored the 30% tax rate for the loss years, and the business planner who did the plan set the tax rate lower than that (5% instead of 30%) for the second and third years because the previous losses would offset taxes in that year.

The 'Include Negative Taxes' Row

In Figures 6-32, 6-33, and 6-34, notice the bottom row in Profit and Loss, "Include Negative Taxes." You can use that row to override the normal treatment and count negative taxes when there is a loss. To count the negative taxes, type TRUE into the annual column, even if the formula shows FALSE because there is no profit.

Taxes and Loss Carried Forward

Specifically, to handle taxes for a business plan that has a long string of losses:

- Business Plan Pro automatically overrides the tax rate to zero for the period of losses. The "Include Negative Taxes" row at the bottom shows as "False."

- If your plan includes early losses and making a profit later on, then you probably have a "loss carried forward" tax advantage that reduces the tax rate when there are profits.

- Therefore your tax rate in the profitable periods should be less than it would have been. This should be a simple educated guess; you are not doing tax accounting here, just planning. Take whatever your tax rate would have been, and make it lower.

- If you insist on detailed mathematical calculations:
  Take the sum of the losses. For example, $100K.

  1. Multiply that by your estimated tax rate when you make profits. For example, $100K * .25 = $25K. Call that the loss carried forward.

  2. Subtract that amount ($25K) from the tax estimate of the first profitable year. For example, if the tax estimate was $50K at an estimated 25% rate, $50K minus $25K is $25K. Do not worry about making this an exact calculation; an estimate is good enough for planning purposes.

  3. Change your estimated tax rate in the profitable year to make the estimated tax equal to the reduced estimate. For example, if the estimated tax was $50K at 25%, and your target tax is $25K, then make your tax rate 12.5% for that first profitable year.

  4. Explain the adjustment in text. An example would be: "Taxes are set at zero during the loss periods. The loss carried forward impact reduces the estimated tax rate during the profitable periods." Include this in the text accompanying the General Assumptions table.

TIPS

Loss Carried Forward

The problem with losses is that tax treatment depends on what happens in the future. If your losses are followed later by profits, then the losses reduce future taxes on profits. This is called "Loss Carried Forward" in tax and accounting jargon.

Business Plan Pro sets the tax rate to zero for losses, but it does not automatically adjust future tax rates for loss carried forward. Remember, this is planning, not accounting.

Sales Forecast

Forecasting is more art than science. Think of it as educated guessing. Like the weather forecast, it is a combination of knowing as much as you can about conditions and guessing what they mean for the future. You can do it. It may be hard to forecast, but it is even harder to run a business without forecasting.

The Sales Forecast in standard Business Plan Pro is simple to understand. It has a group of rows for Sales, and a group of rows for Cost of Sales. Both of these sum to totals that reappear in your Profit and Loss table.

> **TIPS**
>
> ### More on Sales Forecast: Hurdle: The Book on Business Planning
>
> Make sure you read the *Forecast Your Sales* section of your Hurdle book, which explains this in greater detail. Use the Resources button on the tool bar and then click the Books > Hurdle link to read the book in PDF format.

Figure 6-35 shows a sample sales forecast for a pizza restaurant. It has one block of rows for lines of sales, and another block for direct costs. If you have set your plan for a business that has inventory, the direct costs are equivalent to inventory in cost of sales, or cost of goods sold.

FIGURE 6-35: SALES FORECAST

E9	=E3*$B9						
	A	B	C	D	E	F	G
1	Sales Forecast						
2	Sales		Jan	Feb	Mar	Apr	May
3	Individuals		$0	$0	$3,895	$6,813	$7,906
4	Families		$0	$0	$5,645	$9,874	$11,458
5	Take-out		$0	$0	$954	$1,669	$1,936
6	Total Sales		$0	$0	$10,494	$18,356	$21,300
7							
8	Direct Cost of Sales		Jan	Feb	Mar	Apr	May
9	Individuals	45.00%	$0	$0	$1,753	$3,066	$3,558
10	Families	45.00%	$0	$0	$2,540	$4,443	$5,156
11	Take-out	45.00%	$0	$0	$429	$751	$871
12	Subtotal Direct Cost of Sales		$0	$0	$4,722	$8,260	$9,585

The standard forecast is a simple list of sales and cost of sales.

The row names in the cost of sales area are the same as the lines of sales above, in this example. You set or change them using the Edit Row Label command, so you can customize as much as you want. You can add and delete rows, to tailor your sales forecast to your business.

You may notice, in the sample forecast in Figure 6-35, that there are no sales projected for the first two months. This is not unusual in a start-up plan. The new pizza business in the sample expects to start up two months before it actually starts making sales.

Additional Information - Sales Forecast

Cost of Sales - Defined

The Sales Forecast includes Cost of Sales, as well as Sales. Cost of Sales is an important accounting concept. Sales less Cost of Sales results in Gross Margin. Analysts use it to compare different companies and different industries.

Cost of Sales for Types of Business

Cost of Sales is also called Direct Cost, and Cost of Goods Sold, depending on the type of business. Here are some concrete examples:

1. **Retail**. Goods that a retail business purchases and then resells to customers are the classic instance of Cost of Goods Sold. They belong in the Sales Forecast as Cost of Sales.

2. **Manufacturing**. Materials that a manufacturing company buys as raw materials for the manufacturing process are Costs of Goods Sold, or Cost of Sales, or Direct Unit Costs. In this case these terms are virtually interchangeable.

   If you want to include manufacturing labor as costs of Goods Sold, see the section titled "Handling Direct Labor as Cost of Sales" later in this chapter.

3. **Service**. Service businesses have Costs of Sales. Accountants and attorneys have photocopying and research. Transportation businesses have fuel, maintenance, and drivers. News publications have the cost of newsprint and editors.

   If you want to include some salaries as Costs of Goods Sold, see the section titled "Handling Direct Labor as Cost of Sales" later in this chapter.

TIPS

Ask an Accountant

The distinction between cost of sales and operating expenses is important, but sometimes subtle. In many cases the accountants make a determination based on judgement and experience. Your accountant may have an opinion in your case.

The Units-Based Forecast (PREMIER version)

In the PREMIER version of Business Plan Pro, the Sales Forecast can actually be one of two possible forecasts. You select one or the other using the EasyPlan Wizard, either when you start a new plan, or after that, by selecting Plan Setup from the File menu. The first of the two, and the simplest, is called the Value-based Sales Forecast. It has a group of rows for Sales, and a group of rows for Cost of Sales. (This is the only sales forecast included in standard Business Plan Pro.) The second, called the Units-based Sales Forecast, projects Units, Price Per-unit, Sales, Cost Per-unit, and Costs. Figure 6-36 shows an example of a units-based sales forecast (with the same final sales and costs numbers as in Figure 6-35, the standard forecast).

FIGURE 6-36: UNITS SALES FORECAST

E28	=E17*E23					
	A	B	C	D	E	F	G
15	**Sales Forecast**						
16	**Unit Sales**		Jan	Feb	Mar	Apr	May
17	Individuals		0	0	487	852	988
18	Familes		0	0	332	581	674
19	Take-out		0	0	80	139	161
20	**Total Unit Sales**		0	0	898	1,572	1,824
21							
22	**Unit Prices**		Jan	Feb	Mar	Apr	May
23	Individuals		$8.00	$8.00	$8.00	$8.00	$8.00
24	Familes		$17.00	$17.00	$17.00	$17.00	$17.00
25	Take-out		$12.00	$12.00	$12.00	$12.00	$12.00
26							
27	**Sales**						
28	Individuals		$0	$0	$3,895	$6,813	$7,906
29	Familes		$0	$0	$5,645	$9,874	$11,458
30	Take-out		$0	$0	$954	$1,669	$1,936
31	**Total Sales**		$0	$0	$10,494	$18,356	$21,300
32							
33	**Direct Unit Costs**		Jan	Feb	Mar	Apr	May
34	Individuals	45.00%	$3.60	$3.60	$3.60	$3.60	$3.60
35	Familes	45.00%	$7.65	$7.65	$7.65	$7.65	$7.65
36	Take-out	45.00%	$5.40	$5.40	$5.40	$5.40	$5.40
37							
38	**Direct Cost of Sales**		Jan	Feb	Mar	Apr	May
39	Individuals		$0	$0	$1,753	$3,066	$3,558
40	Familes		$0	$0	$2,540	$4,443	$5,156
41	Take-out		$0	$0	$429	$751	$871
42	**Subtotal Direct Cost of Sales**		$0	$0	$4,722	$8,260	$9,585

The illustration shows a units-based sales forecast for the same numbers as in the previous, standard sales forecast. Notice how it multiplies units times price, and units times per-unit cost, to calculate sales and costs of sales.

Switching Between Two Sales Forecasts (PREMIER version)

In the PREMIER version, when you have numbers in the Sales Forecast table (Value-based), and then switch to the other Sales option (Units-based), it may seem like you have lost data. You have not.

There are two separate forecasts embedded within the plan file. When you go from one to the other, you make one active and the other inactive.

You can use this facility to create two Sales Forecasts, then switch between the two, and compare. This can help you develop a sense for how either of the two would affect other areas of the plan.

Average Price Calculation

Business Plan Pro calculates average Price by dividing Sales by Units. Figure 6-37 shows what happens when a Unit-based Sales Forecast contains Prices but no Sales. The average Price of zero in the first-year column looks wrong, because the Price assumption is $25 per unit. However, look again: the average Price is zero, because if there are no sales—as is the case here—then the average price is zero.

FIGURE 6-37: NO SALES, NO PRICE

O20	=IF(O15<>0,O24/O15,0)					
	A	**M**	**N**	**O**	**P**	**Q**
13	Sales Forecast					
14	Unit Sales	Nov	Dec	2004	2005	2006
15	Example	0	0	0	0	0
16	Other	1,815	1,905	14,010	20,000	25,000
17	Total Unit Sales	1,815	1,905	14,010	20,000	25,000
18						
19	Unit Prices	Nov	Dec	2003	2004	2005
20	Example	$25.00	$25.00	$0.00	$0.00	$0.00
21	Other	$50.00	$50.00	$50.00	$50.00	$50.00
22						
23	Sales					
24	Example	$0	$0	$0	$0	$0
25	Other	$90,750	$95,250	$700,500	$1,000,000	$1,250,000
26	Total Sales	$90,750	$95,250	$700,500	$1,000,000	$1,250,000
27						

Without any Unit Sales, the price calculation ends up as zero.

Figure 6-38 shows why Business Plan Pro calculates the average Price from Sales and Units. In this example, volume changes price.

To calculate the average, you divide Total Sales for the year by Total Units for the year. The average Price is not the mathematical average of 12 price assumptions in 12 columns; it is Sales divided by Units. As the example in Figure 6-38 shows, if you made $45,500 in sales on a volume of 2,100 units, the average price is $21.67 per unit.

FIGURE 6-38: AVERAGE PRICE, SECOND CASE

O20	=IF(O15<>0,O24/O15,0)					
	A	L	M	N	O	P
13	Sales Forecast					
14	Unit Sales	Oct	Nov	Dec	2004	2005
15	Example	200	300	700	2,100	2,000
16	Other	1,545	1,815	1,905	14,010	20,000
17	Total Unit Sales	1,745	2,115	2,605	16,110	22,000
18						
19	Unit Prices	Oct	Nov	Dec	2003	2004
20	Example	$25.00	$25.00	$15.00	$21.67	$15.00
21	Other	$50.00	$50.00	$50.00	$50.00	$50.00
22						
23	Sales					
24	Example	$5,000	$7,500	$10,500	$45,500	$30,000
25	Other	$77,250	$90,750	$95,250	$700,500	$1,000,000
26	Total Sales	$82,250	$98,250	$105,750	$746,000	$1,030,000
27						

The price calculation depends on having Unit Sales.

Handling Direct Labor as Cost of Sales

Many companies have salaried employees whose compensation should be included in Cost of Sales. For example, assembly and manufacturing workers in a manufacturing company, or full-time consultants in a consulting company.

If you have the standard version, then you can add direct labor into the Profit and Loss table. You can use the row named "Other Costs of Sales" in the top section of Profit and Loss, inserting rows above it if you need to. Make sure that you do not include these same costs in the Personnel table, because you do not want to count the same spending twice. Figure 6-39 shows an example.

If you have the PREMIER version you can simply set your plan to divide expenses into categories, then put these salaries into the first category. They automatically flow into Cost of Sales, without affecting inventory.

FIGURE 6-39: DIRECT LABOR AS COST OF SALES, STANDARD VERSION

F6	2000				
	A	E	F	G	H
1	Pro Forma Profit and Loss				
2		Mar	Apr	May	Jun
3	Sales	$10,494	$18,356	$21,300	$25,018
4	Direct Costs of Goods	$4,722	$8,260	$9,585	$11,258
6	Pizza Chef Salary	$2,000	$2,000	$2,000	$2,000
7	Other Costs of Goods	$100	$100	$100	$100
8		------------	------------	------------	------------
9	Cost of Goods Sold	$6,822	$10,360	$11,685	$13,358
10	Gross Margin	$3,672	$7,996	$9,615	$11,660
11	Gross Margin %	34.99%	43.56%	45.14%	46.61%
20	Expenses:				
21	Payroll	$15,472	$16,480	$16,480	$16,480
22	Depreciation	$1,250	$1,250	$1,250	$1,250
23	Advertising	$100	$100	$100	$100
24	Rent	$1,500	$1,500	$1,500	$1,500
25	Insurance	$200	$200	$200	$200
26	Payroll taxes	$2,321	$2,472	$2,472	$2,472
27	Other	$100	$100	$100	$100
37		------------	------------	------------	------------
38	Total Operating Expenses	$20,943	$22,102	$22,102	$22,102
39	Profit Before Interest and Taxes	($17,271)	($14,106)	($12,487)	($10,442)
40	Interest Expense	$167	$167	$167	$167
41	Taxes Incurred	$0	$0	$0	$0
52	Net Profit	($17,438)	($14,273)	($12,653)	($10,609)
53	Net Profit/Sales	-166.17%	-77.76%	-59.40%	-42.40%

The illustration shows how a sample company handles direct labor as cost of sales in the Profit and Loss table.

As an option, if you do not have inventory, you can put direct labor into the sales forecast as an additional row. This works only for companies that do not have inventory. In this case too, you should be sure you do not count personnel twice. If you put direct labor into the sales forecast costs area, do not add the same costs into the personnel plan as well.

Advanced Formulas

Your main help includes an example of a simple formula that copies whatever price is in the first column all the way through the whole 12 months and three or five years. Use that and then you can change a price assumption by just changing the first month.

To Learn More About...	Search the Help Index for...
Copying a formula across months and years	Fill Right; Fill Series

Start-up

The EasyPlan Wizard sets each business plan as either a start-up company or an ongoing company. The start-up companies have the Start-up table. This table establishes the starting balances in the Balance Sheet table. Figure 6-40 shows an example of a standard start-up table.

FIGURE 6-40: START-UP TABLE

	A	B
1	Start-up	
2		
3	Requirements	
4		
5	Start-up Expenses	
6	Legal	$300
7	Stationery etc.	$200
8	Expensed Equipment	$2,000
9	Other	$500
10	Total Start-up Expense	$3,000
12	Start-up Assets Needed	
13	Cash Balance on Starting Date	$13,000
15	Other Current Assets	$500
16	Total Current Assets	$13,500
18	Long-term Assets	$0
19	Total Assets	$13,500
20	Total Requirements	$16,500
22	Funding	
24	Investment	
25	Investor 1	$12,000
26	Investor 2	$0
27	Other	$500
28	Total Investment	$12,500
30	Current Liabilities	
31	Accounts Payable	$0
32	Current Borrowing	$2,000
33	Current Liabilities	$2,000
34	Subtotal Current Liabilities	$4,000
36	Long-term Liabilities	$0
37	Total Liabilities	$4,000
39	Loss at Start-up	($3,000)
40	Total Capital	$9,500
41	Total Capital and Liabilities	$13,500

The Start-up table lists assets and expenses before the beginning of the plan.

TIPS

Timing is Everything

Do not count expenses twice: they go in Start-up or Profit and Loss, but not both. The only difference is timing. Do not buy assets twice: they go into the Start-up if you acquire them before the starting date. Otherwise, put them in the Profit and Loss.

Start-up Specifics

- **Start-up Expenses.** These are expenses that happen before the beginning of the plan, before the first month. For example, many new companies incur expenses for legal work, logo design, site selection and improvements, and other expenses. This is a simple list, for which you can both insert and delete rows.

- **Cash Balance on Starting Date.** Business Plan Pro calculates your starting cash with simple arithmetic. Cash goes into your Start-up table as either investment or borrowed money. It goes out as the sum of start-up expenses plus all other starting assets (inventory, other current assets, and long-term assets). What's left over, money raised but not spent, is starting cash.

- **Start-up Assets Needed.** Typical start-up assets are cash (the money in the bank when the company starts), and in many cases starting inventory. Other starting assets are both current and long-term, such as equipment, office furniture, machinery, etc.

Business Plan Pro assigns Assets to fixed categories, because those same categories are also in the Balance Sheet and Cash Flow tables. All companies see rows for Cash, Other Current Assets, and Long-term Assets. Companies that deal with inventory (an EasyPlan Wizard setting) also see a cell for Starting Inventory.

You do not enter cash into your start-up assets directly. Business Plan Pro puts the cash into your plan by taking the sum of financing and subtracting expenses and other assets.

- **Funding.** This includes both Capital Investment and Loans. The investment section is another summary list area, so that you can add or delete rows and rename the row labels to complete your list. The loans section is defined with the same categories used in the Balance Sheet and Cash Flow.
  The only investment amounts or loan amounts that belong in the Start-up table are those that happen before the beginning of the plan. Whatever happens during or after the first month should go instead into the Cash Flow table, which automatically adjusts the Balance Sheet.

- **Total Requirements.** Total Start-up requirements are the simple sum of Start-up Expenses and Start-up Assets.

Since timing is the only distinction between these and normal expenses and assets, the start-up requirements numbers are not as magical and all-encompassing as we might like. As we have explained, standard accounting sets this distinction, so it cannot be helped.

Expenses vs. Assets

Many people can be confused by the accounting distinction between expenses and assets. For example, they would like to record research and development as assets instead of expenses, because those expenses create intellectual property. However, standard accounting and taxation law are both strict on the distinction:

- Expenses are deductible against income, so they reduce taxable income.

- Assets are not deductible against income.

Some people are also confused by the specific definition of start-up expenses, start-up assets, and start-up financing. They would prefer to have a broader, more generic definition that includes, say, expenses incurred during the first year, or the first few months, of the plan. Unfortunately, this would also lead to double counting of expenses and non-standard financial statements. All the expenses incurred during the first year have to appear in the Profit and Loss statement of the first year, and all expenses incurred before that have to appear as start-up expenses.

This treatment is the only way to correctly deal with the tax implications and the proper assigning of expenses to the time periods they belong. Tax authorities and accounting standards are clear on this, so Business Plan Pro has no choice.

What a company spends to acquire assets is not deductible against income. For example, money spent on inventory is not deductible as expense. Only when the inventory is sold, and therefore becomes cost of goods sold or cost of sales, does it reduce income.

 TIPS | **Why You Do not Want to Capitalize Expenses**

Sometimes people want to treat expenses as assets. Ironically, that is usually a bad idea, for several reasons:

- Money spent buying assets is not tax deductible. Money spent on expenses is deductible.
- Capitalizing expenses creates the danger of overstating assets.
- If you capitalized the expense, it appears on your books as an asset. Having useless assets on the accounting books is not a good thing.

One common misconception involves development expenses. Generally, companies want to maximize deductions against income as expenses, not assets, because this minimizes the tax burden. With that in mind, seasoned business owners and accountants always want to account for money spent on development as expenses, not assets. This is generally much better than accounting for this expenditure as buying assets, such as patents or product rights.

Assets look better on the books than expenses, but there is rarely any clear and obvious correlation between money spent on research and development and market value of intellectual property. Companies that account for development as generating assets can often end up with vastly overstated assets, and questionable financials statements. Whenever you have the choice, you should treat development as an expense.

Another common misconception involves expensed equipment. The standard Business Plan Pro Start-up table includes Expensed Equipment among start-up expenses because the U.S. tax authority (Internal Revenue Service, IRS) allows a limited amount of office equipment purchases to be called expenses, not purchase of assets. As of the date this was written, that amount was $17,000 per year. You should check with your accountant to find out whether this rule has changed recently. As a result, expensed equipment takes advantage of the allowance.

After your company has used up the allowance, then additional purchases have to go into assets, not expenses. This treatment also indicates the general preference for expenses over assets, when you have a choice.

Start-up Requirements - Example

Start-up requirements are the simple sum of Start-up Expenses and Start-up Assets.

Figure 6-41 shows the upper portion of the Start-up table for a sample business plan. Start-up Expenses come to a total of $33,750 and Start-up Assets total $499,000. Start-up Requirements in this case are $532,750, the sum of $499,000 plus $33,750.

FIGURE 6-41: START-UP EXPENSES AND ASSETS

Start-up Expenses	
Legal	$1,000
Stationery, etc.	$2,500
Brochures	$5,000
Consultants	$15,000
Insurance	$250
Rent	$500
Research and Development	$1,000
Expensed Equipment	$3,500
Other	$5,000
Total Start-up Expense	**$33,750**
Start-up Assets Needed	
Cash Balance on Starting Date	$494,000
Other Current Assets	$5,000
Total Current Assets	**$499,000**
Long-term Assets	$0
Total Assets	**$499,000**
Total Requirements	**$532,750**

Start-up Total Requirements include Expenses and Assets.

TIPS

Cash Requirements (Cash Balance on Starting Date)

The Cash Requirements cell is labeled Cash Balance on Starting Date because that is what it should be when your plan is done. However, you do not set cash requirements—Business Plan Pro calculates this cell automatically, subtracting the money you spend on expenses and assets from the money you raise as investments or loans.

Start-up vs. Total Requirements

The Start-up table adds Start-up Expenses plus Start-up Assets to create an estimate of Total Requirements. While a useful number, use it as an estimate only:

- It does not include additional funding that enters into the Cash Flow table in the early months of the business. For example, your plan might need to add capital in the third month, or borrow money in the second month. In that case your cost is greater than what shows on the Start-up table.

- It does not automatically check for negative balances in the early months of cash flow (although the EasyPlan Wizard does check later, and suggests that you add cash to compensate for negative balances).

Start-up Liabilities and Capital

Figure 6-42 shows the rest of the Start-up table, the funding/financing section. This is where you enter assumptions for money coming into the business at start-up, as investments and loans.

↑TIPS

Assets = Capital + Liabilities

As always, it is the standard equation in accounting. Assets are always equal to capital plus liabilities. The Start-up table makes sure that is so.

FIGURE 6-42: START-UP LIABILITIES AND CAPITAL

Investment	
Investor 1	$500,000
Investor 2	$32,750
Other	$0
Total Investment	**$532,750**
Current Liabilities	
Accounts Payable	$0
Current Borrowing	$0
Current Liabilities	$0
Subtotal Current Liabilities	**$0**
Long-term Liabilities	**$0**
Total Liabilities	**$0**
Loss at Start-up	($33,750)
Total Capital	$499,000
Total Capital and Liabilities	**$499,000**

The funding portion of the Start-up table plans on money coming into the business as loans and investment.

Start-up Expenses and Start-up Losses

Your Loss at Start-up is always equal to your Start-up Expenses (that is proper accounting). If you had $33,750 as Start-up Expenses, as in Figure 6-41, then you also have $33,750 loss as the Loss at Start-up, shown in Figure 6-42. The signs are reversed, because of accounting convention. The Start-up Expenses show positive, and the Start-up Loss shows negative (frequently shown in parenthesis or a red color).

Types of Start-up Funding

- **Investment** in the Start-up Funding is investment in the company. It ends up as Paid-in Capital in the Balance Sheet. This is the classic concept of business investment, taking ownership in a company, risking money in the hope of gaining money later.

- **Accounts Payable** in Start-up Funding are debts that end up as Accounts Payable in the Balance Sheet. Generally this means credit-card debt. This number becomes the starting balance of your Balance Sheet.

- **Current Borrowing** is standard debt, borrowing from banks, Small Business Administration, or other current borrowing.

- **Other Current Liabilities** are additional liabilities that do not have interest charges. This is where you put loans from founders, family members, or friends. We are not recommending interest-free loans for financing, by the way, but when they happen, this is where they go.

- **Long-term Liabilities** are long-term debt, long-term loans. Look to your Business Plan Pro Glossary for more information on distinguishing between current (or short-term) and long-term.

Understanding the Loss at Start-up

Business Plan Pro calculates the Loss at Start-up by subtracting capital and liabilities from assets, forcing the accounting equation of balance: **Assets = Capital + Liabilities**

TIPS

Expect a Loss at Start-up

The loss at start-up is very common…at this point in the life of the company, you have already incurred tax-deductible expenses, but you do not have sales yet. So you have a loss. Do not be surprised; it is normal.

How Much Cash for Start-up?

Cash requirements is an estimate of how much money your start-up company needs to have in its checking account when it starts. Of course you do not automatically know how much that is, and you cannot calculate it by using just the Start-up table. This is a suggested approach:

1. Fill in your Start-up table with estimates, based on what you know about your business, what you can find out from team members, and what you can find out through business research. Estimate Start-up Expenses and the other Start-up Assets that are not cash.

2. Fill in your initial estimates for Sales Forecast, Personnel Plan, and Expenses in Profit and Loss tables.

3. Look at your Cash Flow chart. Expect the Cash Balance to go into negative numbers. Find out the maximum negative balance for the first year. Write that number down.

4. Come back into your Start-up table and add enough additional cash in loans or investment to make that negative balance in Cash Flow turn positive.

This is a better estimate of Start-up Cash requirements than your original estimate. Then, as you work with your plan, changing estimates in other tables, remember to go back to your start-up requirements to add cash as needed to keep the first year's Cash Balance positive.

Chapter 3: Guided Tour, offers an example of the step-by-step way to estimate the amount you need in starting cash.

TIPS

Shouldn't I Start with More Money?

If you can, yes. Many entrepreneurs decide they want to raise more cash than they need so they have money left over for contingencies.

However, although that makes good sense when you can do it, it is hard to explain that to investors. The outside investors do not want to give you more money than you need, for obvious reasons—it is their money!

Cash Pilot (PREMIER version)

Cash Flow is not intuitive. The Cash Pilot is a graphic tool that gives you special power to deal with the underlying assumptions for Accounts Receivable, Accounts Payable, and Inventory. These are all critical to cash flow. Figure 6-43 shows the Cash Pilot as it starts for the Pizza restaurant used for other examples in this chapter.

FIGURE 6-43: CASH PILOT INITIAL VIEW

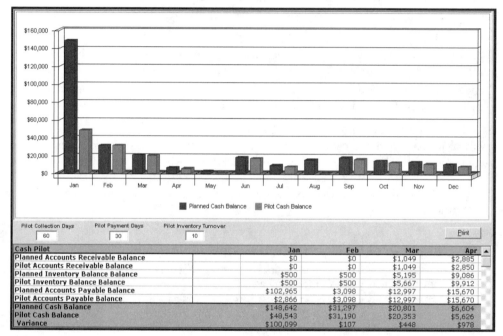

The Cash Pilot gives you a visual tool for managing three key assumptions in your Balance Sheet that affect your cash flow.

TIPS

Accessing the Cash Pilot (PREMIER version)

The Cash Pilot is available in Business Plan Pro PREMIER version only. If you have the PREMIER version installed, you can access the Cash Pilot from the Instructions area in the Cash Flow table.

The key to the Cash Pilot is in the middle section, which presents you with three critical inputs.

1. Collection Days Estimator.
2. Payment Days Estimator.
3. Inventory Turnover Estimator.

Collection Days Estimator

The Collection Days assumption sets the average number of days estimated for collecting bills—Accounts Receivable. Watch how your cash position changes when you change this assumption—the fewer the collection days, the more cash. The reason, of course, is that the higher the collection days estimate, the higher the estimated balance for Accounts Receivable. This balance is critical to Cash Flow.

Of course this calculation is only relevant for companies that have sales on credit, which is one of the plan settings. If your plan does not include sales on credit, collection days in the Pilot has no effect.

Accountants and financial analysts calculate collection days to measure changes in receivables management. They work with average balances for the year and use a standard formula to calculate collection days, which is supposed to be the number of days your company waits between delivering an invoice and collecting the money. The higher the collection days, the higher the average balance of receivables. If collection days is 30, that means you normally have one month's worth of sales on credit in receivables. Collection days of 45 means about a month and a half, 60 means two months.

The Cash Pilot in Business Plan Pro uses simple algebra to reverse that formula and calculate the Accounts Receivable Balance from Sales on Credit and Collection Days. It calculates sales on credit from your percentage sales on credit assumption, multiplied by your sales projection. The accounts receivable balance leads easily to calculations of its cash impact. The payments on accounts receivable are automatically calculated in the Cash Flow table. The details on the Pilot's calculations of Accounts Receivable, including Balances, Payments, and Sales on Credit, are in the Cash Pilot table.

When you increase the average collection days you decrease cash, and vice-versa. The model offers a quick lesson in the relationship between cash flow and accounts receivable.

The Cash Pilot uses a different set of logic to calculate the Accounts Receivables balance for the years. For the first year, the balance is the same as the Ending Balance in the twelfth month. In the second year, the calculation takes the Ending Balance and compares it to Sales on Credit, as a percentage. It also calculates the change in the Collection Days assumption, if any. These ratios are applied to that year's Sales on Credit to estimate the Ending Balance of Receivables. For example, for the first year there were $100K Sales on Credit and an Ending Balance of $40K in Accounts Receivable. If the second year's Sales on Credit are $150K, and there is no change in Collection Days assumptions, then the second year's Ending Balance would be $60K, which is (40/100)*150. If the first year's Collection Days assumption was 60, and the second year's Collection Days was 30, then the resulting estimated balance would be $30K, calculated as (40/100)*150*(30/60).

This revised formula has the advantage of a more accurate reflection of growth. The $40K Ending Balance in the first year indicates month-to-month growth, because the average monthly Sales for the year would be $8,333 (1/12 of $100K) so 60 Collection Days would mean twice that, $16,666, in Accounts Receivable. The Ending Balance of $40K indicates growth, Sales of about $20K per month towards the end of the year. If we calculated the next year's Collection Days based on average Sales without taking this growth into account, the resulting balance estimate would be $12,500 (150/12), a single month's Sales on Credit. Instead, we estimate $30K because the ratio of Sales on Credit and Ending Balance is more important. Sales are growing from $100K to $150K. Even with the improvement in Collection Days from 60 to 30, it would be illogical to see the Accounts Receivable balance fall from $40K to $12,500.

The Pilot uses the same logic to estimate the third year balance by calculating from the ratio between Sales on Credit, second year Ending Balance, and Collection Days assumptions.

Payment Days Estimator

The Payment Days calculations work like the Collection Days, but for Accounts Payable instead of Accounts Receivable. Set the average payment period assumptions with the Cash Pilot. The pilot then calculates the Accounts Payable Balance and that impacts the Payments of Accounts Payable, which affect the Cash Flow. The Accounts Payable Balance is in the Balance Sheet table.

The Payment Days assumption works exactly opposite to the Collection Days. As the payment period increases, so does cash. Business Plan Pro estimates payables balance with an algebraic formula. New Accounts Payable and Payment Days are the independent variables, and the Balance is the unknown. The software takes the Collection Days formula:

$$\text{Payment days} = \text{Average Payables balance} * 365 / \text{New Accounts Payable}$$

and reverses it to calculate the Accounts Payable Balance:

$$\text{Payables balance} = (\text{Payment days} * \text{New Accounts Payable}) / 365$$

This works well for a lot of normal cases. It is an elegant solution. Still, you should be aware that the Payment Days ratio is based on average balance, not ending balance. Therefore, technically, the calculation estimates average balance, not ending balance.

For annual estimates of payables, the Cash Pilot calculates average ratios of accounts payable to sales, adjusting for changes in payment days estimators, instead of using the same algebra as used for monthly calculations.

Inventory Turnover Estimator

For retail, manufacturing, or other product based companies, the Cash Pilot automatically helps you calculate the turnover rates for your company, based on the average monthly balance of inventory. Service companies, which normally do not maintain product inventories, can assume extremely high inventory turnover (100, for example) to create very low inventory balances on the worksheet. The Pilot uses Inventory Turnover and Cost of Unit Sales to calculate alternate Inventory Balances, and those affect the Cash Flow.

You do not need to do complicated inventory turnover assumptions to work with your Cash Flow, or with Business Plan Pro, or with the Cash Pilot. The whole idea of the Cash Pilot is the ability to experiment, so you can type different turnover values into the pilot and see how they affect inventory. The higher the turnover rate, the lower the average inventory. Therefore, the higher the turnover rate, the better the cash flow.

These calculations depend on the nature of turnover, which is a matter of dividing the average inventory balance by the annual cost of goods sold, or cost of sales. A turnover rate of 12 means about one month inventory on average. A turnover rate of 6 means two months, 4 means three months, and 3 means four months. A turnover of 2 is six months' worth of inventory on average, and a rate of 1 means a year's worth of inventory, on average.

As with receivables and payables, Business Plan Pro estimates your Inventory Balance using an algebraic formula based on the business ratio, but reversed and adjusted. Accountants and financial analysts calculate Inventory Turnover, the business ratio, by dividing annual Cost of Sales by the average Inventory Balance. They calculate the average balance by adding starting and ending balances together and dividing by two.

Turnover=cost of sales/inventory balance

The Cash Pilot, on the other hand, needs to estimate your ending Inventory Balance because that is critical to Cash Flow. It knows your Cost of Sales and it knows your Inventory Turnover, because you estimated turnover as an assumption. Therefore, using simple algebra, Business Plan Pro estimates the Inventory Balance using turnover and cost of sales as the known variables, and finds the balance as the unknown. The formula is:

Inventory balance=cost of sales/turnover

This is a good formula for planning, but you should also be aware of some underlying problems:

- The turnover ratio is based on average balance, not ending balance. Therefore, technically, the calculation estimates average balance, not ending balance.
- Business Plan Pro applies the formula to monthly ending balance, not annual balance, so it multiplies cost of sales by 12 to estimate annual sales:

Inventory balance=(cost of sales*12)/turnover

For annual inventory estimates the Cash Pilot does not use the same formula for calculating the ending-year inventory balances in the plan years after the first year.

- For the first year, the balance is the same as the Ending Balance in the twelfth month.
- In the second year, the calculation takes the Ending Balance and compares it to second-year Sales, as a percentage. It also calculates the change in the Turnover assumption, if any. These ratios are applied to that year's Sales to estimate the Ending Inventory Balance.

For example, for the first year there were $100K Cost of Sales and an ending balance of $40K in Inventory. If the second year's Cost of Sales are $150K, and there is no change in Turnover assumptions, then the second year's Ending Balance would be $60K, which is (40/100)*150. If the first year's Turnover assumption was 6, and the second year's turnover was 9, then the resulting estimated balance would be $45K, calculated as (40/100)*150*(6/9).

Business Plan Pro uses the same logic to estimate the third year balance by calculating from the ratio between Cost of Sales, second year Ending Balance, and Turnover assumptions.

TIPS

Fine Tuning your Inventory

Inventory estimates are simple and powerful, but not complex. All the calculations are based on the Cost of Sales portion of your Sales Forecast.

If you need more complex treatment, such as separating finished goods inventory from work in process for a manufacturing company, you can do that with a new table you define yourself. You have a complete spreadsheet application to work with, with hundreds of functions.

Working with the Cash Pilot

Figure 6-44 shows a hypothetical next step with the Cash Pilot, for the example pizza restaurant used in this chapter. In this example we do not have significant sales on credit, so to show the impact of changing Cash Pilot assumptions we took inventory turnover from 10, which was where it started, to 1. That is probably not a realistic estimate for a pizza restaurant, because inventory is mainly foodstuffs, so it would be hard to keep a year's worth on hand. Still it does show how dramatically the Cash Pilot assumptions can affect balances and cash flow.

In this example, the change in inventory assumptions does terrible things to planned cash flow. If the pizza restaurant were keeping a year's worth of inventory on hand, then it would need tens of thousands of dollars of additional working capital. This change shows the importance of the Cash Pilot and the way it can manage cash planning.

FIGURE 6-44: ADJUSTING ASSUMPTIONS WITH CASH PILOT

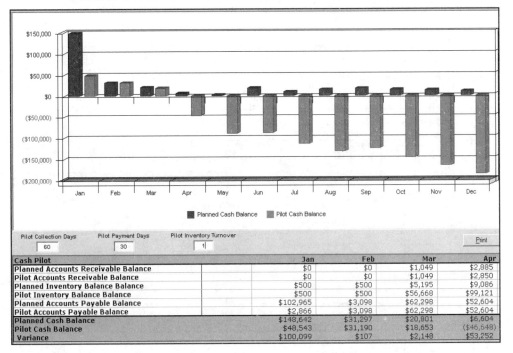

Cash Pilot		Jan	Feb	Mar	Apr
Planned Accounts Receivable Balance		$0	$0	$1,049	$2,885
Pilot Accounts Receivable Balance		$0	$0	$1,049	$2,850
Planned Inventory Balance Balance		$500	$500	$5,195	$9,086
Pilot Inventory Balance Balance		$500	$500	$56,668	$99,121
Planned Accounts Payable Balance		$102,965	$3,098	$62,298	$52,604
Pilot Accounts Payable Balance		$2,866	$3,098	$62,298	$52,604
Planned Cash Balance		$148,642	$31,297	$20,801	$6,604
Pilot Cash Balance		$48,543	$31,190	$18,653	($46,648)
Variance		$100,099	$107	$2,148	$53,252

In this example, the Cash Pilot took inventory from 10 turns per year to 1 turn per year, meaning a year's worth of inventory on average. This is not a realistic assumption, but it illustrates how important these key items are to cash flow. If the inventory were adjusted according to this view, the pizza company has serious cash flow problems.

In Figure 6-45 we adjust the Cash Pilot yet again, this time changing both inventory and payables assumptions to make them more realistic. The initial inventory assumptions were too optimistic, the second set of assumptions way too pessimistic, so this third set is more realistic. Even though inventory is mostly foodstuffs, it is also packaging, and seasonings, and many of its foodstuffs are processed or frozen. Therefore it keeps an average of two months of inventory on hand, in this example, which is a turnover rate of 6. In addition, it needs to pay its vendors faster than 30 days, so that assumption changes to 20 days, on average. You can see the result in Figure 6-45.

FIGURE 6-45: MORE REALISTIC CASH PILOT ASSUMPTIONS

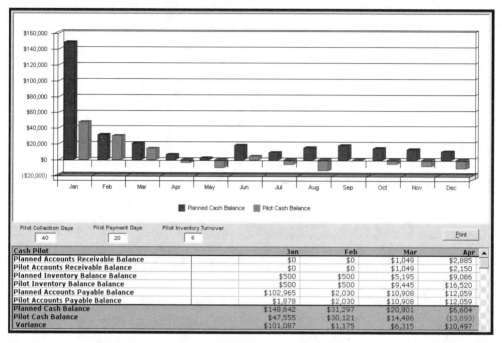

Cash Pilot		Jan	Feb	Mar	Apr
Planned Accounts Receivable Balance		$0	$0	$1,049	$2,885
Pilot Accounts Receivable Balance		$0	$0	$1,049	$2,150
Planned Inventory Balance Balance		$500	$500	$5,195	$9,086
Pilot Inventory Balance Balance		$500	$500	$9,445	$16,520
Planned Accounts Payable Balance		$102,965	$2,030	$10,908	$12,059
Pilot Accounts Payable Balance		$1,878	$2,030	$10,908	$12,059
Planned Cash Balance		$148,642	$31,297	$20,801	$6,604
Pilot Cash Balance		$47,555	$30,121	$14,486	($3,893)
Variance		$101,087	$1,175	$6,315	$10,497

With the more realistic assumptions in this case, the Cash Pilot is an improvement on cash planning, although it still shows negative cash.

As the Cash Pilot assumptions become more realistic, you can choose to replace your previous balance assumptions with the Cash Pilot's balance assumptions instead. Just click the Yes button and the dialog shown in Figure 6-46 appears, offering you the choice of adopting the Cash Pilot estimates.

FIGURE 6-46: ACCEPTING CASH PILOT ASSUMPTIONS

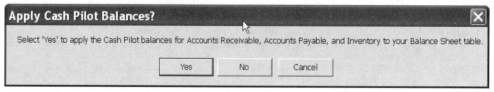

The dialog lets you replace Balance Sheet assumptions with Cash Pilot estimates.

In the pizza restaurant example, after accepting the Cash Pilot revisions as more realistic, the planners would have to go back to cash flow and solve the related cash flow problem. The chart in Figure 6-45 shows that the cash balance is negative when the Cash Pilot estimates replace the originals. More working capital is needed. Accepting the Cash Pilot estimate in this example means a more realistic cash flow, so the plan requires slightly higher borrowing or capital investment. This may seem negative, but it is far better to plan for real needs than to underestimate.

TIPS | **If You Use the Pilot Estimates, You Must Update with Changes**

When the Cash Pilot updates your balance sheet estimates with its estimates, it puts those numbers as numbers, not formulas. Therefore, if you change anything after adopting Cash Pilot estimates, you must go back and confirm the Cash Pilot again. Otherwise, if the Cash Pilot established formulas, then you would lose the ability to experiment with Cash Pilot values, choosing to save them or not.

Background - The Cash Pilot Table

You can access the Cash Pilot table, which details assumptions and formulas, by using the Views > Tables command. The Cash Pilot table does not print as part of your plan unless you specifically link it to some topic, which does not normally happen. It is there just to make assumptions transparent. Figure 6-47 shows a view of that table.

TIPS | **Estimators and Ratios are Different**

We use the estimators as educated guesses, part of our own proprietary mathematical formulas to estimate balances. In the ratios table we calculate the resulting ratios using the standard accounting formulas for ratios, after the fact. They are rarely going to be exactly the same.

FIGURE 6-47: CASH PILOT TABLE

	A	D	E	F
	Table Cash Pilot	Full Columns		Σ $ %
	E10	=IF(PS_Receivables=TRUE,sales*sales_on_credit_percent,0)		
1	**Cash Pilot**	Feb	Mar	Apr
2	Collection Days Estimator	40	40	40
3	Payment Days Estimator	45	45	45
4	Inventory Turnover Estimator	6	6	6
5	**Pilot Cash Flow**	($15,962)	($10,383)	($11,171)
6	**Pilot Cash Balance**	$32,680	$22,297	$11,126
7				
8	**FYI Only: Handling Accounts Receivable**			
9	Previous Accounts Receivable Balance	$0	$0	$1,049
10	Sales on Credit	$0	$1,049	$1,836
11	Cash from receivables	$0	$0	$735
12	Pilot Accounts Receivable Balance	$0	$1,049	$2,150
13				
14	**FYI only: Handling Accounts Payable**			
15	Previous Accounts Payable Balance	$2,965	$4,589	$18,719
16	New Accounts Payable	$3,205	$17,223	$19,041
17	Payments on Accounts Payable	$1,581	$3,093	$10,681
18	Pilot Accounts Payable Balance	$4,589	$18,719	$27,078
19				
20	**FYI only: Inventory**			
21	Previous Inventory Balance	$500	$500	$9,445
22	Inventory Used this Period	$0	$4,722	$8,260
23	Remaining Inventory	$500	($4,222)	$1,185
24	Desired Ending Inventory Balance	$0	$9,445	$16,520
25	Inventory Purchased this Period	$0	$13,667	$15,336
26	Pilot Inventory Balance	$500	$9,445	$16,520
27	Pilot Inventory Purchase	$0	$13,667	$15,336
28				
29	**FYI only: Payables Details**			
30	Payments on this Period's Payables	$0	$0	$0
31	Payments from Initial Balance	$0	$0	$0
32	Payments on Previous Balance	$1,581	$3,093	$10,681

The Cash Pilot table does not normally print as part of the plan. It explains detailed assumptions behind the Cash Pilot. Access it using the Views menu Tables command.

Weak Points in the Math and Formulas

There are some weak points in the way Business Plan Pro calculates these balances. These are the reasons that you might decide to override the formulas and type in your own.

- At several points, the estimators must assume that any month's value is a good approximation of every month's value. The ratios used as calculators are based on annual results, but the calculations come from monthly results. So, for example, the inventory turnover calculations assume your monthly cost of sales is 1/12 of annual cost of sales.
- Estimators rarely match calculated ratio values in the Ratios table. Ratios are calculated after the fact, based on annual numbers. The estimators have a different use and different purpose.

Investment Analysis (PREMIER version)

The Investment Analysis table gives you discounted cash flow analysis including Net Present Value (NPV) and Internal Rate of Return (IRR). Both of these are important financial analysis tools that help a plan present itself in the terms used by the more sophisticated investment analysts. Figure 6-48 shows a sample Investment Analysis.

FIGURE 6-48: INVESTMENT ANALYSIS

N10	=IF(PS_StandardTerm=TRUE,NPV(N14,N8:Q8),NPV(N14,N8:S8))			
	A	N	O	P	Q
3					
4	Initial Investment				
5	Investment	$70,000	$45,000	$100,000	$0
6	Dividends	$0	$0	$0	$0
7	Ending Valuation	$0	$0	$0	$385,000
8	Combination as Income Stream	($70,000)	($45,000)	($100,000)	$385,000
9	Percent Equity Acquired	50%			
10	Net Present Value (NPV)	$87,002			
11	Internal Rate of Return (IRR)	34%			
12					
13	Assumptions				
14	Discount Rate	10.00%			
15	Valuation Earnings Multiple		10	10	10
16	Valuation Sales Multiple		1	1	1
17					
18	Investment (calculated)	$70,000	$45,000	$100,000	$0
19	Dividends		$0	$0	$0
20	Calculated Earnings-based Valuation		$0	$280,000	$520,000
21	Calculated Sales-based Valuation		$280,000	$710,000	$770,000
22	Calculated Average Valuation		$140,000	$495,000	$645,000

The Investment Analysis offers discounted cash flow analyses and a rough estimate of Valuation.

The Estimated Cash Stream

The Investment Analysis starts with the Cash Flow stated in investment terms. That means that an investment is a negative number, and the return is a positive number. In the example, $500,000 is invested at the start of the plan. No money comes out until the fifth year, when the company is valued at $35.6 million.

This example is typical of formal investment analysis. Sales, Profits, Expenses, Assets, and Liabilities are not included in the analysis. The analysis even ignores Cash Flow in this case, because Cash Flow is irrelevant unless it becomes a Dividend.

The example treats the company from the investor's point of view. Namely, there is only one flow into the company that matters, the investment. There are only two flows back out as returns,

Dividends and Equity Valuation. Equity Valuation really matters only when the investor cashes out. Until equity is sold, valuation is just paper money only, not real.

Business Plan Pro creates the cash stream automatically, from the assumptions in your plan. Its formulas pick up on investments and dividend payments during the term of the plan.

TIPS

Buzzwords and Jargon

The NPV and IRR buzzwords are classic examples of MBA jargon. They are not hard to understand or use, so it is worth the effort. Try an Internet search on "IRR" or "NPV" and see how much you find.

The Discount Rate

The Discount Rate is an important element in Discounted Cash Flow analysis. The discount rate is a mathematical estimate of the time value of money and to some extent the risk in an investment.

To understand the discount rate, imagine that somebody offers you the choice between $1,000 delivered today or some greater amount delivered one year from today. Think about how you and other people react to that choice.

There is an old cliché that says a bird in the hand is worth two in the bush. That thought is related. Almost everybody has a preference for now instead of later. Everybody values $1,000 now more than the same amount a year later.

Would you prefer $1,000 now to $1,100 a year from now? What about $1,200 next year? $2,000? $5,000? People differ in their choices between money now, but just about everybody has some amount of additional money that would make them choose to wait. In investment analysis, we use the discount rate to reflect that preference for now over later.

In the example, the Discount Rate is set at 25%. That means $1,000 today is worth approximately $1,250 one year from today. A 10% discount rate would make $1,000 today worth approximately $1,100 a year from today. A 50% discount rate would make it worth $1,500.

Inflation matters to discount rates. The higher the inflation, the higher the discount rate. In an economy with 10% inflation, it takes $1,100 a year from now to equal the value of $1,000 today.

Risk matters. The higher the risk, the higher the discount rate. The bird in hand is worth two in the bush because you might never get the two in the bush.

In the trade-off analysis above, choosing between $1,000 today and $1,250 a year from now, how different do you feel if the promise to pay later comes from a bank, or from an unreliable ne'er-do-well acquaintance? The example sets a Discount Rate of 25%. You type that rate into your business plan as an assumption.

Net Present Value (NPV)

The NPV of an investment stream is the estimated present value of the future stream, at the specified discount rate. Future cash is discounted to its present value.

The formula for NPV in the sample table, Figure 6-48, uses a built-in Business Plan Pro function. The formula in that cell is:

=IF(PS_StandardTerm=TRUE,NPV(N13,N8:S8),NPV(N13,N8:Q8))

The formula applies the NPV function to either the three-year or the five-year cash stream, depending on whether the EasyPlan Wizard setting is for a standard term or a long-term plan.

This analysis depends of course on the assumed valuation for the end of the period. The Valuation assumption is a critical assumption. Business Plan Pro makes a rough estimate based on simplistic assumptions. Use it with caution, and understand how much it depends on those questionable assumptions (more on Valuation below).

The Internal Rate of Return (IRR)

The IRR is the Discount Rate at which the NPV of the Investment is $0. You can experiment with the Investment Analysis included with Business Plan Pro. Set the Discount Rate to the rate shown as IRR, and NPV should be $0.

Analysts use IRR to compare different investments. They expect higher risk investments to show higher IRRs, and generally if the risk is about the same, then the best investment is the one with the higher IRR.

TIPS

Watch the Critical Assumptions

The investment analysis depends entirely on very sensitive critical assumptions: the cash stream depends on ending valuation, which is extremely uncertain. The discount rate makes a huge difference in Net Present Value. Experts learn quickly that they can make huge changes in NPV or IRR with small changes in critical assumptions.

Valuation Estimates

Valuation is what a company is worth, according to stock markets, or buyers and sellers of a business, or tax authorities. Businesses need to determine valuation for tax reasons when ownership changes hands. Ultimately, valuation is not a formula at all, it is as simple as any other commercial transaction: the business is worth as much or as little as buyers will pay for it.

Take this calculated average as a rough estimate at best, subject to the assumptions. It is what we sometimes call a "talking point" in negotiations. Valuation means what the company is worth, what it should sell for if it is sold. Valuation in real business situations is very much more complex than a simple calculation in a spreadsheet.

Think of this the way you might think of the real estate value of a house or some other property. You can talk about it as a formula based on square footage, rooms, bedrooms, or lot size, but the formulas are just a beginning. The actual value depends, however, on many other factors including general economic conditions for the country, specific economic conditions in the local area, the specific neighborhood, neighboring houses, landscaping, sale price of nearby houses, and negotiation effectiveness of the interested parties.

Similarly, the valuation of a business depends not just on simple formulas and multiples, but also general market conditions, specific economics of the business, its location, its branding, its management team, its balance sheet, its customer base, and other factors.

For publicly-traded companies, valuation is the same as their market capitalization: the business' valuation can be determined by multiplying the number of shares outstanding by the value per share.

For privately-held companies, valuation of a business is theoretical until there is a transaction. When the transaction happens, the business is worth whatever the buyers pay for it. You and your business do not necessarily get what you deserve; you get what you negotiate; or what you settle for.

This is important: the valuation estimates in Business Plan Pro are rough estimates only, good starting points for further discussion. Valuation is very much more complex than the simple formulas on this table. Business Plan Pro gives you the earnings multiple and sales multiple formulas for valuation, which are the most common, but not the only formulas.

- The Book Value formula calculates valuation as Assets less Liabilities, just the same as Net Worth. That is supposedly what a business is worth.
- The Liquidation Value formula says the business is worth the liquidation value of its Assets, less Liabilities.
- The Replacement Value formula says the business is worth what it costs to replace it. This comes up for example when a business is purchased by a larger business for the value of its plant, equipment, product line, brand, etc.
- The Times Sales formula is one of two common formulas used for the Business Plan Pro estimate. In the example, the business is worth the Sales Multiple shown in Figure 6-48 as the Calculated Sales-based Valuation. The Valuation Sales Multiple is 1, so the Valuation at the end of the period is $528,000, which is 1 times sales of $528,000.
- The Times Earnings formula is the other of the two most common. Stocks are often quoted in earnings multiples, called PE for "price times earnings" as in 25 times earnings. Earnings in this context is the same as Net Profits, and Business Plan Pro picks this up automatically. The stock's PE ratio is normally quoted as price per share as a multiple of earnings per share. The principal is the same. In the example shown in Figure 6-48, the Earnings Multiple is set as 10, so the Valuation in the last year is $520,000

- Market comparisons (as in real estate) are another very important tool for valuation. Analysts look at actual transactions of similar businesses of similar size.

As we said above, the valuation estimates in Business Plan Pro are rough estimates at best.

Percent Equity Acquired

This row takes your data assumptions input, and gives you a way to confine the investment analysis to some specified portion of equity investment and equity ownership. In this case, the pizza example, the assumption is that the investor ends up with 50% ownership of the pizza restaurant, as shown in the illustration.

TIPS

Spreadsheet Programming

More detailed instructions on programming the Business Plan Pro spreadsheets are found in Chapter 10: Advanced Tables, including details and examples on how to program spreadsheet formulas, programming to link tables, and many other expert features.

Main Help for General How-to-Use Information

Use the Main Help for more information on how to use the software. That is the **Help** facility on your main menu tool bar, as shown here.

FIGURE 6-49: HELP MENU

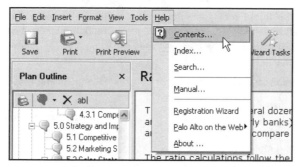

The Business Plan Pro *Help Menu gives you access to several sources of user information.*

This includes information on menus, dialogs, forms, features and functionality. Main Help starts with the Help Menu within Business Plan Pro. Look in the Table of Contents for "Table Mode" to start with Help on tables. Or, as an alternative, just press the F1 key at any time while using Business Plan Pro. You can also search in the Help Index for "Tables," "Table Mode," "Table Options," "Table functions," "Add Tables," "Table Formatting," and of course any menu command in the Table Mode Edit menu, or in the Table Mode Format menu. The table on the next page has some additional details on specific topics in Help.

To Learn More About...	Search the Help Index for...
Adding tables (PREMIER version)	Table, Add Other
Changing row labels, row names	Row labels, Edit
Dealing with locked first column, options for locking and unlocking	Tools, Table Options; Lock Column Headers
Dealing with row headers on top of the columns	Plan Setup; Tools, Table Options; Lock Row Headers
Deleting rows	Delete Data Entry Row
Deleting tables ... taking them out of your outline so they do not print	Plan, Outline: Delete
Exporting to Excel	Export; Excel
Finding detailed row-by-row help	Row-by-row Definitions
General table mode instructions, including how to use the menus, toolbars, etc.	Table Mode; Table Overview
How to break links with topics, so certain tables do not print	Plan, Outline: Delete
How to hide rows so they do not show in printed documents	Row, Format
Inserting new rows	Row, Insert
Inserting tables into your outline	Table, Add Other; Plan, Outline: Insert
Inserting tables from Excel, paste from Excel, import from Excel	Excel, Importing from; Import, Microsoft Excel
Linking data and assumptions from one table to another	Links
Linking tables to topics in the outline, or unlinking them	Plan, Outline: Insert, Delete
Printing tables	Printing; Tools, Table Options; Print, Reports; Print, Table
Setting column headings, Starting Date	Plan Setup
Setting fonts and formats for tables, including all cells or just data entry cells, automatically	Format: Cells, Columns, Fonts
Using the Formula Backstep feature	Formula Backstep
Wizard instructions and examples	Instructions

Your Plan Charts 7

CHAPTER 7: YOUR PLAN CHARTS

In business plans, the more numbers you include, the more charts you need. Charts can illustrate numbers in ways that make immediate visual impact. Given today's technology, you should have the courtesy to illustrate your more important numbers with business charts. This makes it easier for your reader.

Business Plan Pro® includes built-in charts that automatically illustrate the most important numbers in your plan.

Charts vs. Tables

Charts are graphics. Tables are financial numbers displayed in rows and columns. We mention this because in Business Plan Pro tables and charts are distinct and separate objects. Figure 7-1 shows a few of the main charts that automatically link to topics in a standard plan.

FIGURE 7-1: MAIN BUSINESS PLAN PRO CHARTS

Table	Description	Example
Cash	Columns show cash balance and cash flow for next 12 months.	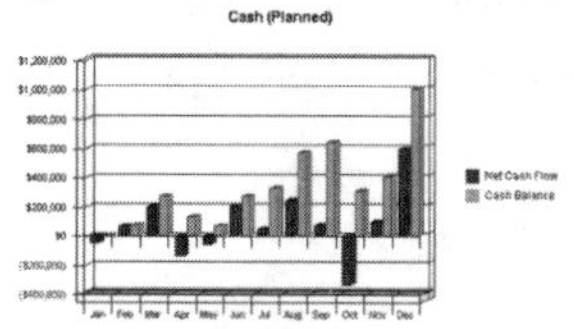
Highlights	Columns show sales, gross margin, and earnings by year.	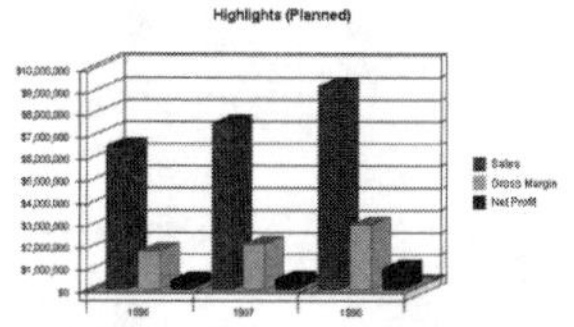
Sales Monthly	Columns show sales for each of the first 12 months.	
Milestones	Track each milestone by start and end dates, budget, and manager.	
Market	Pie shows potential customers in different market segments.	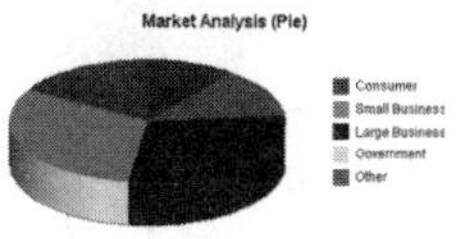
Past Performance (or Start-up)	Columns show highlights of past results for ongoing companies, or start-up balance for start-ups.	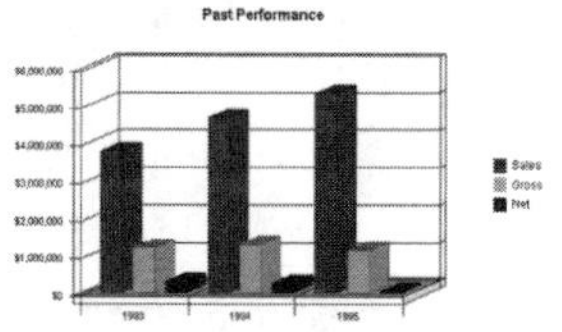

Business Plan Pro *includes more than a dozen pre-programmed charts that illustrate your tables.*

Charts Always Link to Predefined Tables

Business Plan Pro is designed to build business charts automatically, link them to specific numbers, and place them where they belong in your plan document. Because these charts link directly to certain key numbers in the tables, the information shown in the charts is a correct interpretation of the source numbers in your plan.

Figure 7-2 shows an example. The break-even point (circled on the chart) is taken directly from the "Monthly Units Break-even" row shown in the Break-even Analysis table.

FIGURE 7-2: CHARTS LINKED TO TABLE NUMBERS

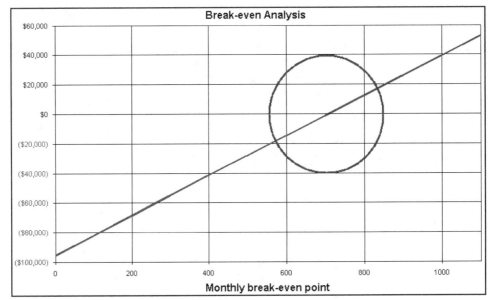

	A	O
1	Break-even Analysis:	
2	Monthly Units Break-even	709
3	Monthly Revenue Break-even	$334,457
4		
5	Assumptions:	
6	Average Per-Unit Revenue	$471.65
7	Average Per-Unit Variable Cost	$336.91
8	Estimated Monthly Fixed Cost	$95,542

As you type in your table numbers, you automatically create your charts.

Use the Tables to Change Numbers in your Charts

The only way you can change any number shown in any chart is by changing the number in the source table. You cannot change the way charts link to specific numbers in your tables.

Modify Chart Appearance

You can change a chart's appearance, placement, or even whether or not it shows up. As you build your business plan, you can change the colors, design, fonts, titles, and even types of charts, but you cannot design new and different charts in Business Plan Pro. Its built-in chart modification features are for the pre-programmed charts only.

Link Charts, Unlink Charts

Certain charts are automatically linked to their corresponding topics. You can link other charts to topics as you want and need, including charts created outside of Business Plan Pro. Also, you can unlink a chart from its topic. Unlinking a chart does not delete it from your file; it just does not print in the plan.

Import Charts

You can import graphics from other software and link them to a topic in your plan, but you cannot design new and different charts within Business Plan Pro.

Other Charts in Plan Outline (PREMIER version)

Business Plan Pro PREMIER provides additional charts. These charts are listed at the bottom of the Plan Outline screen under the heading Other Charts (Not in the Plan Outline).

To Learn More About...	**Search the Help Index for...**
Chart styles, formatting and how to change appearance	Chart Wizard; Chart Designer; Chart Formatting
Import a chart from another program	Graphic; Insert Image
Add a graphic to a topic	Graphic; Insert Image
Link and unlink charts	Plan, Outline: Insert, Delete

Help on How to Use the Charts

This chapter gives an overview of the charts included in Business Plan Pro. Instructions, examples and online Help are provided within the software to explain the mechanics of working with your charts. The following describes how to access these help resources in Business Plan Pro.

Main Help for General How-to-Use Information

Use the main Help for more information on how to use the software. That is the Help facility on your main menu, as shown here.

FIGURE 7-3: HELP MENU

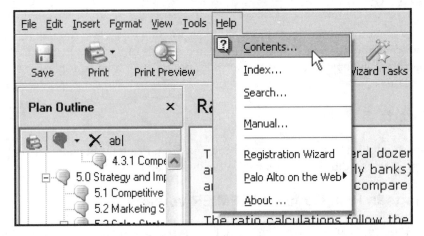

The main Help menu provides several information sources on using Business Plan Pro.

You can also access Help on charts as follows:

- Look in the Help file Table of Contents for "Chart Mode."
- Press the F1 key while looking at a chart to open chart help.
- Search the Help Index for "charts," "chart mode," "chart options," and "customizing chart."

Wizard Instructions

Chart-by-chart instructions are included in the EasyPlan Wizard® instructions window. Figure 7-4 shows an example of the instructions window for the Cash chart.

FIGURE 7-4: WIZARD INSTRUCTIONS FOR A CHART

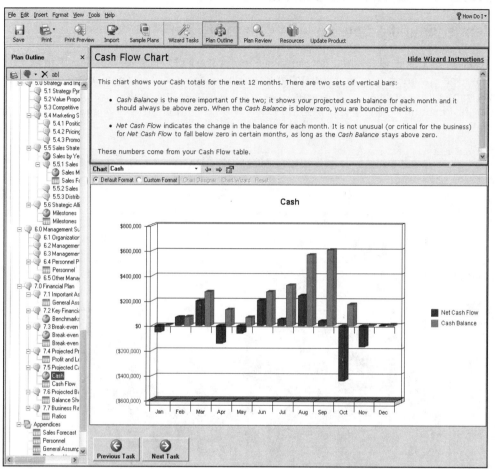

The Business Plan Pro *EasyPlan Wizard includes instructions (highlighted in the illustration) for every chart. This is your main source for information about each chart.*

Additional Chart Details

Understanding the Benchmarks Chart (PREMIER version)

If you select "more detail" in the Plan Setup section of the PREMIER version EasyPlan Wizard, you have the option of including a Benchmarks chart with your plan. The Benchmarks chart shows comparative or relative values for five critical business financial indicators: Sales, Gross Margin %, Operating Expenses, Collection Days, and Inventory Turnover. Figure 7-5 shows an example.

FIGURE 7-5: BENCHMARKS FOR ONGOING COMPANIES

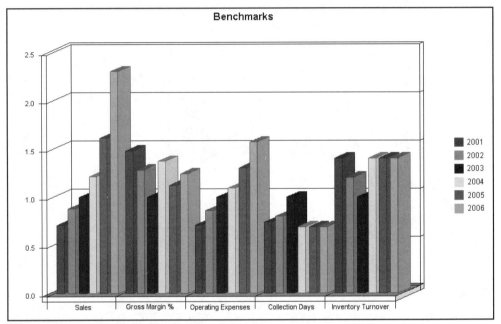

In the Business Plan Pro PREMIER *version, the Benchmarks chart compares past and future financial indicators as index values, showing the amount of change in each one. The illustration shows Benchmarks for an Ongoing company, which has data for six years.*

The Benchmarks chart uses index values to compare different numbers. Specifically, Sales and Operating Expenses are measured in currency value (usually dollars), while Gross Margin is a percent, Collection Days are measured in days, and Inventory Turnover is measured as a number.

The index values compare changes in the numbers, as relative values. The last full year, the last column in the Past Performance table, is always set to 1, and the other years, past and future, are shown as values relative to 1. The bars show relative change, not absolute values.

In the example shown, Sales in 2003 were $5.3 million. Sales for 2001 were $3.8 million, so the red bar in the chart shows up as less than 1, about 70%. Actually, 3.8/5.3 = .72, which is about what the red bar shows. The light blue bar in Sales for the year 2006 is clearly between 2 and 3, so Sales for that year are more than double the $5.3 million from 2003. In the sample plan, the estimate is $12.2 million for 2006, which is 2.3 times $5.3 million.

Then take Gross Margin, which is expressed as percent. In the sample plan, the Gross Margin for 2003 was 21.3%. The chart shows the decline from 31.4% in 2001 (displayed as about 1.5 times the index value of 1 for 2003, and then the projected increase back to 29% in 2004, 24% in 2005, and 26% in 2006. You can see the chart showing relative values. Sales are in millions of dollars, and Gross Margin in percentages, but we can compare the relative level of change for both factors over time.

Benchmarks Chart is Customized in PREMIER to Match Plan Options

The Benchmarks chart displays differently for different EasyPlan Wizard Plan Setups. Figure 7-5 shows how the Benchmarks chart for an ongoing company includes at least six years' of data. Figure 7-6 shows how the Benchmarks for a start-up company has as few as three years, because it does not have past history to compare. Setting your plan for five vs. three years also has an affect. The Benchmarks shows bars for Accounts Receivable only if your Plan Setup includes Accounts Receivable, and it shows bars for Inventory only if your Plan Setup includes Inventory.

Some Numbers Do Not Work with Benchmarks

Because of its dependence on index values, the Benchmarks chart can become useless with unusual sets of numbers. Here are some examples of good numbers that simply do not display well in the Benchmarks chart:

- Business plans whose numbers switch in value, such as from negative to positive. If your Gross Margin is negative for the index year, then the Benchmarks chart simply does not display any useful information. It shows the negative year as 1, and the positive years as negative. That may be annoying, but it is also unavoidable: Business Plan Pro needs to work with index values to compare these factors, and index values behave this way when the index number is negative.

- Business plans that involve huge changes in any one of the five factors probably do not show good benchmarks indicators for the other values. For example, your Sales in the index year is $10,000, but Sales soar to $2 million in the first year, $10 million in the second, and $25 million in the third year. The chart in this case shows a year 3 value of 2,500, because $25 million is 2,500 times greater than $10,000. With one of the benchmark values showing a maximum of 2,500, the others probably likely do not show at all.

Unlink Benchmarks Chart When it Does Not Work

If the Benchmarks chart does not work for you, do not use it. And do not worry about not using it. Find the text topic linked to the Benchmarks chart and unlink that chart so it does not print.

You can also delete the entire topic if you want. Normally Business Plan Pro PREMIER version links the Benchmarks chart to the Key Financial Indicators topic.

FIGURE 7-6: BENCHMARKS FOR START-UP COMPANIES

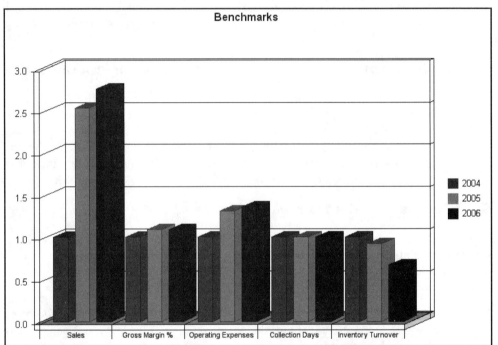

The Benchmarks chart for the Start-up company has fewer years, because there is no past history to compare.

The Break-even Chart

The Break-even chart, shown in Figure 7-7, is a business plan staple, but can also present problems in some cases. By default, Business Plan Pro gets break-even numbers from the Sales Forecast and Profit and Loss tables, but the numbers in break-even are not used by any other charts and tables, so you can also input your own assumptions to see the resulting chart. Unfortunately the break-even depends on averaging inputs over your whole business, which makes it less useful for some businesses that have very diverse product lines.

FIGURE 7-7: BREAK-EVEN CHART

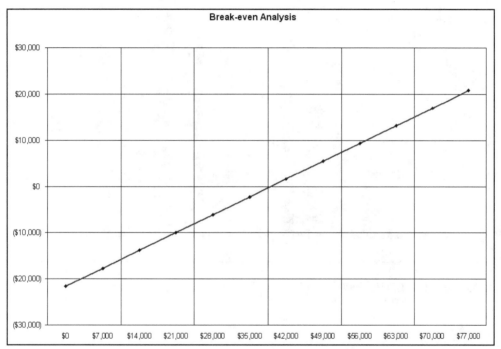

The break-even chart shows how sales affect profits, given some general assumptions for a hypothetical average month. It does not necessarily fit with all plans, so if it does not work for your plan, do not include it.

The Sales Monthly Chart

This chart is linked to your Sales Forecast table. Figure 7-8 shows an example of the sales for each row in a sample restaurant plan.

FIGURE 7-8: SALES MONTHLY CHART

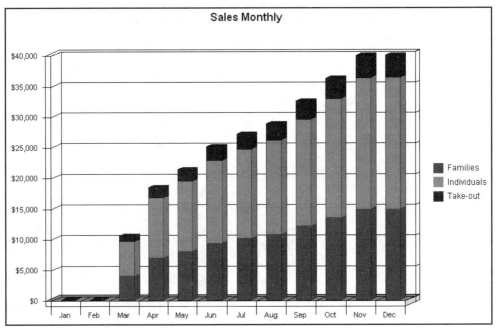

This first chart of a series shows the monthly sales bar chart illustrating the hypothetical plan. This is the chart you use most often.

The Organizational Chart (PREMIER version)

The organizational chart normally links to the topic named "Organizational Structure." If you do not want to use it you can ignore it, and unlink the chart from the topic, so it does not print.

Figure 7-9: Organizational Chart

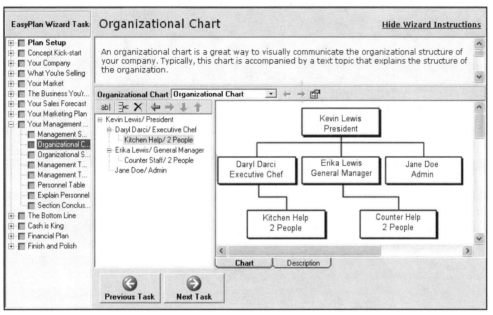

Use this chart feature in the PREMIER *version to include an organizational chart as part of your chapter on management.*

For more detailed help on working with this built-in chart, search the Help Index for "Organizational chart."

Make it Your Plan

Remember, nothing about Business Plan Pro is carved in stone...you can modify the charts' appearance, ignore the built-in charts, or make your own charts with other software and import them into your plan...it is your plan.

This page intentionally blank.

Print and Publish

CHAPTER 8: PRINT AND PUBLISH

Distributing your plan to the appropriate people and in the appropriate format can be critical to the success of your business plan or, more importantly, your business. Business Plan Pro® *provides you with numerous options for printing your plan, or parts of your plan, and the tools to distribute it.*

Business Plan Pro *is also capable of printing additional documents like the Concept Kick-start, the Loan Document, and the Summary Memo.*

And if you are looking to publish electronically as well, there is www.secureplan.com.

Overview – Form Follows Function

Business Plan Pro is designed to print a good-looking plan including cover page, legal page, table of contents, and appendices. The printing is automatic and so is the formatting. You can manage options with the Print Options form. If you are printing to a color printer, the plan includes color graphics.

The standard format is professional. You could do more with a lot more effort—page layout, extensive graphics, etc.—but you certainly do not have to. We have seen the standard format do fine with investors, bankers, and even at graduate-level business plan contests. No serious business plan evaluation process is going to reject a plan developed and printed in Business Plan Pro for formatting or print related problems.

You do have other options. You can also post your finished plan to a website, either your own site or the password-protected secure site at www.secureplan.com. And you can save your plan as an Adobe Acrobat electronic document, as a Business Plan Pro Word Document, as a Rich Text Format document (.rtf), or as plain text for emailing. This chapter looks at output options, including the process of printing, and a review of related business plan documents and tools, such as the presentation and the summary memo.

The form and output of your business plan should match its business purpose. Every document deserves the basic respect of grammar, spelling, and basic editing. A business plan submitted to a venture capital firm for instance, should have a better presentation than what you normally expect for an internal plan developed for in-house use only. Plans used for venture contests generally require more formality, and perhaps more flair, than plans used internally. Banks care less about flair and more about collateral.

Some companies put a great deal of attention into the presentation and formatting of even internal plans. For example, we were involved in a three-year business plan for Apple Japan in the early 1990s that ended with a professionally-designed annual plan logo and hundreds of copies of the plan printed with a full-color cover. On the other hand, we have also seen some entrepreneurial business plans that were so full of fancy graphics and color illustrations that they made investors nervous. In this context too, form should follow function. The plan is a business document.

The presentation of the plan document, including such variables as covers, coil binding, and quality of paper, depend mainly on your own good judgment. There is also a growing trend for plans online, such as at www.secureplan.com, a secure and password-protected site. Joe Tanous, a venture capitalist, told us his firm "does not accept business plans on paper anymore." He said that stance was not unusual, and is becoming more common.

Plan Review

Before you publish or distribute your business plan, always run it through a final edit. Read it over again. Have someone else read it for you. Sometimes you do not see errors because you are too close to them.

FIGURE 8-1: THE PLAN REVIEW

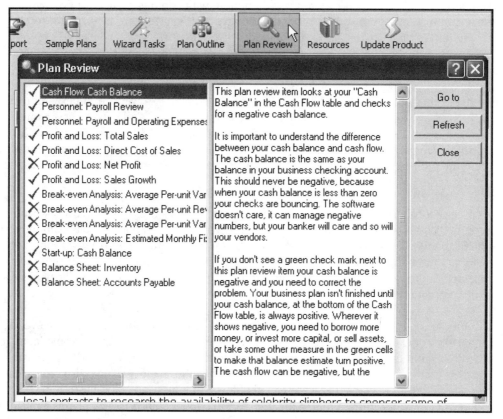

Access the Plan Review from the icon button or from the EasyPlan Wizard Tasks' Finish and Polish section.

- Business Plan Pro has a built-in tool, the Plan Review, shown in Figure 8-1, which reviews your plan, text and tables, for completeness and common errors. We strongly recommend that you use the Plan Review before you distribute your business plan.

- Run the spell checker from the toolbar or the Tools menu, but do not trust it implicitly. A correctly spelled wrong word is not flagged as an error.

- Check the numbers in your tables and charts. Make sure they match each other and match the number references in your text.

Printing Your Plan

Business Plan Pro is designed to format and print a business plan as easily as possible, using the Print commands from your File menu, as shown in Figure 8-2.

FIGURE 8-2: FILE > PRINT MENU

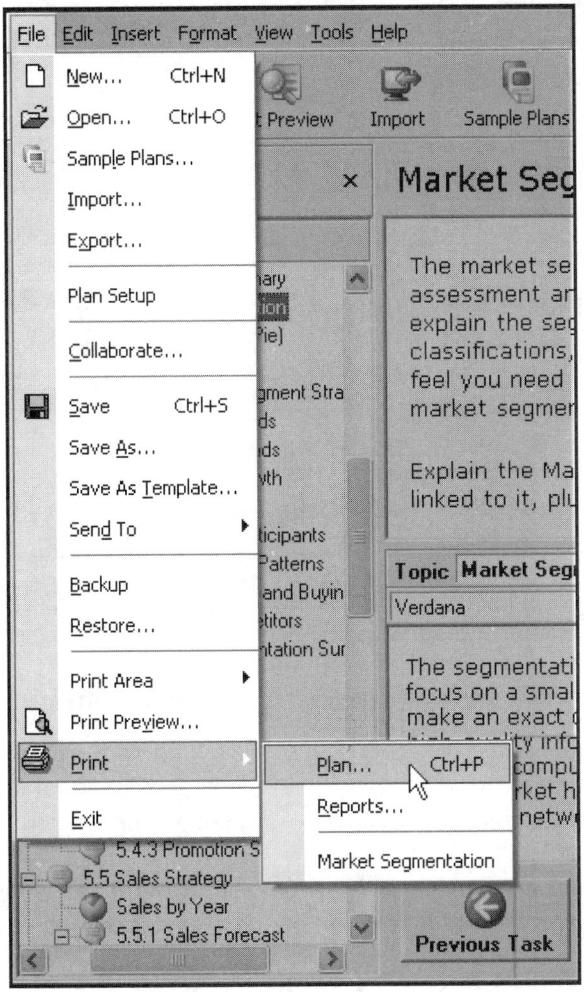

The Print Menu sub-menu options, which is discussed in more detail in the following section of this chapter.

Help   For step-by-step procedures, click the dialog Help buttons or the Help menu.

Print Dialog

The print dialog box shown in Figure 8-3 displays when you choose the File > Print command.

FIGURE 8-3: PRINT DIALOG

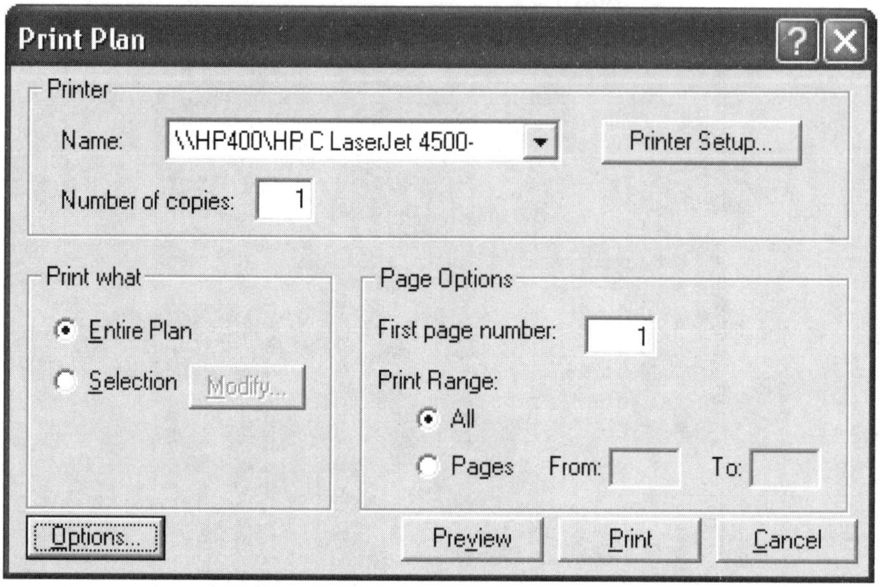

The Print Dialog box lets you specify what you wish to print. The default setting prints the entire plan with all linked tables and charts.

If you are printing your entire plan, you can accept the default settings.

- If you wish to print only specific pages, adjust the settings in the Print Range portion.
- If you wish to print only certain topics, choose the Print what > Selection button. It displays an outline list in which you use the check boxes to select the sections to print (described in the following section of this chapter).
- If you wish to print supporting pages with your plan (Cover Page, Table of Contents, table Appendices, etc.), click on the Options button (described later in this chapter).

📌 TIPS · Select Topics Before You Print

There are lots of reasons to print just selected topics: you might want just a company summary, or the sales and marketing topics and tables, or maybe just the topics that have monthly financials printed in the appendices.

Use the Print > Print what option to select topics rather than printing the whole plan.

Print Options

From within the main Print dialog, the Options button lets you be even more specific as to the portions of your plan you wish to print. Figure 8-4 shows the Print Options form.

FIGURE 8-4: PRINT OPTIONS FORM

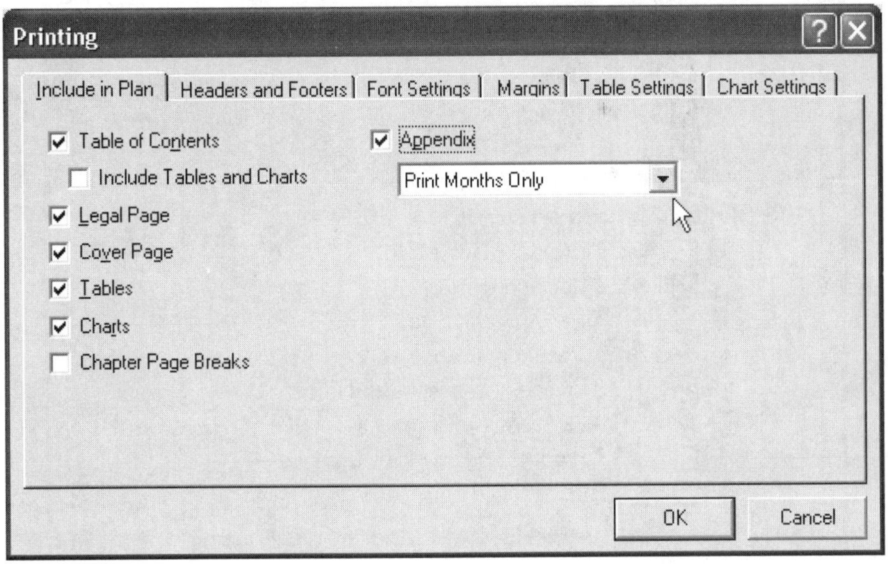

Use the Print Options form to select portions of your plan to print. The default setting to is print all selections.

This form also contains tabbed sections that let you:

- Customize header and footer information to print at the top and bottom of each page of your printed plan.
- Adjust the font style/font size settings for your printed document.
- Adjust the margin settings to print.
- Choose between several different table print layouts (Table Settings).
- Choose to print charts in black and white (Chart Settings).

Printing Selected Topics Only

If you wish to print only selected topics, the Selection setting in the Print dialog displays the full topic outline and all linked tables and charts. Mark the topic(s) to print. Figure 8-5 shows the Selection dialog.

FIGURE 8-5: SELECT TOPICS TO PRINT

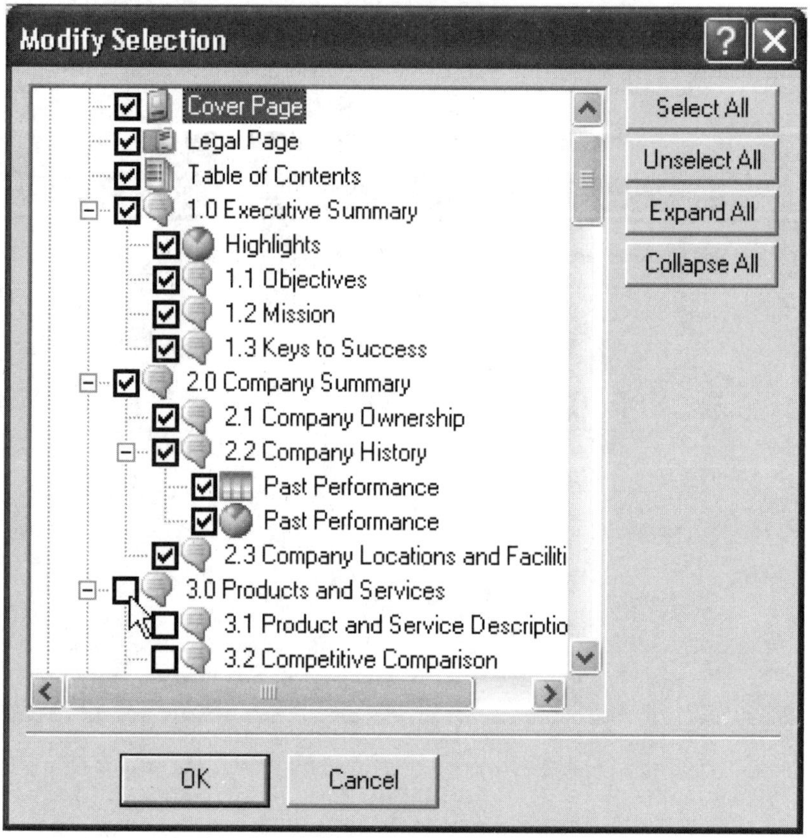

Scroll through the topic outline and mark the topic(s) you wish to print.

How to Select Topics to Print

- **Select All** = All topics and linked tables/charts.
- **Unselect All** = No items selected to print.
- **Expand All** = Displays all levels of the outline.
- **Collapse All** = Shows only the highest level topics in outline.

Print Preview

Before you print your plan, it is a good idea to look at it first on the screen and confirm that it contains all the sections you want and that the page formatting is correct. The Print Preview option lets you do this. Figure 8-6 shows an example of the Print Preview screen.

FIGURE 8-6: PRINT PREVIEW SCREEN

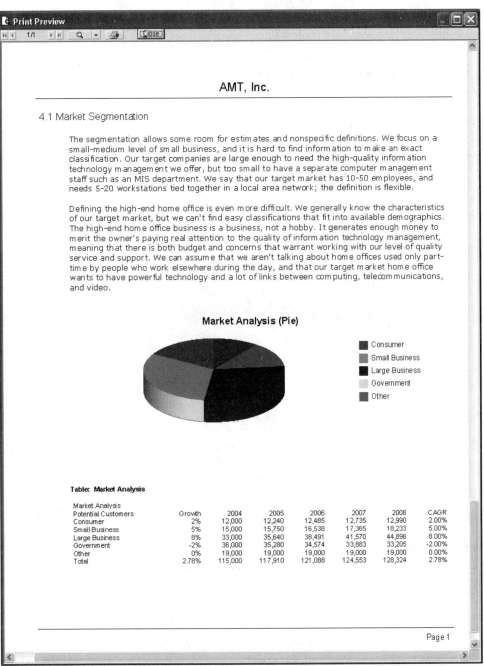

The Print Preview shows you what the printed plan will look like.

Print Menu

One of the great strengths of Business Plan Pro is its ability to print a beautiful business plan complete with Cover Page, Table of Contents, Legal Page, tables, charts, and Appendices.

Select the File > Print command to print your business plan. From there you can also access a wide range of print options.

Print Document – Options

Different types of planning documents can be printed. They are already formatted to include specific plan information for different needs. The following describes them in detail. Figure 8-7 shows the Print sub-menu options.

FIGURE 8-7: PRINT SPECIAL DOCUMENTS

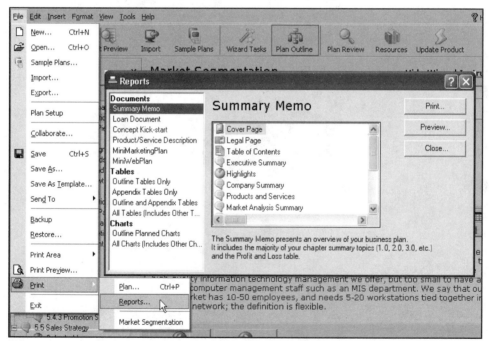

Choose to print the document that best meets your current needs.

Plan

This menu opens a dialog box to print some or all of your business plan. You can specify topics, linked tables and charts, Cover Page, etc. The default setting is to print the entire plan file, including Cover Page, Table of Contents, Legal Page, and monthly table Appendices.

Reports

Business Plan Pro is already programmed to select certain topics and print those selections conveniently, as specialized plan documents. The contents of each report are listed below. Each report also includes a Cover Page, Legal Page and Table of Contents.

Summary Memo

The Summary Memo presents an overview of your business plan for investors, friends, colleagues, business partners, or family. It includes the majority of your summary topics and the Profit and Loss (Income Statement) table.

- Executive Summary
- Highlights (chart)
- Company Summary
- Products
- Market Analysis Summary
- Strategy and Implementation Summary
- Competitive Edge
- Management Summary
- Financial Plan
- Projected Profit and Loss (topic, table, and appendix)

Loan Document

The Loan Document is more financially oriented than the Summary Memo document, and it is often presented to bankers or venture capitalists with an introductory cover letter. The Loan Document does not replace the business plan, it is just a summary. However, it is sometimes appreciated by the venture capitalist or banker.

- Executive Summary
- Highlights (chart)
- Company Ownership
- Financial Plan
- Projected Profit and Loss (topic table, and appendix)
- Projected Cash Flow (topic, table, appendix, and chart)
- Projected Balance Sheet (topic table, and appendix)

Concept Kick-start

The Concept Kick-start presents a brief overview of your business concept. It is a great document to pass on to close colleagues, friends, or family as a tool for communicating your basic business concept; however, we do not recommend distributing this document for funding purposes.

- Objectives
- Mission
- Break-even Analysis (topic, table, and chart)

Product/Service Description

The Product/Service Description presents a brief overview of what you are selling. Again, like the Concept Kick-start, this is a great document to share with close colleagues, friends or family as a tool for communicating your basic business concept. It can sometimes help to share a document like this or the Concept Kick-start to see if there is a viable business idea there.

- Products/Services
- Product/Service Description
- Competitive Comparison
- Sourcing
- Technology
- Future Products

Mini Marketing Plan

The Mini Marketing Plan describes your overall marketing plan, strategy, tactics, and marketing programs. This is a great document to share with your marketing team. Most likely, your marketing team uses this document to prepare a full-length marketing plan to describe strategy, tactics, and marketing programs in further detail.

- Market Analysis Summary
- Market Segmentation
- Market Analysis (table and pie chart)
- Target Market Segment Strategy
- Market Needs
- Market Trends
- Market Growth
- Competitive Edge
- Marketing Strategy
- Positioning Statement
- Pricing Strategy
- Promotion Strategy
- Distribution Strategy
- Sales Strategy
- Sales Forecast (topic, table, and appendix)
- Sales Monthly (chart)
- Sales by Year (chart)

The contents of these reports differs slightly in the PREMIER version, as it has more topics, tables, and charts.

MiniWeb Plan

The MiniWebPlan describes your overall Internet strategy. This report option will only display when you select "yes" to a Website from the Plan Setup in the EasyPlan Wizard.

Printing Tables

The File > Print > Reports command lets you print tables. Figure 8-8 shows the Outline Tables list in the Print Reports dialog.

FIGURE 8-8: PRINT TABLES FROM REPORTS

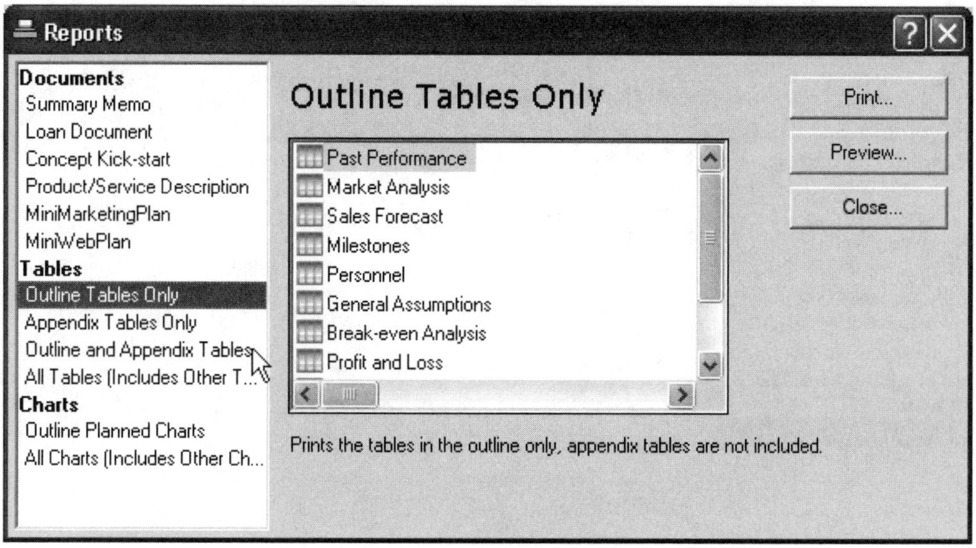

You can print all plan tables using the Print > Reports form. This option gives you more control over table output.

TIPS

Print Tables Separately

To print the current table only, choose File > Print > Table Name. The table name automatically displays. Highlight the table name to print.

Printing Charts

The File > Print > Reports command includes the option to print charts. Figure 8-9 shows the charts list from the Print Reports dialog.

FIGURE 8-9: PRINT CHARTS FROM REPORT WRITER

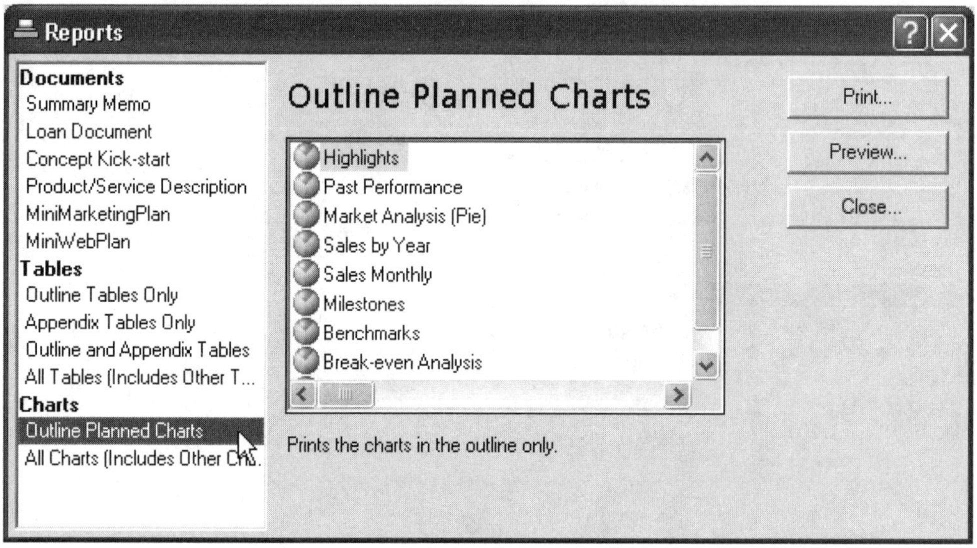

You can also print a single chart directly from Chart view, as a single graphic. This option gives you more control over chart output.

TIPS

Print Charts Separately

Print the current chart by choosing File > Print > Chart Name. The chart name automatically displays from the menu. Highlight the chart name to print.

Export

The Export command is part of the File menu, as shown in Figure 8-10.

FIGURE 8-10: FILE > EXPORT MENU AND EXPORT WIZARD

The File > Export menu opens the Export Wizard. Click Next to continue.

The Export command saves a business plan in one of the following different formats:

1. Business Plan Pro Word Document (.doc) file.
2. Microsoft Excel® Workbook (.xls) file.
3. Adobe Acrobat® Portable Document Format (.pdf) file.
4. Rich Text Format (.rtf) file.
5. Hypertext Markup Language (.htm) pages for use on the World Wide Web.
6. Palo Alto Software Plan Component (PREMIER version) (.pdp) file.

Help For step-by-step procedures, click the dialog Help button or the Help menu.

The exported file can contain the entire text outline or the spreadsheet. Figure 8-11 shows the Export dialog.

FIGURE 8-11: EXPORT OPTIONS DIALOG

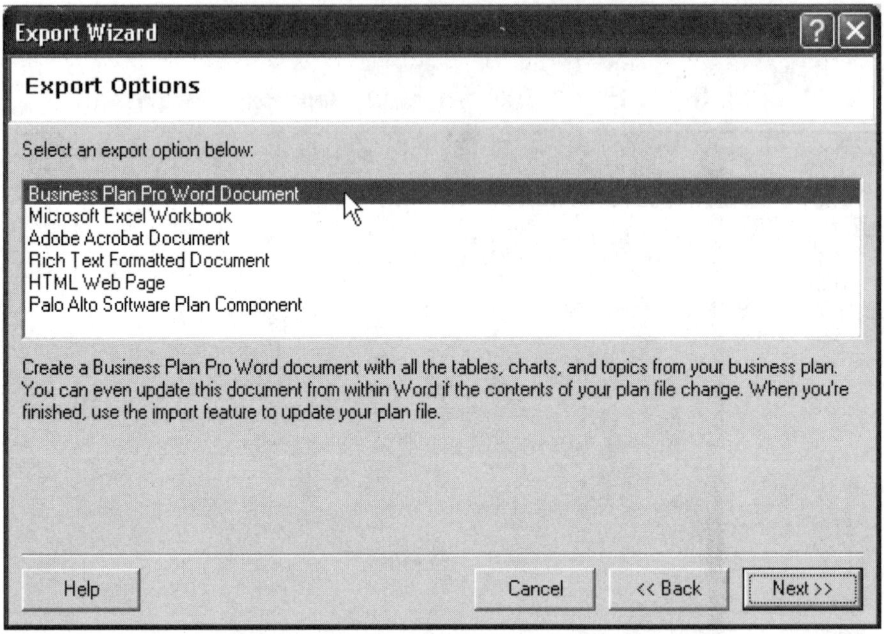

The Export command lets you save your plan file to several different formats for use with word processing, spreadsheet, and other programs. The Plan Component command shown is a PREMIER version feature (see Appendix C of this manual).

- Use File > Export.
- Choose which format to export and click Next.
  - If you export as a Business Plan Pro Word Document, you can open the .doc file in Microsoft Word with enhanced features and a special Palo Alto Software menu that allows dynamic interactivity with BPP. The file retains all of its text formatting, including tabs and indents.
  - If you export as .xls, you create an Excel Workbook that contains all your plan tables.
  - If you export as .pdf, your plan can be read onscreen using the Acrobat Reader or your Internet Browser. The pages in the .pdf file display the same as if they were printed. This is a read-only file.
  - If you export as .rtf, the file can be opened in any word processing program such as MS Word, Write, and Works, and retains most of the original formatting, including font style, font size, bold, underline, and italic.
  - If you export as .htm, individual html-coded pages are created for each page of your plan.
  - If you are a PREMIER version user and export as a .pdp Plan Component, this file can be imported directly into another business plan.

FIGURE 8-12: EXPORT CONTENT SELECTION

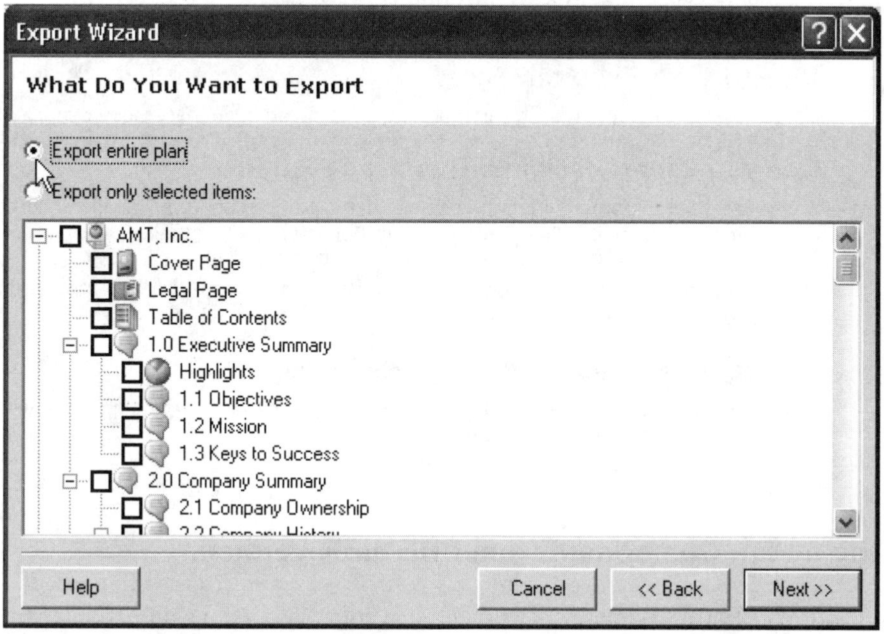

You can chose to Export the entire plan, or selected topics, tables and/or charts.

The Wizard lets you choose to export your entire plan, or click the button for selected items. You choose which topics, tables and/or charts to export by scrolling through the list and clicking in the check boxes next to each item.

FIGURE 8-13: EXPORT DIRECTORY CHOICE

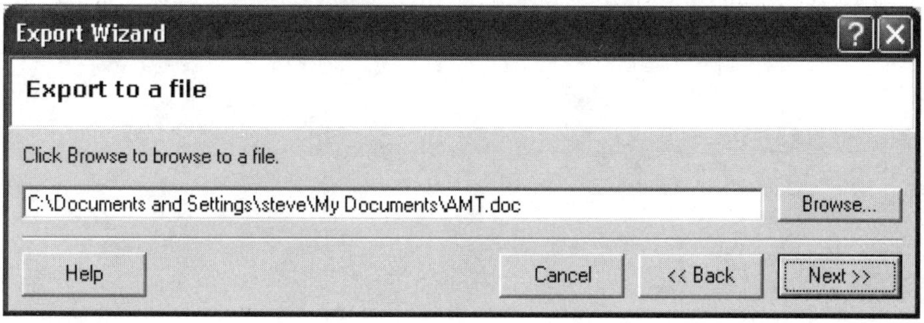

The default filename for the .doc file is the same as your business plan file. This .doc file is also stored in the default directory, unless you specify differently.

Once you have selected what you want to export, follow the Export Wizard screens in choosing a file directory, as shown in Figure 8-13, and finishing your export.

Directory for Exported Files...

Unless you specify otherwise, your exported file is saved in your My Documents folder.

Can you Import back into Business Plan Pro?

These are different formats from the original plan file (.bpd) and are limited in how they can be imported back into Business Plan Pro. For instance, text topics can be re-imported from a Business Plan Pro Word Document. In the PREMIER version, Excel tables can be re-imported into User-defined tables. However, you can use the Windows clipboard to copy and paste text back into your business plan.

No Technical Support for Exported files

Our technical support facilities do not include help working with exported files or with modifying them using other software.

Exporting a Plan Component from PREMIER Version

Business Plan Pro PREMIER version has an additional command, Plan Component, which allows you to export all or part of the plan to another Business Plan Pro user. See Appendix C of this manual for more information.

?

To Learn more about...	Search the Help Index for...
Export Plan Component-PREMIER version	Export, Import, Collaborate

The PowerPoint Presentation

When a business plan is part of new financing, either debt financing or new investment, the process frequently involves a streamlined presentation. Investors expect it. Mainstream venture capitalists, angel investors, and investment clubs normally consider new investments using a process that includes a presentation event. The entrepreneurs, key members of the management team, have limited time to show the investors their business opportunity. Normally they do that using a slide presentation. These days, that most often means a PowerPoint® presentation using a projector connected to a computer.

The Presentation

The business plan presentation is valuable for presenting a plan to investors. Although it is based on the plan, and describes the plan, it is a different medium and should be different from the plan.

Business Plan Pro includes several PowerPoint templates for a standard business plan presentation. We partnered with **PresentationPro, Inc.** to deliver professional, graphically sharp presentation templates for your business plan. Click the Resources button > Make it Happen > Present > Presentation Templates for more information and access to these templates.

- Agree Template
- Big Cash Template
- Premier Template
- Screens Template
- Target Template

While the details and specifics depend on you, your plan, and your audience, a standard business plan presentation includes about 7-20 slides covering some or all of the following (details on how to move information from the business plan to PowerPoint are in Chapter 9: Working with Microsoft Office):

- Title slide. You can do "My Company Business Plan" or some other title.
- Highlights. The Highlights chart from Business Plan Pro, displayed as large as possible, words to be added by the presenter, in person.
- The Market. The Market (pie) chart from Business Plan Pro.
- The Market Need. Use bullet points from either the Mission or the Market Analysis text topics.
- Competitive Advantage. Use bullet points from this section in your plan's chapter on Strategy.
- Sales Forecast. Show the chart from Business Plan Pro. Talk about the details.
- Management Team. Names and positions of the top people. Fill in the rest verbally.
- Financial Plan. Highlights only, in bullet points.

- <u>Benchmarks</u>. Business Plan Pro PREMIER version's Benchmarks chart gives you good talking points.
- <u>Break-even</u>. The Business Plan Pro chart, first year, important for discussion.
- <u>First-year Cash</u>. Just the chart, from Business Plan Pro.
- <u>Specific Objectives</u>. Bullet points only, taken from the first chapter of the plan.
- <u>Milestones</u>. If possible show the Milestones chart only.
- <u>Investment Analysis</u>. Bullet points only, taken from the PREMIER version's Investment Analysis table.
- <u>Keys to Success</u>. Bullet points, from this topic in the first chapter.
- <u>Next Steps</u>. Always a good idea, end the discussion with next steps, assuming a positive outcome.

Like a business plan, a business plan presentation is a specialized tool. Most of these presentations need to summarize an entire business plan in a streamlined 7-20 slides for a talk that lasts about 30 minutes.

- It uses graphics to illustrate main points. The slide displays the chart only, so the presenter fills in the details.
- It uses bullet points and key phrases only. They are reminders and placeholders, not complete thoughts.
- It is all summary. The text is large and there is not much of it. Charts tell most of the story.

A good presentation is about results. It is short and exciting. It makes its key points quickly and well. It needs to be optimized for the business purpose, avoid details, and stick to highlights.

Always, even when details are important, keep the text large and the graphics simple. People do not read details from a presentation.

This kind of optimized tool is not done automatically by computer software, and particularly not by business plan software. The format is different, the purpose is different, so the tool itself must also be different. There is no way a business plan document can automatically create a PowerPoint presentation without ending up with a poor presentation, too much text, too many numbers, and not enough summary.

Chapter 9: Working with Microsoft Office explains how to create this kind of presentation in PowerPoint using your plan developed with Business Plan Pro to provide the content.

Web Options as Output

The Internet and the World Wide Web offer attractive alternatives to distributing a document as a printed physical copy. The advantages include immediate availability, always having the latest copy online, and multiple access 24 hours a day, 7 days a week.

www.secureplan.com

Business Plan Pro includes the facility to publish a business plan directly to a secure, password-protected website provided by Palo Alto Software. The commands for uploading onto a secure website are built into the software. Click the File > Send To > SecurePlan.com command.

Select SecurePlan.com and a welcome screen displays, similar to that shown in Figure 8-14.

FIGURE 8-14: SECUREPLAN.COM WELCOME SCREEN

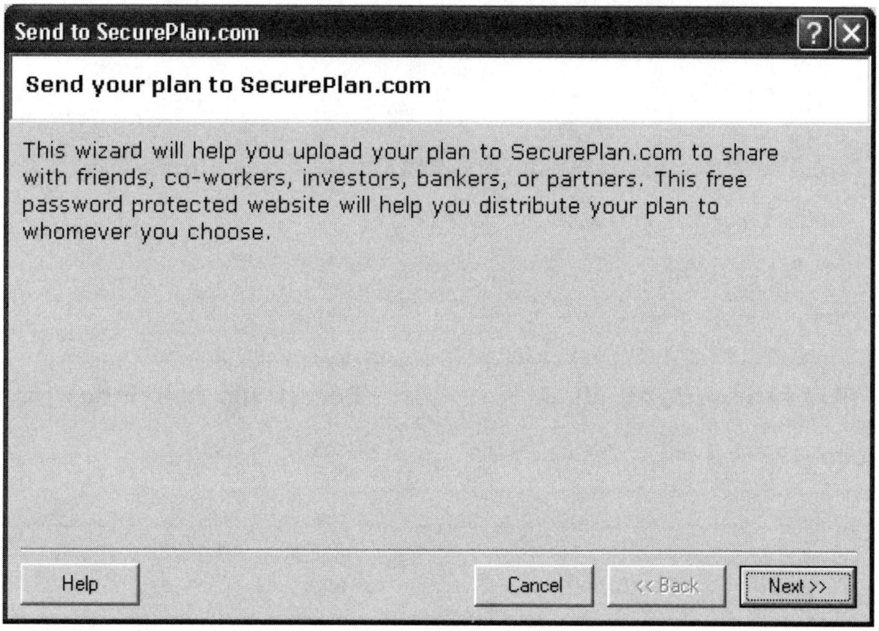

These screens walk you through the process of uploading your business plan to a secure website.

- Click the **Next >>** button to continue.

You are then asked to establish your SecurePlan.com account, as shown in Figure 8-15.

Help For step-by-step procedures, click the dialog Help button or the Help menu.

FIGURE 8-15: ESTABLISH A SECUREPLAN.COM ACCOUNT

Send to SecurePlan.com

Create a SecurePlan.com account

Enter your email address below to create a SecurePlan.com account. A password for your account will be automatically generated and sent to the email address you enter here.

Email: Me@myemail.com

| Help | | Cancel | << Back | Next >> |

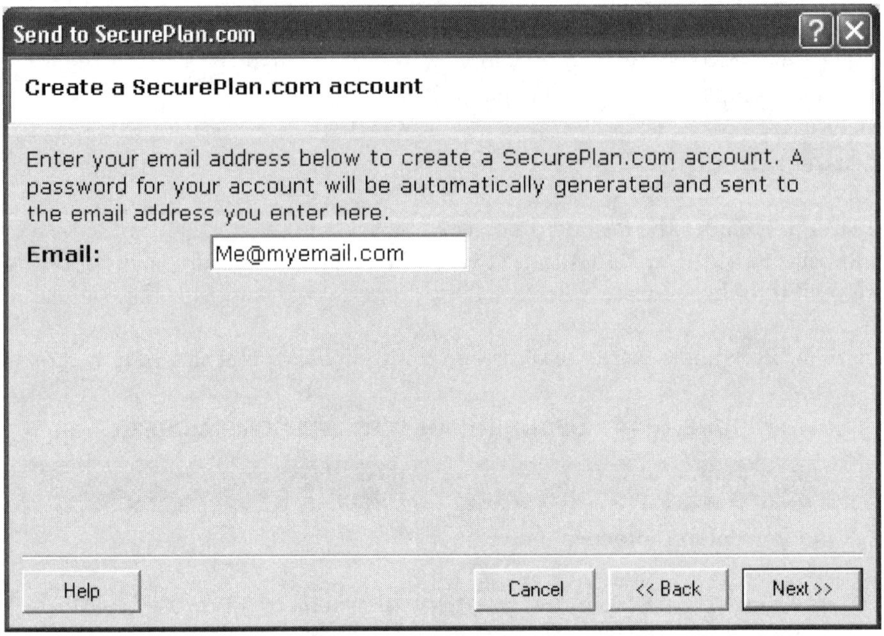

Your SecurePlan.com account is password protected.

Once your account is established, additional screens take you through the steps to upload your business plan to your secured website page.

To Learn more about...	**Search the Help Index for...**
Password protected website for sharing your business plan	SecurePlan.com

Working with Microsoft Office®

CHAPTER 9: WORKING WITH MICROSOFT OFFICE®

We know Microsoft Office well. Business Plan Pro® *began in the late 1980s as Business Plan Toolkit®, a collection of templates for Microsoft Excel and Microsoft Word.*

The template product won many awards, including a "best of breed" recommendation by PC World and Newsweek in 1994. The template is still available, in updated versions, for Macintosh users.

Comparison

Microsoft Office

Microsoft Office® (Office) includes Microsoft Word® (Word), a powerful word processor, Microsoft Excel® (Excel), a spreadsheet, Microsoft PowerPoint® (PowerPoint), a presentation maker, and other applications. They can share data and have a similar interface. The Office platform starts with its powerful tools and also serves as a de facto standard for exchanging documents.

The main Office tools are application programming languages, more than applications. Excel, for example, is a blank spreadsheet; it does nothing unless you program it with formulas.

Business Plan Pro

Business Plan Pro, in contrast, focuses on doing one thing very well: developing a business plan. Its advantages for this one task include content, ease of use, and the value of business time. Where Excel is a blank applications language to be programmed, Business Plan Pro is already programmed with business plan financials. Where Word is a blank document, Business Plan Pro starts with a suggested business plan outline. It has instructions and examples on every topic.

The time and ease of use elements are based on two main points: the spreadsheet work and the document formatting work. Furthermore, its content is unique.

TIPS

Business Plan Pro as a Head Start

If you are an expert user of Microsoft Office, Business Plan Pro is an information-rich, helpful, guided development tool that serves as an excellent head start. You can work through the main points of your plan, and the main financial analysis, then move it to Microsoft Office for fine tuning.

Spreadsheet – Comparison

Microsoft Excel

Anybody who has business and spreadsheet knowledge can develop a business plan using Microsoft Office. However, developing a complete set of linked, financially and mathematically correct tables is a long and painstaking job.

Business Plan Pro

Business Plan Pro, on the other hand, gives that same expert a starting point of completely developed, tested, and documented tables. This can save 40, 60, maybe 100 hours of spreadsheet work. Furthermore, in the Business Plan Pro PREMIER version, the tables are built into a flexible interface with spreadsheet-programming capability for adding tables as needed, and linking those added tables to the standard ones. It is essentially the best of both worlds, a developed spreadsheet that can be modified and linked.

Document – Comparison

Microsoft Word

While Microsoft Office is a powerful tool for developing the document, in most cases even the expert needs to manually merge text, tables, and charts together. The Word document is the source, the Excel tables and charts the illustrations. When numbers change, charts and tables need to be merged into the document again.

Business Plan Pro

Business Plan Pro includes built-in content representing years of expertise; it provides a wealth of know-how in its content-driven expert software. Help and instructions are available throughout, and the EasyPlan Wizard walks you through the planning process from start to finish.

Comparison Summary

Perhaps the best news, as a conclusion to this comparison, is that a Microsoft Office user does not have to choose. Business Plan Pro is built to work with the Office tools, so you can take full advantage of the business plan head start, then move your plan over to Office for finish and polish—you do not have to, of course, but there is that option. Furthermore, you can pull your work from Word and Excel into Business Plan Pro.

TIPS

No Technical Support for Working in Microsoft Office Programs

Palo Alto Software cannot provide technical support for programming in Word, Excel, or PowerPoint. Each is a very powerful application programming language, that gives you many opportunities to make mistakes and create errors. Make backups often.

Working with Microsoft Word

Word is one of the most popular and powerful word processing tools available. It is a generally-accepted standard for transferring documents between different users. Business Plan Pro can work with Word a couple of ways:

- You can transfer text from Word into the text portions of Business Plan Pro.
- You can use the enhanced export to a Business Plan Pro Word Document, open the file in Word, then import text changes back and forth between the two programs.

Transferring from Word to Business Plan Pro

A clean text document developed in Word can be copied and pasted into Business Plan Pro. However, many Word documents include features not compatible with your business plan text.

- Business Plan Pro handles bullet and numbered lists like the Internet does, different from Word.
- Business Plan Pro has its own business formats that cannot deal with the multiple columns, text boxes, or frames created in Word.

There are two ways to paste imported text with non-compatible formatting removed:

Edit > Paste Special

The Edit > Paste Special commands are one approach to importing text into your plan:

- Paste Special > Filtered Text: Removes Word-specific codes, and pastes only the fomatting, styles, and coding that are Business Plan Pro compatible. This is the recommended Paste Special option.
- Paste Special > Formatted Text: Pastes all text, coding, and formatting from Word into the plan topic; you then use the text and HTML formatting features in Business Plan Pro to clean up your topic information.
- Paste Special > Unformatted Text: Removes all the text formatting styles and the Word behind-the-scenes coding and pastes as "text only." You then must reformat all your text within Business Plan Pro.

Notepad

Another approach (used with earlier versions of Business Plan Pro) is to open the Word document in Notepad (a Microsoft document application included with Microsoft Windows). Notepad opens Word documents in a similar way to the Edit > Paste Special > Unformatted Text command that cleans the text of the additional features not compatible with Business Plan Pro.

?

To Learn more about...	Search the Help Index for...
Edit > Paste Special	Paste Special
Notepad	Notepad

Enhanced Export to a Business Plan Pro Word Document

If you are using Microsoft Word 2000 or newer, you can export your business plan file (including topic outline and all linked tables and charts) to a Business Plan Pro Word Document (.doc) file.

The Business Plan Pro Word Document is more powerful than a standard Word document. A special Palo Alto Software menu within Word lets you update both programs. You can make changes to tables and charts in Business Plan Pro, then udpate the .doc file with those changes. The text content from a Business Plan Pro Word Document can also be imported back into Business Plan Pro.

If you are using a version of Word that is older than 2000 you use the Rich Text Format Document Export option to export your plan to an .rtf file, but once there, it is not interactive with Business Plan Pro, and text cannot be directly imported.

The Export Wizard dialog walks you through the process of exporting. Figures 9-1 shows the Export Outline dialog. This dialog lets you export the entire plan (topics, tables, and charts), or mark only specific sections. Figure 9-2 shows the Export Wizard dialog where you enter the filename and location to store your .doc file.

FIGURE 9-1: EXPORT OUTLINE DIALOG

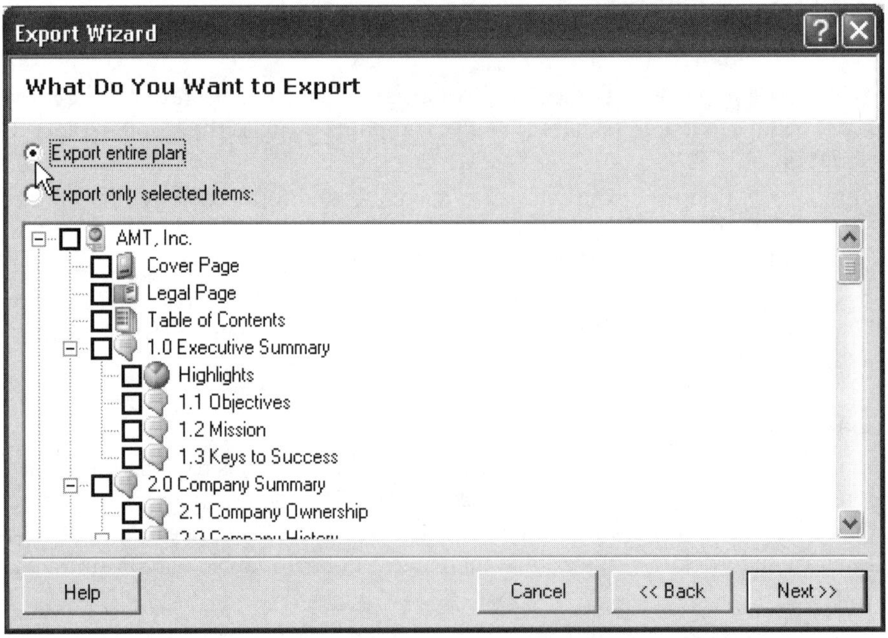

The Export Wizard lets you choose to export some or all of your plan outline.

Help For step-by-step procedures, click the dialog Help button or the Help menu.

FIGURE 9-2: EXPORT TO FILE DIALOG

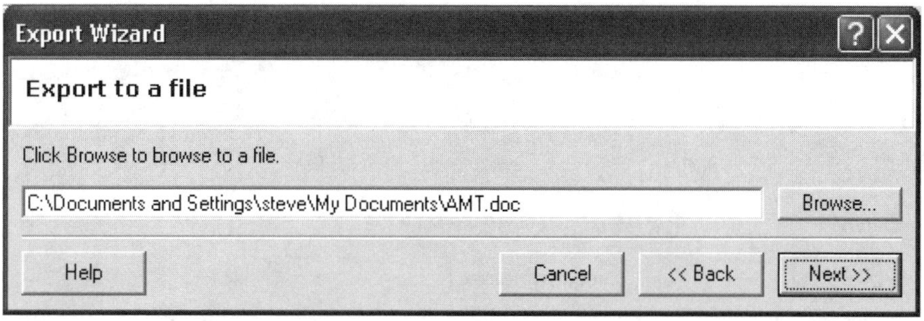

Export Wizard [?][X]

Export to a file

Click Browse to browse to a file.

| C:\Documents and Settings\steve\My Documents\AMT.doc | Browse... |

| Help | | Cancel | << Back | Next >> |

The default filename for the .doc file is the same as your business plan file. This .doc file is also stored in the default directory, unless you specify differently.

Follow the steps in the Export Wizard to complete the export process.

To Learn more about...	Search the Help Index for...
Exporting to Business Plan Pro Word Document	Export; Word Document; Microsoft Word

TIPS

Using Word Outline Facility After Export

After you export a finished plan to a BPP Word Document, you can set MS Word to outline view using the Word outline facility.

The heading styles help you manage the document by logical hierarchy, in the outline view.

Working in both Program Files

Once the Business Plan Pro Word Document file has been created using the export function, you can share information between the .doc file and your Business Plan Pro business plan file. For example, if you made adjustments to your Sales Forecast in Business Plan Pro, you can "refresh" the table information in the .doc file. If you make topic edits in the .doc file, you can "refresh" the topic text in the Business Plan Pro file. Figure 9-3 shows how the Palo Alto Software menu Refresh Topic command links the two program files together.

FIGURE 9-3: THE PALO ALTO SOFTWARE MENU IN MS WORD

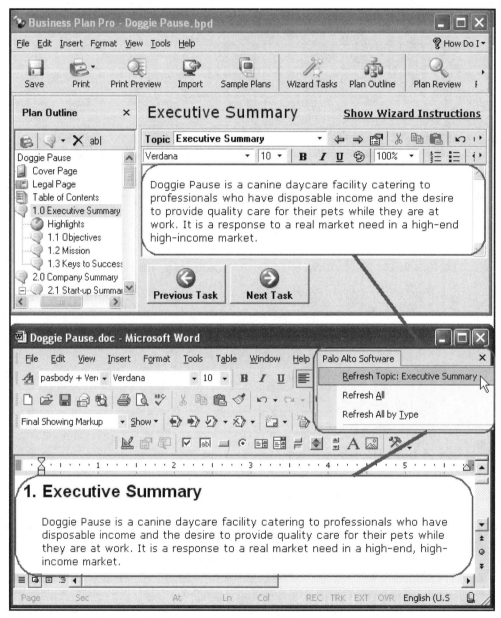

When you Export to a Business Plan Pro Word Document, BPP adds a Menu list to Word that lets you dynamically update the .doc file with changes made in Business Plan Pro.

When to Export to Word

You might consider exporting to Word if you need:

- More sophisticated graphics directly integrated into the plan document.
- More sophisticated formatting options.
- Integration with other external documents or worksheets.

For example, Business Plan Pro is frequently used as an instructional tool for business school classes. Business Plan Pro is capable of supporting a graduate-level print job for classes or competitions. However, when specific types and styles of formatting are required as a condition of the class or competition, exporting to Word gives a plan the extensive formatting options available in this word processing program. The Business Plan Pro Word Document is also appropriate in some larger businesses where Word compatibility is needed with other business plans and related documents.

When Not to Export to Word

If you have doubts, do not export. The Business Plan Pro automatic format is approved and endorsed by real business readers including bankers, Small Business Development Centers (SBDCs), and investors. Your business plan is not going to be more successful just because of formatting options in Word. Focus on the content, not the format, and let Business Plan Pro handle the output for you.

Exported Tables Cannot be Imported Back into Business Plan Pro

The exported Business Plan Pro Word Document becomes data in Microsoft Word. You can use whatever Word features you want to modify and manipulate the file. However, tables exported into a Word document are no longer live. The tables export as Word tables, and the charts are included in the Word file as graphics.

If you export to a Business Plan Pro Word Document and then need to change assumptions in tables, you must make your changes in Business Plan Pro first, then use the Refresh command to update the table view in the .doc file.

To keep the Word version of your plan and still change the financial data in a version older than Word 2000, you could export tables to Excel and then merge the resulting Excel tables into the modified Word document, using Microsoft Office functions and features. That has to take place in Office, not Business Plan Pro.

Importing from a Business Plan Pro Word Document

Topic edits made in the .doc file can be imported back into Business Plan Pro. Because of the linked formulas between tables in Business Plan Pro, changes made to tables in the .doc file cannot be imported back into Business Plan Pro.

The Import Wizard lets you choose the full outline or selected topics. Figure 9-4 shows the plan outline from the Import Wizard dialog.

FIGURE 9-4: THE IMPORT OUTLINE

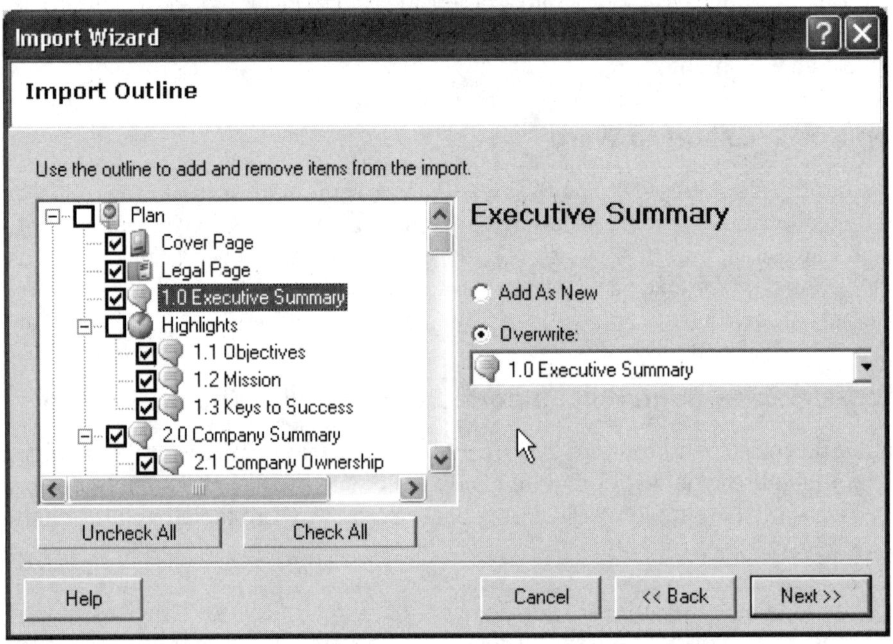

The Import Outline allows you to chose to import all or some of the text topics.

The Import Wizard dialog gives you the option to overwrite the topic that currently exists in Business Plan Pro with the edited topic from the Business Plan Pro Word Document, or add it to the plan outline as a new topic.

Help   For step-by-step procedures, click the dialog Help button or the Help menu.

When to Import from a Business Plan Pro Word Document

If you have made edits to topics after exporting to the .doc file, it is recommended that you import back into your original Business Plan Pro plan file to keep it updated.

Working with Microsoft Excel

Business Plan Pro has built-in linked tables (covered in Chapter 6: Your Plan Tables, and Chapter 10: Advanced Tables), which are quite compatible with Microsoft Excel. They are programmed using the same spreadsheet programming you use in Excel. Unlike the standard Excel spreadsheet, these tables are already programmed, full of help, and carefully documented. Important formulas are locked to prevent inadvertent errors. Furthermore, you can complete a full business plan without doing any Excel programming; just type in your numbers. However, if and when you need them, the underlying spreadsheet capabilities are there.

Exporting from Business Plan Pro to Excel

Business Plan Pro exports its tables to a complete Excel workbook, with all range names, formulas and calculations accessible.

1. Choose File > Export.
2. The Export Wizard dialog opens, asking for file name and folder. Be careful to note the file name (it should end with .xls) and the directory for the file you are creating.

FIGURE 9-5: EXPORT TO EXCEL

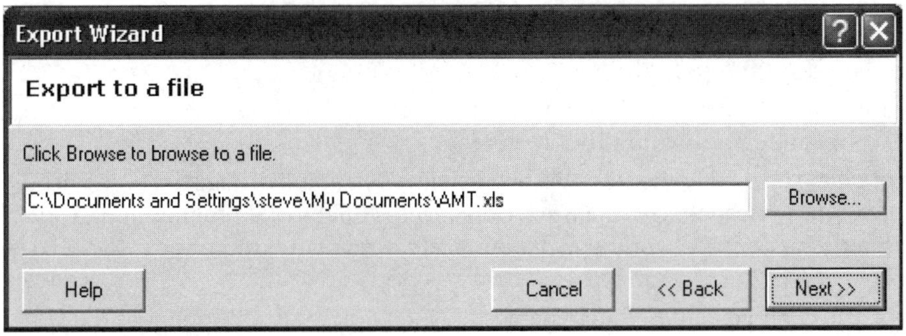

You can export the entire Business Plan Pro *spreadsheet to an Excel workbook.*

Help   For step-by-step procedures, click the dialog Help button or the Help menu.

Recommended Steps after Export to Excel

Open the exported file in Excel and use the Save As command to save it immediately in the latest Excel format, with a different file name.

- If you work with Excel 2002, for example, save it as a standard Excel .xls formatted file.
- This avoids many file format problems, makes your files more robust, and gives you a backup of your file as it was before you started working with it.
- Giving it a different file name preserves the original exported file as a reference.

Caution after Export to Excel

While your tables are inside Business Plan Pro, they are protected several ways—beginning with worksheet and formula locks—to avoid accidental errors. After export to Excel, those protections are gone, so be careful. The export to Excel can be the business-planning equivalent to getting "enough rope to hang yourself."

Since Excel is an application programming language, after you export your Business Plan Pro tables to an Excel workbook, you can do anything Excel allows. That includes changing formulas and deleting necessary range names or worksheets, which are changes that destroy the workbook you started with.

For this reason, Palo Alto Software does not offer free technical support once Business Plan Pro tables are exported to Excel.

Working with the Exported Tables in Excel

- Always keep the original exported file unchanged, so you can refer to it. If you want to start again from the original export, open the original file and use the Excel Save As command to create a copy of it with a new file name.
- Make sure you see the sheet tabs. They are named to match your tables. For example, the Profit and Loss table is in a sheet named "P&L," the Sales Forecast is in a sheet named "Sales Forecast," and so forth.
- Confirm that the sheet tabs are unlocked. In Excel, use the Tools > Protection > Unprotect Sheet command (a password is not required).
- Do not delete or modify the Logistics worksheet. Deleting the Logistics worksheet effectively destroys your workbook. The Logistics worksheet is full of vital programming variables that are used throughout the workbook. If you delete it, you get hundreds of #REF and #VALUE errors.
- Do not delete range names. Range names are vital to formulas throughout the workbook. You can add new ones, but do not delete existing ones. The result is #REF and #VALUE errors.
- You can use the Go To command in the Edit menu to view the range name references.
- Make sure you show row and column headings and watch for hidden rows and columns.
- If your plan settings did not show inventory, for example, then your exported worksheet does not show rows for inventory.
- If your business plan did not break expenses by categories, you have many rows in your Profit and Loss sheet hidden.
- The hidden rows are still in the worksheets, but hidden. Watch the row numbers to catch the hidden rows. Use the Excel format commands to unhide rows. The Format menu includes a Row command, and the Row command includes an Unhide command.

- Generally, each worksheet is one business plan table, but watch for multiple options within a single worksheet. Specifically:
  - The PREMIER version Sales Forecast includes two sales forecasts, the value-based and the units-based. One of the two has your numbers and the other is blank.
  - The Personnel worksheet in PREMIER version has several personnel plans. One of them has your data and the others are blank.
- Do not delete the unused tables, select the rows you do not use and run the Hide command under Rows in the Format menu. Deleting the extra tables causes #REF errors.
- Always keep the original exported file safe so you can refer to it. If you want to go back and start again, use the Save As command again.

Import from Excel to Business Plan Pro

Copy and Paste

When copying from Excel and pasting into Business Plan Pro, you should be aware of the following:

1. You cannot paste into black (locked) cells.
2. The key tables have unprotected data entry cells for the monthly columns.
3. The first-year total column is locked.
4. The annual columns for years two to five, are unlocked.
5. To paste from Excel, you have to copy blocks with the same structure, no more than 12 columns at a time for the monthly data.

Please remember some of the important tips and traps for pasting from Excel to Business Plan Pro:

- A simple copy and paste from Excel to Business Plan Pro copies values only, not formats or formulas. To copy and paste spreadsheet information completely, you need to use the Paste Special command in Business Plan Pro and choose Paste All to paste both formulas and formats.
- If you paste a formula from one worksheet containing an erroneous reference, you get a #REF error in the target worksheet. That is true in both Excel and Business Plan Pro.
- Copy a formula =XYZ (referring to a range name not already in Business Plan Pro) from Excel and paste it into Business Plan Pro. Business Plan Pro behaves like Excel does by creating a new range named XYZ located in a position relative to the target cell.
- Copy the formula =sales from an Excel worksheet and paste it into Business Plan Pro. Since Business Plan Pro already has a range named =sales, it creates a new range named =sales_2 and gives the target cell the formula =sales_2. To make the cell refer to the Business Plan Pro range named sales, you have to edit the formula manually.

Import to User-Defined Table (PREMIER version)

Excel workbooks can be imported into a user-defined table in Business Plan Pro PREMIER. The user-defined table is listed at the bottom of the Plan Outline and can be linked to a topic and included in your printed plan. The Import dialog lets you select the sections within the worksheet to import. Figure 9-6 gives an example.

FIGURE 9-6: IMPORT FROM EXCEL TO USER-DEFINED TABLES

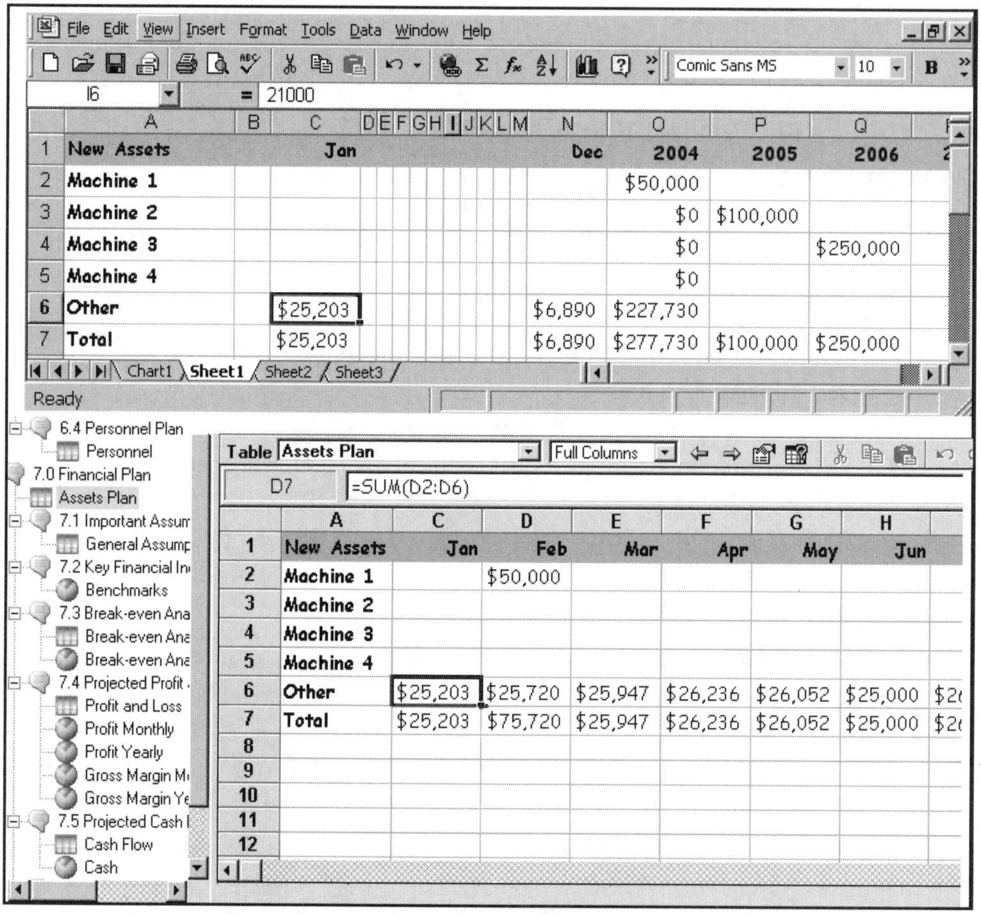

The Excel worksheet on the top was pasted into a user-defined table on the bottom.

Working with Microsoft PowerPoint

TIPS

PowerPoint is a Different Medium

A business presentation is a different medium. It is about a business plan, but is not the same as a business plan.

Do not try to directly include portions of your plan—stick to graphics, and bullet point summaries. Even a mission statement should be modified for use in PowerPoint. Refer to key points only, not the full text.

Before working with PowerPoint, please be sure you read through the Chapter 8: Print and Publish discussion on developing presentations to go along with your business plan. Business Plan Pro includes specialized templates for PowerPoint, and Chapter 8 includes details on the style and content of the PowerPoint presentation.

As that chapter states, a business plan presentation is a specialized communication. Most of these presentations need to summarize an entire business plan in a streamlined set of 7-20 slides for a talk that lasts about 30 minutes.

- It uses graphics to illustrate main points. The slide displays the chart only, so the presenter fills in the details.
- It uses bullet points and key phrases only. They are reminders and placeholders, not complete thoughts.
- It is all summary. The text is large and there is not much of it. Charts tell most of the story.

A good presentation is about results. It is short and exciting. It makes its key points quickly and well.

It needs to be optimized for the business purpose. Normal business plan presentations have to say what they can in 30 minutes. They avoid details and stick to highlights. Some special occasion presentations, in contrast, need to go into great detail on specific points. Always, even when details are important, keep the text large and the graphics simple. People do not read details from a presentation.

This kind of optimized presentation tool is not created automatically by computer software, and particularly not by business plan software. The format is different, the purpose is different, so the tool itself must also be different. There is no way a business plan document can automatically create a PowerPoint presentation without ending up with a poor presentation, too much text, too many numbers, and not enough summary.

You can, however, use your Business Plan Pro business plan to provide the important content for the presentation.

Importing to PowerPoint from Business Plan Pro

Export First to a Business Plan Pro Word Document

In the following example, we first exported our business plan to a Business Plan Pro Word Document, then used Word and PowerPoint together to create the business presentation. The advantage is that the export to Word gives us a manageable document with graphics and tables easily available for copy and paste. If we stay in Business Plan Pro, we have to export each graphic as a separate file, then import those files into the PowerPoint presentation. Export to a BPP Word Document is quicker. This export is explained earlier in this chapter. Figure 9-7 shows an example of developing a slide presentation from an exported business plan.

FIGURE 9-7: DEVELOPING POWERPOINT SLIDES

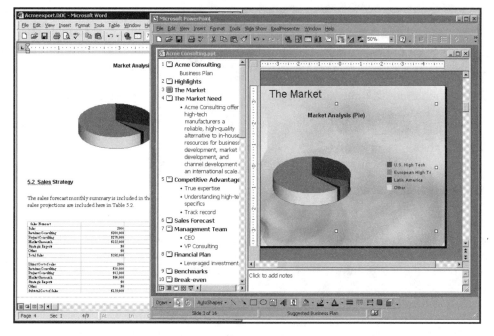

The background is a Word .doc file produced from a Business Plan Pro Word Document *plan export. The foreground is a PowerPoint presentation.*

Use PowerPoint Presentation Templates

Business Plan Pro includes five PowerPoint business plan templates that can help you deliver your business plan in a clear, concise, professional, graphically sharp presentation. Click the Resources button and choose Make it Happen > Present > Presentation Templates. Choose any of the bullet list links. The template opens in PowerPoint and you can then copy/paste text, tables and charts from your exported Business Plan Pro Word Document (as described earlier).

FIGURE 9-8: POWERPOINT PRESENTATION TEMPLATES

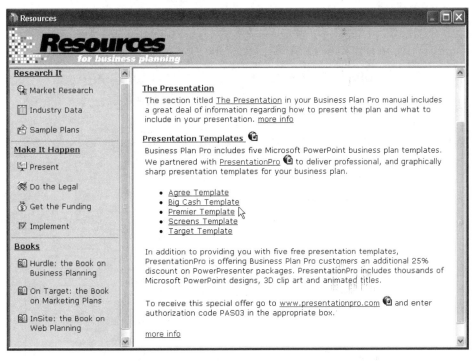

Business Plan Pro *has five PowerPoint presentation templates included in Resources.*

Remember: the Medium has Changed

Remember the purpose of a PowerPoint presentation. You want summaries in the presentation, not detail. Contents should change to reflect the different medium of communication.

- Summarize, do not quote. For example, do not include the whole mission statement, include key bullets.
- Use graphics as talking points.
- Less text is better. Do not copy your business plan texts into your PowerPoint presentation. Make bullets that summarize in a few words.
- Generally, PowerPoint text should not go below 18 points. If you need smaller than that to make the text fit, you probably have too many words.

Import PowerPoint Graphics into Business Plan Pro

Business Plan Pro does not offer a direct import from PowerPoint. You can, however, import a graphic image created from PowerPoint into Business Plan Pro. An example is an organization chart, which PowerPoint does well.

To make an organization chart for your business plan using PowerPoint, and include it as an illustration in the plan:

1. Use PowerPoint to create the organization chart. Figure 9-9 shows the PowerPoint facility (in Office 2002) for an automatic Organization Chart.

FIGURE 9-9: POWERPOINT ORGANIZATION CHART

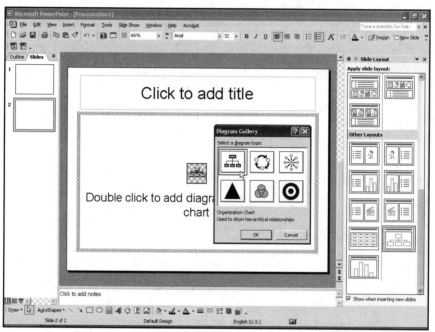

The PowerPoint Organization Chart template is a useful tool for developing an organization chart to include in your plan.

2. Use the rulers in PowerPoint to resize the graphic to fit well into the Business Plan Pro page. A width of 5" is usually a good size.
3. Save the Organization Chart as a graphic file using the PowerPoint Save As command. PowerPoint gives you the option of saving just the single slide, not the whole presentation. Use the dialog options in PowerPoint to save the graphic as either *.jpg, *.gif, *.bmp, or *.wmf file.
4. Within Business Plan Pro, find the target topic for the organization chart from the Plan Outline screen and highlight it to open it in Topic view.
5. Position your cursor in the text screen where the image is to display.
6. Right-click with your mouse to open the pop-up menu. Select Insert > Image from the menu options.
7. Locate the graphic file created in PowerPoint and select from the dialog box, as shown in Figure 9-10.

FIGURE 9-10: INSERT GRAPHIC IMAGE IN A TEXT TOPIC

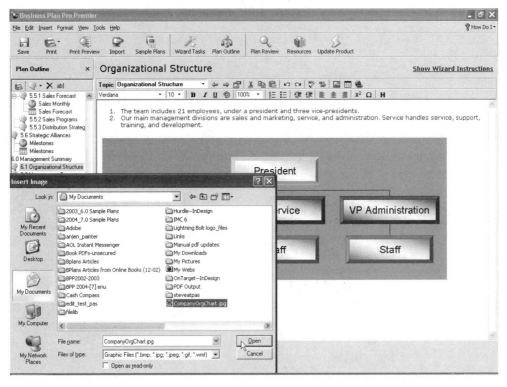

Locate the .gif, .jpg, .bmp, or .wmf, graphic image to insert into your text topic.

 TIPS

Insert Image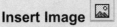

You can also use the Insert Image button from the toolbar to access the dialog box.

Notes on Graphics:

Graphics need to fit on to a standard 8 1/2" x 11" paper for printing. Also, some printers may not have enough memory to print a large graphic along with text and other images on a single page. Consult your print manual for more information.

TIPS

Build an Organizational Chart (PREMIER version)

Use the Insert > Organizational Chart command to build into a text topic. Instructions on how to build an organizational chart within Business Plan Pro can be found in the Help index.

This page intentionally blank.

Advanced Tables

10

Excel® is a registered trademark of Microsoft Corporation.

CHAPTER 10: ADVANCED TABLES

Chapter 6: Your Plan Tables, covers the standard tables. This chapter covers additional programming and customization.

The best way to learn this is by doing it. This chapter takes you through a series of examples. It starts with simple examples that offer practical tips. It also includes details of more complex formulas, as well as explanations of formulas you might want to add or change.

This level of customization is provided for those users who may want it. It is not necessary in order to create a solid business plan.

Customizing Formulas in Tables

Business Plan Pro® gives you extensive spreadsheet-like programmability for your financial tables. Although your tables do not need to be programmed, they are built into a very powerful spreadsheet tool that includes a complete Microsoft Excel®-compatible spreadsheet which supports sophisticated financial functions that calculate your loan payments, depreciation, and investment analysis. All of this power is available even while working within the financial analysis.

Furthermore, you can build your own customized spreadsheets within Business Plan Pro directly (PREMIER version), linking them to the thoroughly tested and documented tables already there.

Examples – Custom Formulas

We go through some examples of Business Plan Pro spreadsheet formulas. To follow along with the examples:

- Open Business Plan Pro.
- Use the Sample Plan Browser to open a business sample plan file (the AMT Computers sample plan is a good one, although not all the examples and illustrations show exactly that plan).
- If your tables do not show the row and column headings, use the Tools menu, and choose Options > Tables.
- Set your tables to show row and column headings.

Example: Absolute Reference in a Formula

Relative Value

The default reference for a spreadsheet formula is "relative" to its current location. If you copy a formula to another column, the reference in the formula changes accordingly.

Absolute Value

Sometimes you do not want some or all of a formula to change its reference. In those cases, we use the $ in the formula, which makes it "absolute," regardless of which cell the formula is copied to.

In Figure 10-1, the formula highlighted in column C is: =$B38*C23 The $ makes the reference to B38 an absolute reference to column B.

FIGURE 10-1: SAMPLE FORMULA WITH ABSOLUTE VALUE

C38	=$B38*C23			
	A	**B**	**C**	**D**
13	Sales Forecast			
14	Unit Sales		Jan	Feb
22	Unit Prices		Jan	Feb
23	Systems		$2,000.00	$2,000.00
24	Service		$75.00	$69.00
25	Software		$200.00	$200.00
26	Training		$37.00	$35.00
27	Other		$300.00	$300.00
28				
29	Sales			
30	Systems		$170,000	$230,000
31	Service		$15,000	$13,800
32	Software		$30,000	$40,000
33	Training		$5,365	$5,425
34	Other		$48,000	$52,800
35	Total Sales		$268,365	$342,025
36				
37	Direct Unit Costs		Jan	Feb
38	Systems	80.00%	$1,600.00	$1,600.00
39	Service		$30.00	$60.00
40	Software		$120.00	$120.00
41	Training		$11.10	$11.10
42	Other		$90.00	$90.00

In this example, Cell C38 shows a formula with an absolute value for column B.

If you chose to copy that formula to cell D38, the formula could become: =$B38*D23. The reference to C23 moved one column to the right, but the reference to column B in $B38 did not change. In our example, the only portion of the formulas that is "absolute" is the reference to column B. If we copied the formula down a row, the row reference changes "relative" to its new location. The new formula in cell C39 becomes =$B39*C24. In that case, the B column remains absolute because of the $, but the row number adjusts to the change in location.

To create an absolute reference for both column and row, we use the $ sign for both. In that situation, if our formula had been created as: =$B$38*C23 and we then copied it to C39, both column and row number would have remained absolute, making the formula =$B$38*C24.

Example: Automatic Price Formula for Sales Forecast

In this example, we create a price formula so that every cell in the row looks to the first cell for the correct number. In Figure 10-2 you see a portion of the Sales Forecast table of the AMT Computers sample plan.

FIGURE 10-2: SALES FORECAST FORMULA

	A	B	C	D	E
	D23	=C23			
13	Sales Forecast				
14	Unit Sales		Jan	Feb	Mar
15	Systems		85	115	145
16	Service		200	200	200
17	Software		150	200	250
18	Training		145	155	165
19	Other		160	176	192
20	Total Unit Sales		740	846	952
21					
22	Unit Prices		Jan	Feb	Mar
23	Systems		$2,000.00	$2,000.00	$2,000.00
24	Service		$75.00	$69.00	$58.00
25	Software		$200.00	$200.00	$200.00
26	Training		$37.00	$35.00	$39.00
27	Other		$300.00	$300.00	$300.00
28					

This simple formula makes the price in column D equal to whatever price is already in column C.

Cell D23 is selected. The formula for cell D23 is: **=C23**

If you copy that formula into the rest of the 12 monthly columns (Edit > Fill > Right command), then whenever you change the assumption in the first month, that change automatically ripples through the whole system.

⚲TIPS

Locked Cell Error

As you copy the formula in D23 and paste it in the following cells to its right along the row, you cannot paste into cell O23. That produces a "locked cell" error.

O23 is locked because it calculates average price for the year by dividing total revenue by total units sold.

This example shows basic spreadsheet programming. The formula in D23 makes that cell equal to whatever is in C23.

- Select D23.

- Hold down the shift key while D23 is selected and then press the right arrow key a few times. That automatically selects a range of cells to the right along the row.
- Use the Edit > Fill > Right command to copy D23 across the row. If your selection includes O23, which is locked, you get the locked cell error message (described in a previous tip).

Example: Variable to use as Percent of Sales (P&L Example)

Business Plan Pro uses named ranges as variable names as much as possible, to simplify reading and working with formulas. There are several dozen built-in range names that work from any table in Business Plan Pro. These are named to make them easier to include within a formula. For example, the Sales Forecast table uses a range name "Sales" as a variable, which is the sum of sales for that column.

However, you do not have to be in the Sales Forecast to use the "Sales" range name. Figure 10-3 shows how you can use this built-in English-language range as a variable to create a formula to make all the cells in a given row of the Profit and Loss table calculate as a percent of sales.

FIGURE 10-3: PERCENT OF SALES IN PROFIT AND LOSS

C6	=$B6*Sales			
	A	B	C	D
1	Pro Forma Profit and Loss			
2			Jan	Feb
3	Sales		$268,365	$342,025
4	Direct Cost of Sales		$176,010	$237,561
5	Production Payroll		$9,500	$9,500
6	Royalties	10%	$26,837	$34,203
7			------------	------------
8	Total Cost of Sales		$212,346	$281,263
9	Gross Margin		$56,019	$60,762
10	Gross Margin %		20.87%	17.77%

Notice the use of the named range "Sales" as a variable in the formula shown, also the $B6 which always refers to the B column when used in any other column.

The example shows a Profit and Loss table with cell C6 selected. The formula for C6 calculates that cell by multiplying the variable with the range name "Sales" by the value in B6. As with a previous example, the reference to B6 uses the **$B6** to make sure that the reference to column B is absolute, and the reference to row 6 is relative. That formula was written into C6 first, then copied to cells D6:N6 and P6:S6.

Example: Programming a Sales Forecast Growth Rate in Column B

Figure 10-4 shows a sample sales forecast in which a growth rate assumption, in column B, automatically calculates sales projections for annual sales in the second and third year.

FIGURE 10-4: GROWTH RATE VARIABLE IN SALES

P16	=Round(O16*(1+$B16),0)						
	A	B	C	N	O	P	Q
13	**Sales Forecast**						
14	**Unit Sales**		Jan	Dec	2004	2005	2006
15	Systems		85	275	2,251	3,134	4,323
16	Service	20.00%	200	343	3,128	3,745	7,500
17	Software		150	490	3,980	5,000	6,500
18	Training		145	200	2,230	4,000	8,000
19	Other		160	200	2,122	2,500	3,000
20	**Total Unit Sales**		740	1,508	13,711	18,388	29,323

This formula sets a growth rate in column B that impacts the annual numbers in columns P and Q.

The formula in P16 (in the figure above) calculates service unit sales in 2005 by applying the growth rate in column B. The phrase **$B16** in that formula always refers to the absolute value in the B column.

Round to Nearest Whole Number

The formula described in Figure 10-4 also uses the **ROUND** function to round the result to the nearest whole number. For example, the formula "=Round(3/5,0)" calculates to the whole number 1, while the formula "=Round(2/5,0)" calculates to the value 0.

Example: Make a Cell a Percent of any Other Cell (P&L Example)

You can create formulas to calculate a cell using the value of another cell. Figure 10-5 shows an example of a formula that calculates a cell to be 50% of the value of another cell. In cell C15, the formula is =.5*C14 . The value in C14 is 5,000, so the value in C15 is 2,500, exactly 50% of 5000.

FIGURE 10-5: ONE ROW A PERCENT OF ANOTHER

	C15	=0.5*C14			
	A	**B**	**C**	**D**
1	Pro Forma Profit and Loss			
2			Jan	Feb
13	Sales and Marketing Payroll		$24,000	$24,000
14	Ads		$5,000	$5,000
15	Catalog		$2,500	$3,000
16	Mailing		$3,000	$11,800
17	Promo		$0	$0
18	Shows		$0	$0
19	Literature		$0	$7,000
20	PR		$0	$0
21	Seminar		$1,000	$0
22	Service		$2,000	$1,000
23	Training		$450	$450
24			------------	------------
25	Total Sales and Marketing Expenses		$37,950	$52,250
26	Sales and Marketing %		14.14%	15.28%

The formula makes the catalog expense 50% of advertising expense.

Example: Sales Commission Formula (Personnel Example)

Figure 10-6 shows a commission structure that can be built into the Personnel Plan. The formula for cell D28 shows in the edit bar in that figure. It applies whatever percent is typed into column B in that row to the Gross Margin for that same month.

FIGURE 10-6: SETTING COMMISSIONS FOR PERSONNEL

	D28	=6000+($B28*Gross_margin)					
	A	**B**	**C**	**D**	**E**	**F**	
15	Personnel Plan						
16	Production Personnel		Jan	Feb	Mar	Apr	
23	Fulfillment		$1,500	$1,500	$1,500	$1,500	
24	Other		$0	$0	$0	$0	
25	Subtotal		$9,500	$9,500	$9,500	$9,500	
26							
27	Sales and Marketing Personnel						
28	Manager	1.00%	$6,744	$6,835	$6,985	$8,940	
29	Technical sales		$5,000	$5,000	$5,000	$5,000	
30	Technical sales		$3,500	$3,500	$3,500	$3,500	

The formula in the edit bar shows how spreadsheet programming sets the commission rate for the sales manager.

Range Names

Just as the formula in Figure 10-3 uses "Sales" as a named range, you can use dozens of other named ranges as variables. These include Sales, Earnings, Inventory, Gross_margin, etc.

Range Names are Relative

Range names automatically adjust for different columns. The formula **=Sales** in column G shows the value of sales in column G. That same formula in column D shows the value of sales in column D.

Errors Using Range Names

#VALUE

Range names produce errors when used improperly. For example, the range named "Sales" starts in column C and spreads across multiple columns. The formula **=Sales** in column B produces a #VALUE error because there is no valid value for that column.

However, a range name that occupies a single cell can be used as a variable anywhere in the financials. For example, because the range "Starting_year" occupies a single cell, you can use the formula **=Starting_year** anywhere in the financials without getting a #VALUE error.

Pasting Range Names

When you copy a formula using a range name and paste it into a new table, Business Plan Pro automatically changes it by adding an underscore character and a number. It has to make this change to keep track of new range names.

For example, paste the formula "=sales" into a new worksheet and Business Plan Pro pastes "=sales_2" instead.

You can go back and change this, but the default happens that way. This handling is necessary because the named ranges are in different worksheets.

List of Range Names

A complete list of the built-in range names for Business Plan Pro can be found in Appendix A of this manual.

Linking Tables

Reading Built-in Links

Click on any cell in the Sales row of the Profit and Loss table and look at its formula. It is linking from the Sales Forecast, with some spreadsheet logic (the IF portion) to specify which of the various Sales Forecasts is active.

Building Your Own Links

You can use the spreadsheet power to build your own links to fit your planning needs. Here are some examples.

Examples – Linking Tables

Example: Link from Sales Forecast to Profit and Loss

Assume that AMT plans on paying royalties equal to 10% of sales of software. We can build a formula that does this automatically. That formula is demonstrated in Figure 10-7. We take a row in Profit and Loss named "Royalties" and link it to the row in the Sales Forecast that contains software sales.

FIGURE 10-7: LINK FROM SALES TO PROFIT AND LOSS

C6	='Sales Forecast'!C25*0.1			
	A	C	D	E
1	Pro Forma Profit and Loss			
2		Jan	Feb	Mar
3	Sales	$268,365	$334,025	$415,635
4	Direct Cost of Sales	$176,010	$231,161	$293,112
5	Production Payroll	$9,500	$9,500	$9,500
6	Royalties	$20	$20	$20
7		------------	------------	------------
8	Total Cost of Sales	$185,530	$240,681	$302,632
9	Gross Margin	$82,836	$93,345	$113,004
10	Gross Margin %	30.87%	27.95%	27.19%

The formula for royalties takes 10% of row 25 in the Sales Forecast.

The formula for cell C6 in the Figure 10-7 is: ='Sales Forecast'!C25*0.1

You can type that formula into your Profit and Loss table, or you could follow these steps:

1. Use the Edit > Row Label command to change the row label from "Other" to "Royalties."
2. Select the January cell for the Royalties row (our example shows cell C6). This is the target cell for the link formula.
3. Type the equals sign = (without quotation marks or parentheses) into the cell.
4. Go to the Table pull-down list and choose the Sales Forecast table.
5. Find the cell for January sales of software (in the example, cell C25) and select it. This is the source cell.

    Your formula edit bar should at this point show the formula **='Sales Forecast'!C25**

6. To make royalties equal to only 10% of sales of software, we type into the formula ***0.1**
7. Press the ENTER key.

You are probably looking at Profit and Loss at this point (cell C6 in our example). Your formula should now be correct: **='Sales Forecast'!C25*0.1**

To put this same link across the entire row:

- Copy the January royalties formula (cell C6) and Paste into remaining months (cells D6:N6), and years two and three (P6:Q6) or years two through five in a longer plan (P6:S6).

Cell References in Linked-tables Formula Examples

We refer to specific cells as they appear in our example. Your settings may show differently. Use the cell address as a general reference and adjust to match your table view.

Example: An IF Function in Profit and Loss linked to a Sales Row

Figure 10-8 shows an expense row from Profit and Loss linked to a sales row, using a simple IF function. The formula checks whether training sales (cell C33 of the Sales Forecast) are greater than $10,000. If they are, then the seminar expense is $5,000. If not, then the seminar expense is $2,000.

FIGURE 10-8: THE IF FUNCTION IN A LINKING FORMULA

	A	C	D	E	F	G	H	I	J
C21	=IF('Sales Forecast'!C33>10000,5000,2000)								
1	Pro Forma Profit and Loss								
2		Jan	Feb	Mar	Apr	May	Jun	Jul	Aug
18	Shows	$0	$0	$0	$0	$0	$0	$3,200	$0
19	Literature	$0	$7,000	$0	$0	$0	$0	$0	$0
20	PR	$0	$0	$0	$1,000	$0	$0	$0	$0
21	Seminar	$2,000	$2,000	$2,000	$2,000	$5,000	$2,000	$2,000	$2,000
22	Service	$2,000	$1,000	$1,000	$500	$2,500	$500	$500	$500
23	Training	$450	$450	$450	$450	$450	$450	$450	$450
24		---------	---------	---------	---------	---------	---------	---------	---------
25	Total Sales and Marketing Expenses	$38,450	$54,250	$41,950	$50,450	$59,450	$52,450	$54,650	$51,450
26	Sales and Marketing %	14.33%	16.24%	10.09%	7.19%	9.23%	10.79%	15.08%	16.81%

The IF function in this example sets seminar expense to vary according to Sales Forecast numbers.

Follow these steps to create the formula link in your own plan:

1. Select the target cell (cell C21 in the Profit and Loss).
2. Type: **=IF(**
3. Choose the Sales Forecast table from the pull-down menu.
4. Find the source cell in the Sales Forecast table (cell C33) and click to select it. The edit bar shows the formula as: **=IF('Sales Forecast'!C33**
5. Type the rest of the formula into the edit bar, as shown in the example: **>10000,5000,2000)**
6. Press the <ENTER> key.
7. Use the Edit > Fill > Right command to copy the formula to the rest of the unprotected cells in the row.

Building Power Variables

Power variables in a spreadsheet are cells whose values affect many other cells. For example, in Business Plan Pro PREMIER you might set the growth factors shown in Figure 10-9 in a new table, then link to those growth factors in your financials. That gives you the power to change the forecast rapidly, do sensitivity analysis, and scenarios. This example adds rows to the General Assumptions table.

FIGURE 10-9: POWER GROWTH VARIABLES

O8	=1*PRODUCT(C8:N8)						
	A	L	M	N	O	P	Q
1	General Assumptions						
2		Oct	Nov	Dec	2004	2005	2006
3	Plan Month	10	11	12	1	2	3
4	Current Interest Rate	10.00%	10.00%	10.00%	10.00%	10.00%	10.00%
5	Long-term Interest Rate	10.00%	10.00%	10.00%	10.00%	10.00%	10.00%
6	Tax Rate	30.00%	30.00%	30.00%	30.00%	5.00%	5.00%
7	Sales on Credit %	10.00%	10.00%	10.00%	10.00%	10.00%	10.00%
8	Sales Growth	1.0150	1.0150	1.0150	1.1956	1.1500	1.1250
9	Cogs growth	1.0080	1.0080	1.0080	1.1003	1.0900	1.0800
10	Expense growth	1.0075	1.0075	1.0075	1.0938	1.0850	1.0750
11	Calculated Totals						
12	Payroll Expense	$16,480	$16,480	$16,480	$188,912	$241,680	$250,164
13	Sales on Credit	$3,617	$3,988	$3,992	$27,942	$70,730	$77,061
14	New Accounts Payable	$24,782	$26,458	$6,673	$203,356	$403,390	$437,037
15	Inventory Purchase	$18,115	$19,789	$0	$127,016	$321,010	$347,176

For this illustration we insert rows in the General Assumptions table and set up the power growth variables shown. The 2004 annual factors are automatic, based on monthly assumptions and the formula shown.

The second columns (column B) of the Sales Forecast, Personnel Plan, and Profit and Loss are empty without protection so that you can program your own power variables. Once those variables are available, program the main tables to link into them.

Figure 10-10 shows a view of how the Profit and Loss table looks in the monthly section with power variables linked in from the Assumptions table. The formula shown in the illustration, for example, applies the growth factor to a monthly expense item. Notice the use of the "$10" absolute reference, which is convenient for copying that formula to other rows in the expense area. You can use similar links to growth factors in the Sales Forecast and Personnel Plan (not shown).

FIGURE 10-10: POWER VARIABLES IN PROFIT AND LOSS

E27	=D27*Assumptions!E$10					
	A	B	C	D	E	F
1	Pro Forma Profit and Loss					
2			Jan	Feb	Mar	Apr
3	Sales		$0	$0	$10,494	$18,356
4	Direct Costs of Goods		$0	$0	$4,722	$8,260
6	Pizza Chef Salary		$0	$0	$2,000	$2,000
7	Other Costs of Goods		$0	$0	$100	$100
8			------------	------------	------------	------------
9	Cost of Goods Sold		$0	$0	$6,822	$12,360
10	Gross Margin		$0	$0	$3,672	$5,996
11	Gross Margin %		0.00%	0.00%	34.99%	32.66%
20	Expenses:					
21	Payroll		$12,000	$13,120	$15,472	$16,480
22	Depreciation		$1,250	$1,250	$1,250	$1,250
23	Advertising		$100	$101	$102	$102
24	Rent		$1,500	$1,500	$1,500	$1,500
25	Insurance		$200	$202	$203	$205
26	Payroll taxes	15%	$1,800	$1,968	$2,321	$2,472
27	Other		$100	$101	$102	$102
37			------------	------------	------------	------------
38	Total Operating Expenses		$16,950	$18,241	$20,040	$22,111

The spreadsheet programming makes all expense rows grow at the same rate assigned by the power variables. The formula for E27 shows in the illustration. The formula for cell F27, for example, is =E27*Assumptions!F$10.

Figure 10-11 shows a portion of the same business plan's Profit and Loss table in the annual area, to the right. As with the monthlies, the power growth assumption is built into the formula. The formula for cell P27 is =O27*(Assumptions!P$10) . The row number 10 is absolute, but the column letter P is not because the R column is also used for the following year. The sales and personnel tables have similar formulas (not shown).

FIGURE 10-11: POWER GROWTH IN ANNUAL COLUMNS

P27	=O27*Assumptions!P$10					
	A	M	N	O	P	Q
1	Pro Forma Profit and Loss					
2		Nov	Dec	2004	2005	2006
3	Sales	$39,885	$39,920	$279,415	$321,327	$361,493
4	Direct Costs of Goods	$17,948	$17,964	$125,737	$144,597	$162,672
6	Pizza Chef Salary	$2,000	$2,000	$20,000	$22,000	$24,200
7	Other Costs of Goods	$100	$100	$1,000	$1,100	$1,210
8		-----------	-----------	-----------	-----------	-----------
9	Cost of Goods Sold	$20,048	$20,064	$146,737	$167,697	$188,082
10	Gross Margin	$19,837	$19,856	$132,678	$153,630	$173,411
11	Gross Margin %	49.73%	49.74%	47.48%	47.81%	47.97%
20	Expenses:					
21	Payroll	$16,480	$16,480	$188,912	$241,680	$250,164
22	Depreciation	$1,250	$1,250	$15,000	$35,000	$35,000
23	Advertising	$108	$109	$1,251	$1,357	$1,459
24	Rent	$1,500	$1,500	$18,000	$19,530	$20,995
25	Insurance	$216	$217	$2,502	$2,714	$2,918
26	Payroll taxes	$2,472	$2,472	$28,337	$30,745	$33,051
27	Other	$108	$109	$1,251	$1,357	$1,459
37		-----------	-----------	-----------	-----------	-----------
38	Total Operating Expenses	$22,133	$22,136	$255,252	$332,384	$345,045

The formula in cell P27 shows in the edit bar. All the expense rates are set to grow at the same power-variable rate.

When the power variables are programmed into the tables, you can make changes and evaluate assumptions very quickly. The quick change of assumptions in Figure 10-12 generates the different financial picture shown in Figure 10-13.

FIGURE 10-12: CHANGING THE POWER ASSUMPTIONS

O8	=1*PRODUCT(C8:N8)						
	A	K	L	M	N	O	P	Q
1	General Assumptions						
2		Sep	Oct	Nov	Dec	2004	2005	2006
3	Plan Month	9	10	11	12	1	2	3
4	Current Interest Rate	10.00%	10.00%	10.00%	10.00%	10.00%	10.00%	10.00%
5	Long-term Interest Rate	10.00%	10.00%	10.00%	10.00%	10.00%	10.00%	10.00%
6	Tax Rate	30.00%	30.00%	30.00%	30.00%	30.00%	5.00%	5.00%
7	Sales on Credit %	10.00%	10.00%	10.00%	10.00%	10.00%	10.00%	10.00%
8	Sales Growth	1.0500	1.0500	1.0500	1.0500	1.7959	1.5000	1.3500
9	Cogs growth	1.0350	1.0350	1.0350	1.0350	1.5111	1.3000	1.2500
10	Expense growth	1.0200	1.0200	1.0200	1.0200	1.2682	1.3500	1.5000
11	Calculated Totals						
12	Payroll Expense	$16,480	$16,480	$16,480	$16,480	$188,912	$241,680	$250,164
13	Sales on Credit	$3,245	$3,617	$3,988	$3,992	$27,942	$70,730	$77,061
14	New Accounts Payable	$23,150	$24,832	$26,515	$6,736	$203,717	$416,779	$479,610
15	Inventory Purchase	$16,442	$18,115	$19,789	$0	$127,016	$321,010	$347,176

This illustration shows a very different set of assumptions, but the change involved just a few power variables.

In Figure 10-13 the formula for cell P27 shows how the formula has not changed, but the values shown have. The different growth factor created significant change automatically. Look for the change showing in the expense areas.

FIGURE 10-13: CHANGE IN PROFIT AND LOSS

P27	=O27*Assumptions!P$10				
	A	M	N	O	P	Q
1	Pro Forma Profit and Loss					
2		Nov	Dec	2004	2005	2006
3	Sales	$39,885	$39,920	$279,415	$707,301	$770,608
4	Direct Costs of Goods	$17,948	$17,964	$125,737	$318,286	$346,773
6	Pizza Chef Salary	$2,000	$2,000	$20,000	$22,000	$24,200
7	Other Costs of Goods	$100	$100	$1,000	$1,100	$1,210
8		------------	------------	------------	------------	------------
9	Cost of Goods Sold	$20,048	$20,064	$146,737	$341,386	$372,183
10	Gross Margin	$19,837	$19,856	$132,678	$365,916	$398,424
11	Gross Margin %	49.73%	49.74%	47.48%	51.73%	51.70%
20	Expenses:					
21	Payroll	$16,480	$16,480	$188,912	$241,680	$250,164
22	Depreciation	$1,250	$1,250	$15,000	$35,000	$35,000
23	Advertising	$122	$124	$1,341	$1,811	$2,716
24	Rent	$1,500	$1,500	$18,000	$24,300	$36,450
25	Insurance	$244	$249	$2,682	$3,621	$5,432
26	Payroll taxes	$2,472	$2,472	$28,337	$38,255	$57,382
27	Other	$122	$124	$1,341	$1,811	$2,716
37		------------	------------	------------	------------	------------
38	Total Operating Expenses	$22,190	$22,190	$255,614	$346,477	$389,860

Changing the power variables as shown in Figure 10-12 produces a radically different financial picture shown here.

TIPS

Tradeoffs in Analysis

Here you have some classic tradeoffs: the more you build in the power variables that change multiple assumptions, the faster the analysis, but the less real and detailed the analysis. Generally powerful and fast changes are great for strategic planning, and detail is great for normal business planning. You can create what you need.

Customized Formulas and Tables
Insert New Tables (PREMIER version)

With the PREMIER version of Business Plan Pro, you can insert a brand new empty table into your business plan, linking it to a topic. This lets you develop your own tables and add them to your business plan. Once you have inserted a new table, you can also link any cell in a new table into the entry areas of any of the main tables. The next example shows the use of a blank table.

Monthly Headings in a New Table

Linking information via formulas is convenient, and you can do that with dates and the date function automatically built into Business Plan Pro. Figure 10-14 shows an example.

FIGURE 10-14: MONTH AND YEAR HEADINGS IN A NEW TABLE

C2	=date(PS_StartingYear+1,PS_StartingMonth,15)				
	A	B	C	D	E	F
1						
2			Jan-05	Feb-05	Mar-05	Apr-05

- The range name "PS_StartingYear" variable is a four-digit number for the starting year of the plan.
- The range name "PS_StartingMonth" variable is a number between one and 12, the starting month of the plan.
- The date function **=date(year,month,day)** works with both these variables to give you dates according to the starting dates of your plan.
- The Date and Number format options are available in the Format > Cells menu.

Example: Linking Inserted Table to Sales Forecast

Figure 10-15 shows one example, linking from a new table into the Sales Forecast table.

FIGURE 10-15: LINK FROM USER-DEFINED TABLE INTO SALES

P15	='User 1'C40				C40	=SUM(C35:C39)		
	A	O	P			A	B	C	D
13	Sales Forecast				34	Total estimated unit sales	2004	2005	2006
14	Unit Sales	2004	2005		35	Consumer	120	153	187
15	Systems	2,251	3,134		36	Small Business	555	709	1,034
16	Service	3,128	6,000		37	Large Business	1,485	2,138	2,887
17	Software	3,980	5,000		38	Government	51	65	87
18	Training	2,230	4,000		39	Other	40	69	128
19	Other	2,122	2,500		40	Total	2,251	3,134	4,323
20	Total Unit Sales	13,711	20,634						

The example here shows how the User-defined table links back into the Sales Forecast table. You can add tables if you have the PREMIER version.

Here is how it is done in detail:

- Select the target cell in the Sales Forecast. In the example, cell P15 is selected. That cell contains the projection for unit sales of systems in 2005.
- Type the equals sign, = into the cell (without quotation marks, parentheses, etc).
- Use the Table pull-down list to go to the user-defined table that contains the source cell (in this example, it is User 1).
- Click on the source cell. In the example, that is cell C40. The formula becomes ='User 1'!C40
- Press <ENTER>.

Example: Pasting from an Excel Worksheet to a Blank Table

You can copy a range from an Excel worksheet and paste it into a user-defined table. Figure 10-16 shows an example of the Excel worksheet and the Business Plan Pro user-defined table. If you want to preserve the formulas within the worksheet, it is an easy multi-step process.

FIGURE 10-16: PASTING TO USER-DEFINED TABLES FROM EXCEL

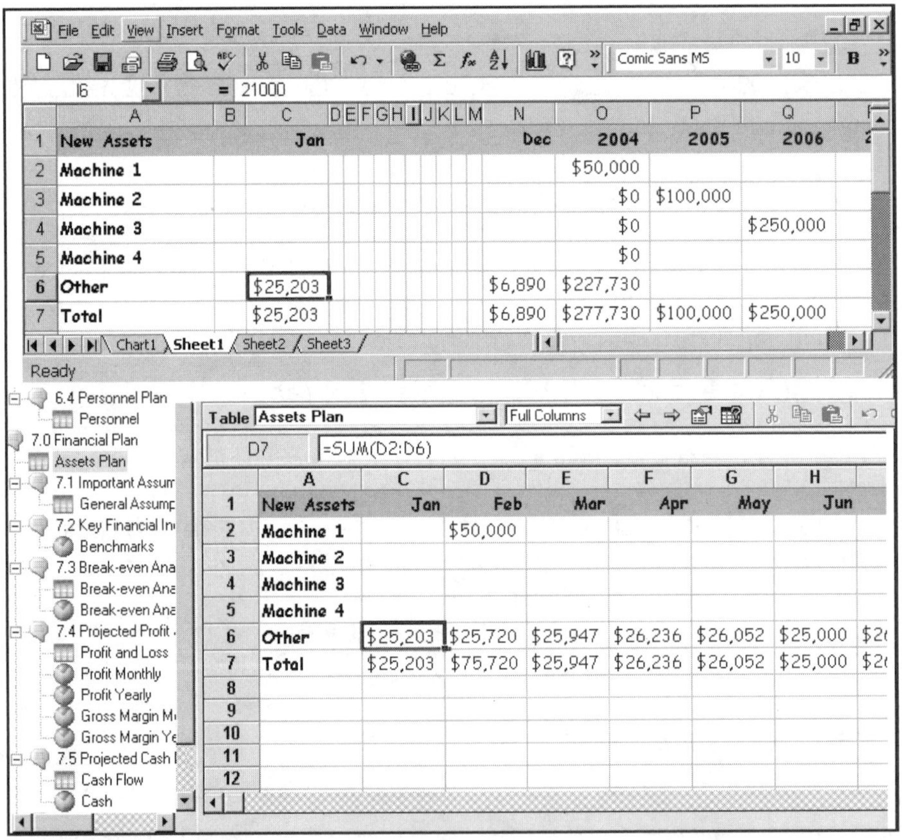

The Excel worksheet on the top was pasted into the Business Plan Pro *user-defined table on the bottom.*

1. In Microsoft Excel (the example was developed with Excel 2000), make sure that the spreadsheet area you want to paste contains only unprotected cells.
2. If you have any doubts, select the area you want to copy and paste, then use the Format menu, Cells command, and Protection tab to make sure those cells are not protected.
3. Within Excel, select and copy the source area you want to use in Business Plan Pro.
4. Select Business Plan Pro. Use the Plan Outline Insert tool from the toolbar to insert a new table attached to a topic. Select the cell you want to have as the upper left cell in the target range. Remember, those cells should be unprotected in Excel.
5. Use Edit > Paste Special > Paste All command. Your Excel spreadsheet is now pasted into your Business Plan Pro user-defined table.

Tips on Pasting from Excel to Business Plan Pro

If you do work with this paste process, please remember these important tips and traps for pasting from Excel to Business Plan Pro:

- A Copy and Paste from Excel to Business Plan Pro copies values only, not formats or formulas. To copy and paste spreadsheet information completely, use the Paste Special command in Business Plan Pro and chose Paste All to paste both formulas and formats.
- If you paste a formula from one worksheet containing an erroneous reference, you get a #REF error in the target worksheet. That is true in Excel, and it is also true when you paste from Excel into Business Plan Pro. For example:
- If you copy the formula =C9 from cell C10 in Excel into cell C1 in Business Plan Pro (or Excel), you get a #REF error. Business Plan Pro wants to reinterpret the formula to refer to the relative row number, 9 is 1 less than 10, but when you paste into row 1 you do not have the possibility of a lower row number.
- Copy a formula =XYZ (referring to a range name not already in Business Plan Pro) from Excel and paste it into Business Plan Pro. Business Plan Pro behaves like Excel does in this instance. It creates a new range named XYZ located in a position relative to the target cell.
- Copy the formula =Sales from Excel and paste it into Business Plan Pro. Business Plan Pro creates a new range named =Sales_2 and give the target cell the formula =Sales_2. To make the cell refer to the range named Sales, you have to edit the formula manually.

TIPS

No Links to External Files

The Business Plan Pro spreadsheet is so compatible with Microsoft Excel that almost any function or formula that works in Excel works in Business Plan Pro. However, Business Plan Pro cannot link formulas to external files outside of the plan. Excel can do this, but Business Plan Pro cannot.

Protected Cells Remain Protected after Copying

If you copy protected cells from Excel to Business Plan Pro, they remain protected. You cannot access them to change them after they are copied.

Example: Linking Sales Forecast from the Market Forecast Table

For this example, the AMT computer store wants to develop a more detailed Sales Forecast for computer systems drawing from information, including its projected market size and its projected market share.

Figure 10-17 shows a customized AMT sample plan user-defined table.

FIGURE 10-17: USER-DEFINED TABLE, PART 1

	A	B	C	D	E	F	G
	B6	=Market!C7					
1		2004	2005	2006	2007	2008	
2	Consumer	12,000	12,240	12,485	12,735	12,990	
3	Small Business	15,000	15,750	16,538	17,365	18,233	
4	Large Business	33,000	35,640	38,491	41,570	44,896	
5	Government	36,000	35,280	34,574	33,883	33,205	
6	Other	19,000	19,000	19,000	19,000	19,000	
7							
8							
9	Estimated sales per segment, in percent, per year						
10	Consumer	10.00%	12.50%	15.00%	20.00%	25.00%	
11	Small Business	20.00%	20.00%	25.00%	30.00%	30.00%	
12	Large Business	15.00%	20.00%	25.00%	30.00%	35.00%	
13	Government	0.56%	0.74%	1.01%	1.36%	1.86%	
14	Other	0.84%	1.46%	2.69%	4.60%	8.41%	
15							

The formula shown in the edit bar picks up information from the Market Analysis table.

- Although the system continues to refer to this table as User 1 for linking purposes, we can rename it in the plan topics. For example, we could call it "Detailed sales assumptions" instead of "User 1."
- The top row contains years. Cell B1 has the formula =PS_startingYear which refers to a named range within Business Plan Pro. C1 contains the formula =B1+1.
- The cells in this section of the table link to the Market Analysis table, which contains projected total market numbers for different market segments. The cells in Figure 10-17, from A2 through F6, refer to the Market Analysis table. That means that if you decide to change the Market Analysis table for any reason, you do not have to retype.

TIPS

For more detail on Forecasting

Please refer to *Part 4: Forecasting* in **Hurdle: the Book on Business Planning**. The book offers detailed tips on how to develop forecast numbers using a combination of research, analysis, common sense, and educated guessing. Click the Resources button > Books > Hurdle to read the book in PDF format.

Example: Total Sales Based on Percent of Total Market

In the second table block shown in Figure 10-18, we project the percent of total market expected to purchase systems within each given year. As with the total potential market projections, these are a combination of research, analysis, common sense, and educated guessing.

These cells do not use formulas; they are assumptions typed manually into the cells.

Calculated Unit Sales

The third block of cells calculated the estimated unit sales for the geographic market. For each market segment, it multiplies percent of total by total market to calculate projected total sales for the segment.

The illustration shows the formula for cell B18. It multiplies the unit number in B2 times the percentage in B10, and uses the Business Plan Pro ROUND function to round that calculation to even numbers.

FIGURE 10-18: USER-DEFINED TABLE, PART 2

B18	=ROUND(B10*B2,0)				
	A	B	C	D	E	F
2	Consumer	12,000	12,240	12,485	12,735	12,990
3	Small Business	15,000	15,750	16,538	17,365	18,233
4	Large Business	33,000	35,640	38,491	41,570	44,896
5	Government	36,000	35,280	34,574	33,883	33,205
6	Other	19,000	19,000	19,000	19,000	19,000
8						
9	Estimated sales per segment, in percent, per year					
10	Consumer	10.00%	12.50%	15.00%	20.00%	25.00%
11	Small Business	20.00%	20.00%	25.00%	30.00%	30.00%
12	Large Business	15.00%	20.00%	25.00%	30.00%	35.00%
13	Government	0.56%	0.74%	1.01%	1.36%	1.86%
14	Other	0.84%	1.46%	2.69%	4.60%	8.41%
16						
17	Total estimated unit sales	2004	2005	2006	2007	2008
18	Consumer	1,200	1,530	1,873	2,547	3,248
19	Small Business	3,000	3,150	4,135	5,210	5,470
20	Large Business	4,950	7,128	9,623	12,471	15,714
21	Government	202	261	349	461	618
22	Other	160	277	511	874	1,598
23	Total	9,512	12,346	16,491	21,563	26,648

In the example, the estimated unit sales are produced by multiplying market by percent penetration.

The ROUND Function

The formula shown in Figure 10-18 rounds the calculation to the nearest whole number:

$$=ROUND(B10*B2,0)$$

Here are more examples of how this function works:

- =ROUND(B10*B2,1) rounds to a single decimal.

- =ROUND(B10*B2,-2) rounds to the nearest hundred.

- =ROUND(B10*B2,-3) rounds to the nearest thousand.

Market Share and Sales

The detailed market model then continues into its fourth section, which contains percentage assumptions of AMT's share of the local market. Figure 10-19 demonstrates this.

The final section of the model multiplies the total market projected sales by the assumed AMT percentage market share, in order to project AMT sales of systems. The final numbers in row 40 of that model are then linked back into the Sales Forecast, which was associated with Figure 10-14 earlier in this discussion.

FIGURE 10-19: USER-DEFINED TABLE, PART 3

B40	=SUM(B35:B39)				
	A	B	C	D	E	F
18	Consumer	1,200	1,530	1,873	2,547	3,248
19	Small Business	3,000	3,150	4,135	5,210	5,470
20	Large Business	4,950	7,128	9,623	12,471	15,714
21	Government	202	261	349	461	618
22	Other	160	277	511	874	1,598
23	Total	9,512	12,346	16,491	21,563	26,648
25						
26	Estimated share per segment, in percent, per year					
27	Consumer	10.00%	10.00%	10.00%	10.00%	10.00%
28	Small Business	18.50%	22.50%	25.00%	27.50%	30.00%
29	Large Business	30.00%	30.00%	30.00%	30.00%	30.00%
30	Government	25.00%	25.00%	25.00%	25.00%	25.00%
31	Other	25.00%	25.00%	25.00%	25.00%	25.00%
33						
34	Total estimated unit sales	2004	2005	2006	2007	2008
35	Consumer	120	153	187	255	325
36	Small Business	555	709	1,034	1,433	1,641
37	Large Business	1,485	2,138	2,887	3,741	4,714
38	Government	51	65	87	115	155
39	Other	40	69	128	219	400
40	Total	2,251	3,134	4,323	5,763	7,235

In this third view of the sample, this company's unit sales are estimated by taking total market units and estimated market share.

The SUM function

The formula calculates exactly as it seems: the sum of the cells included in the summation range. These SUM formulas are common in spreadsheets, and throughout Business Plan Pro as well. The SUM formula is used to sum unit sales, total sales, and total cost of sales. It is used to sum rows in the Personnel Plan, in the Profit and Loss, the Cash Flow, and Balance Sheet.

There is an illustration of the SUM function in Figure 10-19, showing the formula for cell B40 of the same worksheet, which sums the range (B35:B39). The actual formula is: =SUM(B35:B39)

Example: Assets and Depreciation

Although we recommend a much simpler treatment of assets and depreciation, Figure 10-20 shows a user-defined table (PREMIER version) that uses depreciation functions to help manage assets.

FIGURE 10-20: TRACKING ASSETS AND DEPRECIATION

C11	=SYD($C$3,15000,10,1)				
	A	**B**	**C**	**D**	**E**	**F**
1	New Assets	2004	2005	2006	2007	2008
2	Machine 1	$50,000				
3	Machine 2	$0	$100,000			
4	Machine 3	$0		$250,000		
5	Machine 4	$0				$500,000
6	Other	$227,730	$300,000	$150,000	$100,000	$100,000
7	Total	$277,730	$400,000	$400,000	$100,000	$600,000
8						
9	Depreciation					
10	Machine 1	$4,000	$4,000	$4,000	$4,000	$4,000
11	Machine 2		$15,455	$13,909	$12,364	$10,818
12	Machine 3			$40,000	$40,000	$40,000
13	Machine 4					$72,727
14	Other	$45,546	$105,546	$135,546	$155,546	$175,546
15	Total	$49,546	$125,001	$193,455	$211,910	$303,091

This user-defined table (PREMIER version) tracks assets and depreciation in detail. Note the use of the SYD depreciation function in the edit bar, for cell C11.

In this case, capital assets are so important to the business' overall financial position that we used a user-defined table to track them directly. We also used the built-in depreciation functions to handle depreciation automatically:

- We depreciate Machine 2 with the sum of the years digits (SYD) depreciation method, a built-in depreciation function compatible with Microsoft Excel depreciation functions. The syntax is as shown: **=SYD(purchase price, salvage value, years of life, period)**
- We copied that formula over to the rest of the row to calculate depreciation for that machine for five years.
- We depreciated Machine 1 according to the straight-line method, another built in function. The syntax for that function is: **=SLN(purchase price, salvage value, years or life)** which means that the actual formula in cells B10:F10 is: **=SLN($B$2,10000,10)**
- We purchase Machines 3 and 4 according to the assumptions shown in the illustration, using the depreciation functions as well. Machine 3 gets straight-line depreciation and Machine 4 gets SYD depreciation.
- For the last line, which summarizes all other capital expenses for the various years, we depreciate by taking 20% of the value of the purchase in each year, for each of the successive years. The underlying assumption is that all purchases are assets good for five years, depreciated straight line at 20% per year, with no salvage value.

TIPS

Depreciation Details

Depreciation detail demands a lot of fine tuning for very little change in the resulting numbers. It also depends on tax rules. Meanwhile, your sales forecast has more uncertainty on a higher scale. The depreciation example shows how to do depreciation detail and why you probably should not bother. This is planning, not accounting.

?

To Learn More About...	Search the Help Index for...
Inserting a blank table-PREMIER version	Insert table; Table, Add Other

Balance Sheet – Adding Detail (PREMIER version)

The Business Plan Pro standard Balance Sheet is streamlined and powerful. It does not include the row-by-row detail found in many company accounting balance sheets. This simplification is a valuable feature of Business Plan Pro, because it relates to the use of the financials in business planning. More detail in the balance sheet means we have to have more detail in the cash flow. Cash is the most critical element; you need a strong Cash Flow, that is easy to understand and work with.

Additional Assets or Liabilities

The previous section offers an example of developing additional detail on long-term assets, with particular attention to the details of depreciation. Figure 10-20 shows an example. You can do the same kind of detailed tracking for liabilities or different levels of assets. In any case, insert a table to track in detail and then link the results back into the main tables.

"Goodwill" as an Accounting Concept

When a company purchases another company for more than the value of its assets—which is quite common—the difference is recorded as an asset named "Goodwill." This is not a general term for the value of a brand, for example, but a very specific accounting term.

For example, if one business buys another business for $1 million, then it needs to show the $1 million spent as an asset. If there are only $500 thousand in real assets, the accounting result should be $500,000 in real assets purchased and another $500,000 in "Goodwill."

Goodwill is normally amortized over 5 to 40 years, depending on variables determined by the accountants. In Business Plan Pro you record the amortization of Goodwill as depreciation. If you need to set it apart from other depreciation, then use a user-defined table.

Sensitivity Analysis (PREMIER version)

Change your assumptions, and record the changes that result. How sensitive is your business plan to lower levels of sales? Higher costs? More time waiting to collect the money? That is sensitivity analysis.

A spreadsheet like the one now built into Business Plan Pro is a very powerful tool for sensitivity analysis. Make the changes and record the impact.

Example: Sensitivity Analysis

Figure 10-21 shows a useful sensitivity analysis done with a single new table inserted into the plan as a place to record changing results (PREMIER version). To do this with your plan, first insert a new table and then change assumptions and record the impact.

In the case shown here, the assumptions are in the Cash Pilot table. Change the main assumptions in that table and record the minimum cash balance from the Cash Flow.

FIGURE 10-21: SENSITIVITY ANALYSIS SAMPLE

	A	B	C	D	E	F	G
	E11						
1	Cash flow sensitivity analysis						
2	Alternative scenarios	1	2	3	4	5	
3	Collection days	30	45	60	45	45	
4	Inventory turnover	7	7	7	5	3	
5	Payment days	30	30	30	30	30	
6	Minimum balance	$146,594	$3,115	($297,666)	($443,507)	($1,339,796)	
7							
8							

This user table records results of a cash flow sensitivity analysis.

Develop Your Own Sensitivity Analysis

You can see from the example in Figure 10-21 that the possibilities of sensitivity analysis are virtually unlimited. You can use different power variable settings (Figures 10-9 to 10-13), different plans and plan names, or other options to change assumptions and record the results.

Sensitivity Analysis is "What-If"

There is not a big difference between sensitivity analysis and "what-if" analysis. When experts talk about sensitivity, they generally mean a more rigorous and organized analysis of how some variables change when other variables change. When business people talk about sensitivity, they often mean the same thing as "what if" analysis; that is, for example, what happens to cash flow if sales drop?

Dealing with Scenarios (PREMIER version)

Many business plan situations involve different scenarios. The simplest and in many aspects the most powerful way to manage scenarios is with different plans. Each plan is a complete file on its own, and each plan contains a scenario. The normal way to develop scenarios as separate plans is to finish the main plan as the most likely scenario, then use the File > Save As command to save it again with a different name, and make the new one a different scenario. For example, when the main plan is done, save it first as "pessimistic" and then lastly as "optimistic," and manage each of those offshoots as separate scenarios.

Two Built-in Sales Scenarios (PREMIER version)

Chapter 6 explains how the EasyPlan Wizard in PREMIER version gives you the choice of sales forecasts, either value-based or units-based, for every plan. It does not explain that you can also use these two forecasts to manage optional scenarios. That was not the original intention, but it works. Try it. Figure 10-22 shows you how the EasyPlan Wizard switches between the two forecasts.

FIGURE 10-22: SWITCHING BETWEEN SALES FORECASTS

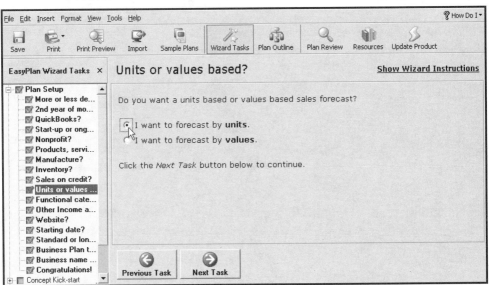

In PREMIER version the EasyPlan Wizard lets you switch between two sales forecasts, one structured more simply than the other. You can use this facility to build two scenarios into your plan.

You can see, as you try it, that each of the forecasts is separate, and whichever is selected links automatically into the Profit and Loss table. Normally you make a choice of structure at the time that you set up your plan. As a special case, however, you can manage two forecasts by making both of the two options significant.

Multiple Personnel Scenarios (PREMIER version)

As with the Sales Forecast, the Business Plan Pro PREMIER version offers several different Personnel Plan options. They switch automatically with the EasyPlan Wizard. Try it:

- Tell the EasyPlan Wizard you do not want to divide expenses by categories, and you get a standard personnel forecast as a simple list.
- If you divide by categories, your personnel goes to a different forecast, broken into four expense categories. The data here is completely different from the simple plan where expenses are not broken into categories.
- If you choose to plan personnel with the "Personnel by People" method, you have yet a third forecast for personnel.
- You can switch between these different personnel plans by changing options with the EasyPlan Wizard. The data stays with each personnel plan.

Subscriptions or Churn Rate Forecasts (PREMIER version)

📌 TIPS

Who Needs a Subscription Sales Model?

Whenever a business sells subscriptions, memberships, or similar services that involve continuing monthly payments, that is a subscription model. It takes some special analysis to separate the running months' revenue from new customers. Subscriptions may be sold annually, but the related sales are essentially monthly.

Figure 10-23 shows the first portion of a subscription sales model, also called Churn Rate model. It calculates subscriber sales for a $19.95 monthly membership business. The EasyPlan Wizard sets the Sales Forecast for a units-based forecast, not value-based. In the units area, one row shows new subscribers, one row shows cancellations (attrition), and one shows total subscribers. In the unit prices, a subscriber pays $19.95 monthly and a cancellation causes a single-month credit. You can see the resulting Sales Forecast.

FIGURE 10-23: SUBSCRIPTION SALES (CHURN RATE)

D16	=ROUND($B16*C18,0)						
	A	B	C	D	E	F	G
13	**Sales Forecast**						
14	**Unit Sales**		Jan	Feb	Mar	Apr	May
15	New subscriptions		100	150	250	300	400
16	Cancellations	3.00%	0	3	7	15	23
17	Total subscribers		100	247	490	775	1,152
18	Subscriber Months		100	247	490	775	1,152
19	**Total Unit Sales**		300	647	1,237	1,865	2,727
20							
21	**Unit Prices**		Jan	Feb	Mar	Apr	May
23	Cancellations		$0.00	($19.95)	($19.95)	($19.95)	($19.95)
25	Subscriber Months		$19.95	$19.95	$19.95	$19.95	$19.95
26							
27	**Sales**						
29	Cancellations		$0	($60)	($140)	($299)	($459)
31	Subscriber Months		$1,995	$4,928	$9,776	$15,461	$22,982
32	**Total Sales**		$1,995	$4,868	$9,636	$15,162	$22,524
33							

This example shows a Sales Forecast for a subscription model. Customers subscribe for a year but the Sales enter the business as subscriber months.

You can see in this figure how the cancellation formula uses a percentage assumption (3%, in Column B) so you can vary the assumption to see the impact of different cancellation rates. The formula showing in the illustration uses the ROUND function to set the cancellations to single user numbers.

This is another good example of an input variable programmed into column B of the Sales Forecast. That makes changing assumptions easier. You can change the rate of cancellation in this sales forecast by changing that single cell.

Subscriber months are fairly easy for monthly projections, but the system gets more complex when you need to translate subscriber months into annual forecasts. Figure 10-24 shows a detailed treatment of the subscription or churn Sales Forecast for the years, instead of months. Some of the formulas require detailed explanation.

FIGURE 10-24: SUBSCRIPTION (CHURN) MODEL YEARS FORMULAS

P18	=((N17+P17)/2)*12			
A	**N**	**O**	**P**	**Q**
13 Sales Forecast				
14 Unit Sales	Dec	2004	2005	2006
15 New subscriptions	700	4,700	10,000	12,500
16 Cancellations	108	497	2,557	4,346
17 Total subscribers	4,203	20,757	11,646	19,800
18 Subscriber Months	4,203	20,757	95,097	243,343
19 Total Unit Sales	9,214	46,711	119,300	279,989
20				
21 Unit Prices	Dec	2004	2005	2006
23 Cancellations	($19.95)	($19.95)	($19.95)	($19.95)
25 Subscriber Months	$19.95	$19.95	$19.95	$19.95
26				
27 Sales				
29 Cancellations	($2,155)	($9,915)	($51,003)	($86,710)
31 Subscriber Months	$83,850	$414,102	$1,897,180	$4,854,685
32 Total Sales	$81,695	$404,187	$1,846,177	$4,767,975
33				

For the annual subscriptions, each subscriber is 12 subscriber months. Notice that rows 22, 24, 28, and 30 are hidden.

- The new subscriptions estimate in 2005 (cell P15) is an input estimate. Be careful, if you are doing this kind of a forecast, to build in the growth. In this forecast the 10,000 new subscribers model may look ambitious, but at the end of the first year the business was picking up 700 new subscribers per month. At that rate the next year would bring in 8,400 subscribers (700*12). Therefore the 10,000 estimate is not as ambitious as it might seem at first glance.

- Cancellations in cells P16 and Q16 are also estimates, based on a percentage of cancellations from the subscriber base. How many people will cancel in a given year? If your business has history you might be able to turn to that history to estimate. If not, you might be able to research cancellations from other, similar business (publicly traded, perhaps, that have to release such information). In either case, you need to make these assumptions clear and row 16 is how you do that.

- Cell P17 presents total subscribers at the end of the year, as a result of the formula: =N17+P15-P16 . The cell N17 in that formula contains the total subscribers at the end of the last month of the previous year. Cell P15 contains new subscribers for the year, and P16 contains dropouts. This is not the number used to calculate revenue, but it is still an important number for marketing, and benchmarking. A subscription business needs to know how many subscribers it adds and loses. Many similar businesses, subscription-based or not, need to estimate their monthly "churn," as this is sometimes called.

- The formula in P17 needs to be adjusted for Q17, because of the impact of the annual numbers in column O. The correct formula for **Q17 is =P17+Q15-Q16** .

- The formula for cell P18 needs to account for subscription months. These are paying months, and they are critical to calculating revenue. If you have 1,000 subscribers for a full year, they contribute 12,000 subscriber months. The formula in P18 is =((N17+P17)/2)*12 . This formula takes the average between the total subscribers at the beginning of the year, and total subscribers at the end of the year, and multiplies that average subscribers by 12 to calculate subscriber months.

This is not a perfect calculation. It creates a reasonable estimate. You could make that exact by developing another complete year of months. This approximation is good enough for planning purposes, however. In the end, no matter how detailed you make your future estimates, they are still estimates. We prefer to leave that fact obvious by not trying to bury estimated guesses in overwhelming detail.

As with row 17, there is a difference between column P and column Q in these formulas because of the impact of the annual column O intervening. The correct formula for cell Q18 is
$$=((O17+Q17)/2)*12 .$$

The effect of taking averages for these columns is appropriate to the level of certainty in predicting subscriptions two and three years into the future.

📌 TIPS   Hiding Unused Rows with Zero Values

Figure 10-24 shows a good example of hiding rows you do not need. Although this Sales Forecast needs to keep track of new subscribers and total subscribers, there are no price or sales implications. We used the Format > Hide Row command to hide those rows that we did not need.

Tax Rate Lookup (PREMIER version)

Business Plan Pro includes a lookup function to deal with tax rates, if you want to make them more complex. Figure 10-25 shows a formula that compares the lookup value to the lookup table and calculates a rate as a result. This is a simple model of a detailed tax table.

FIGURE 10-25: TAX LOOKUP TABLE

B9	=VLOOKUP(B1,B3:C7,2)			
	A	**B**	**C**	**D**
1	**Lookup Value:**	**$125,000**		
2				
3	**Lookup Table:**	**($50,000,000)**	**0.00%**	
4		**$0**	**5.00%**	
5		**$100,000**	**10.00%**	
6		**$250,000**	**20.00%**	
7		**$1,000,000**	**30.00%**	
8				
9	**Lookup Result:**	**10.00%**		
10				

The illustration shows the formula for the lookup as an example of how the formula works.

Figure 10-26 shows how a lookup formula can go into the tax rate assumption so that as profits go up, so do the tax rates.

FIGURE 10-26: LOOKUP IN ACTION

AE6	=VLOOKUP('P&L'!Q53,'User 2'!$B$3:$C$7,2)				
	A	**N**	**O**	**AD**	**AE**
1	**General Assumptions**				
2		**Dec**	**2004**	**2005**	**2006**
3	Plan Month	12	1	2	3
4	Current Interest Rate	9.00%	9.00%	9.00%	9.00%
5	Long-term Interest Rate	8.50%	8.50%	8.50%	8.50%
6	Tax Rate	20.00%	20.00%	25.00%	30.00%
9	Other	0	0	0	0
10	**Calculated Totals**				
11	Payroll Expense	$8,750	$105,000	$115,500	$127,050
13	New Accounts Payable	$11,664	$144,703	$157,477	$168,719
14	Inventory Purchase	$0	$0	$0	$0

The lookup formula in the tax rate changes rates automatically depending on the level of profits.

Additional Resources

?

To Learn More About...	Search the Help Index for...
Adding tables, inserting tables, user-defined tables	Table, Add Other; Insert Table
Spreadsheet functions	Functions
Formulas to link from one table to another by referring to data	Links
Range names, variables in range names, referring to range names in formulas	Range names
Locked cells, data entry cells, cell formats	Locked cells; Data cells; Format, Cells
Accessing locked row and column headers for direct editing and modifications	Tools: Table options
Depreciation and financial functions	Financial functions
Import/Export a table	Import; Export; Microsoft Excell

Conclusion: It is Your World

There is no reason why using a business plan software package should limit your ability to customize your business plan. You can stick with the default or make it as sophisticated as you need. In the end, it is your plan. The software is a tool, but you are the craftperson who uses that tool.

This page intentionally blank.

Working with Quicken® 11

Quicken® is a registered trademark of Intuit Corporation.

CHAPTER 11: WORKING WITH QUICKEN®

*Quicken bookkeeping and Business Plan Pro®
are a good compliment to each other. Planning and
accounting deal with the same underlying business
numbers, but from different directions.*

*Planning looks from today ahead into the
future, while accounting looks from today
backwards into the past. A good business does both
well. The two applications have different purposes,
but both are related to the proper running of a
business.*

Customers who run both Quicken and Business
Plan Pro *can share information between the two
programs. The examples in this chapter show you
how.*

Import MiniPlan to Business Plan Pro

The Quicken software program includes a special tool called the MiniPlan that is designed to work with Business Plan Pro. The MiniPlan gives you a head start with your initial assessment, including summary, objectives, keys to success, initial market analysis, and break-even analysis.

Some users develop a MiniPlan first, then move to Business Plan Pro. If you have not already done a MiniPlan, do not bother—it is built into Business Plan Pro as the Concept Kick-start section of the EasyPlan Wizard Tasks. If you have done a MiniPlan in Quicken, then instead of retyping that material, you can import it directly into your business plan. Figure 11-1 shows the first step:

FIGURE 11-1: IMPORTING THE MINIPLAN

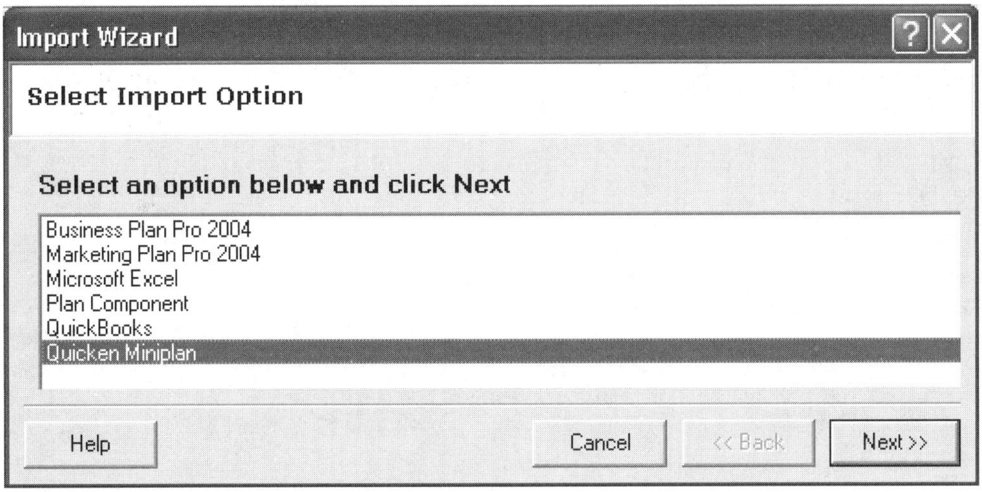

You can import your MiniPlan from Quicken.

- Follow the dialogs to find your MiniPlan and include it in your business plan.

The result is an automatic input, so you do not have to redo what you have already typed. Your business plan then absorbs the following sections from the MiniPlan: Executive Summary, Objectives, Keys to Success, Market Analysis, Break-even Analysis.

Matching the Chart of Accounts

One core element of every bookkeeping or accounting system is the chart of accounts. The chart of accounts is a list of categories of assets, liabilities, capital, sales, costs of sales, and expenses. Quicken calls these categories.

Set Categories in Both Applications

Match the categories between your Quicken bookkeeping and your business plan. This builds a better link between planning and results. It makes your plan more realistic, and your results more valuable for decision making.

Categories in Quicken

In Quicken, you set the categories as you work with your checking, invoices, bills, etc.

Categories in Business Plan Pro

In Business Plan Pro, you create the categories for your Sales Forecast and Profit and Loss tables using the Edit > Insert Row and Edit Label commands. Insert rows first, then use the Edit Label command to give the row a name.

> **TIPS**
>
> **Recommended Sequence**
>
> Generally it is easier to develop your categories in Quicken first and then match them in Business Plan Pro. The Quicken categories relate more directly to your bookkeeping needs. You then match them in Business Plan Pro.

Profit & Loss – Expense List Comparison

In the following illustrations, you can see how the order of expenses is different between Quicken and Business Plan Pro.

Quicken – Profit & Loss Expenses

Figure 11-2 shows the Profit and Loss Statement produced by Quicken.

FIGURE 11-2: QUICKEN PROFIT AND LOSS REPORT

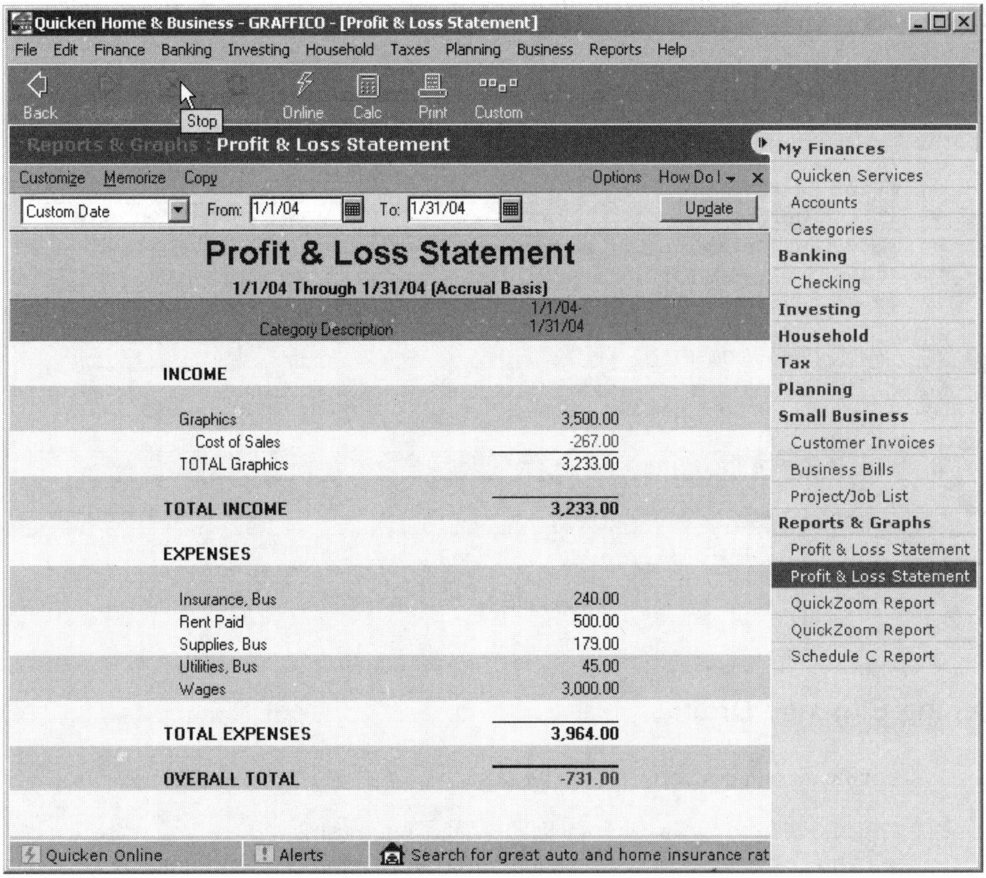

The order of the Quicken report depends on the categories you establish in your Quicken files.

Business Plan Pro – Profit & Loss Expenses

Figure 11-3 shows the Profit and Loss statement in Business Plan Pro.

FIGURE 11-3: BUSINESS PLAN PRO PROFIT AND LOSS

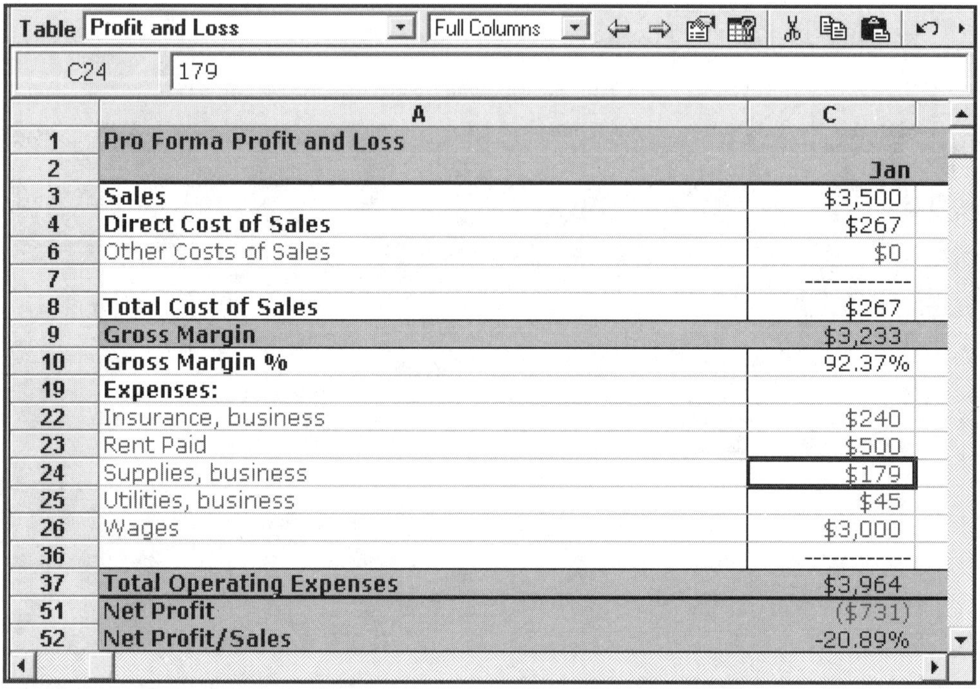

Table	Profit and Loss	Full Columns										
C24	179											

	A	C
1	Pro Forma Profit and Loss	
2		Jan
3	Sales	$3,500
4	Direct Cost of Sales	$267
6	Other Costs of Sales	$0
7		------------
8	Total Cost of Sales	$267
9	Gross Margin	$3,233
10	Gross Margin %	92.37%
19	Expenses:	
22	Insurance, business	$240
23	Rent Paid	$500
24	Supplies, business	$179
25	Utilities, business	$45
26	Wages	$3,000
36		------------
37	Total Operating Expenses	$3,964
51	Net Profit	($731)
52	Net Profit/Sales	-20.89%

This illustration shows the corresponding Business Plan Pro *Profit and Loss table. Rows 20 and 21, which contain no data, are hidden by the Format > Row > Hide command.*

Matching Expense Order

There are normally differences between the two lists:

- Quicken organizes expenses in alphabetical order, while Business Plan Pro organizes according to however you choose to name the rows. Therefore we recommend that you keep your Business Plan Pro expenses in alphabetical order, to match.
- Business Plan Pro separates interest and taxes so it can show Profit Before Interest and Taxes. Quicken does not separate these items. Interest and taxes appear in reports as operating expenses. To make the Business Plan Pro format match the Quicken statements, follow these steps:

1. On your General Assumptions table, set tax rates and interest rates to zero. This makes your Business Plan Pro tax and interest rows also zero.
2. On the Profit and Loss table in Business Plan Pro, use the Format > Row > Hide command to hide those rows.
3. Use operating expense rows, in proper alphabetical order, to estimate interest and taxes. Your business plan now matches the Quicken statements.

- Business Plan Pro normally gets its personnel expenses from the Personnel Plan and puts them at the top of the list of operating expenses, in a row named "Payroll." Quicken, on the other hand, treats wages as another operating expense. If you want to match the Quicken statements more closely in Business Plan Pro, you have several options:
  1. Ignore your Personnel Plan table, unlink it from the plan, and use Format > Row > Hide to hide the Payroll row in your business plan. Add another row in operating expenses for wages, and type your estimates directly into that row. Keep wages in alphabetical order to match the Quicken report.
  2. If you want to use the Personnel Plan table in your plan, you can. Payroll shows automatically. Expenses are not in exactly the same order in Business Plan Pro, because Payroll is at the top, regardless of alphabetical order. However, the bottom line numbers still match.
  3. You can also make the formats match closely, without losing the Personnel Plan table. Add a row in operating expenses that subtracts payroll, hiding both the automatic payroll row and the one that subtracts the same amount; then add another operating expense row in correct alphabetical order, name it "Wages" to match Quicken, and put the formula "=payroll_expense" into that new row.

- Business Plan Pro must have depreciation estimates in the row named Depreciation. It needs to know about depreciation for Cash Flow calculations. Therefore, if you handle depreciation in your Quicken bookkeeping as an expense, then you must also include depreciation in the business plan, and include it in the row already named Depreciation. Even if that puts depreciation out of order in the business plan, when compared to the Quicken plan, it is still needed for proper cash flow planning.

TIPS   **Bringing Planning and Accounting Together**
Quicken and Business Plan Pro have different but related purposes. The key to bringing them together is being able to match your Quicken bookkeeping to your Business Plan Pro worksheets. This gives you a very powerful tool for budgeting and revisions.

Managing the Balance Sheet

Your Balance Sheet in Quicken is almost always more complicated than in Business Plan Pro. Consider the Business Plan Pro Balance Sheet table as a summarized, streamlined version which is ideal for business planning. Do not expect it to be exactly the same because the Quicken Balance Sheet depends on expanding into more detail.

You should be able to reconcile the two formats by summarizing Quicken details with Business Plan Pro.

Total Assets:

Start with total assets, and divide them first into the summarized categories in Business Plan Pro. Here are some helpful details:

- Cash, in Business Plan Pro, should include all of your business' liquid assets: all checking and savings accounts managed by the business, plus money-market funds, and money in real cash (coins and bills).
- Accounts Receivable and Inventory are summaries. You do not need to divide them into detail in Business Plan Pro, because you have Quicken for the detailed management.
- Other Current Assets (also called Short-term Assets) is a holding place for whatever else you have as current assets. For simplification's sake, hold all depreciation for long-term assets (even if you do have current assets that are depreciated, and you do not have long-term assets). Remember the difference between planning vs. tax reporting and detailed accounting.
- Make sure the totals add up. When in doubt, look for current assets and long-term assets, adjusted for inflation. Fit the asset base into the Business Plan Pro categories.

Total Liabilities:

Next, make sure your total liabilities match, then divide them into the Business Plan Pro Balance Sheet using these hints:

- Accounts payable are all of your bills due. Include liabilities like credit card balances.
- Current Borrowing is for bank loans, bank lines of credit, accounts receivable financing, inventory financing, and credit card balances if you do not include them in Accounts Payable.
- Other Current Liabilities is for all other liabilities that do not fit into the first two categories. This is where you put all interest-free debt, such as loans from founders, or accrued taxes (if you do not have them in Accounts Payable).
- Make sure the liabilities total matches your Quicken total. If not, then the numbers are not right. Business Plan Pro mainly handles totals, so just divide the details into the right categories.

Finally, make the capital match as well. Paid-in Capital is actual money invested. Earnings are current-period earnings, as in the present year. Retained Earnings are whatever is required to make capital equal to assets minus equity.

Working with QuickBooks®

CHAPTER 12: WORKING WITH QUICKBOOKS®

QuickBooks is the small business standard for bookkeeping and accounting. Far more small businesses keep books with this application than with all others combined.

If you use QuickBooks Pro or QuickBooks Premier for your bookkeeping, you can also work easily with a business plan in Business Plan Pro® that matches the bookkeeping system in QuickBooks. You can import your sales, cost of goods, and expense categories automatically, so you do not have to retype. You can also use past data from QuickBooks as a starting point for estimating future results.

Remember, however, that planning is different from accounting. Business Plan Pro gives you a starting point for future estimates, not a substitute for detailed accounting statements of past results.

Import from QuickBooks Pro (or Premier)

Business Plan Pro has an Import function that lets you pull major categories and useful information from your QuickBooks file into your plan file (this applies only to the QuickBooks Pro 2002 or QuickBooks Premier 2002 or newer versions).

TIPS

Import for forecasting and categories, not exact past amounts.

The QuickBooks import does not attempt to duplicate your bookkeeping or accounting functions, and it does not give you exact duplicates of your QuickBooks statements. It does give you categories and close approximations that you can use to forecast the future.

The Import function:

- Imports QuickBooks categories for sales, costs of goods, expenses, and other income and expenses.
- Matches major categories only. Accounting information for subcategories is summarized in the major categories.
- (Optional) Applies growth rates to past amounts to provide estimations of future amounts for planning purposes. The approximate amounts are only slightly different from accounting totals.
- (Optional) Imports the most recent balance and puts it in the Past Performance table, then uses it to estimate the ending balance of the last period before the plan starts.

TIPS

Bringing Planning and Accounting Together

QuickBooks and Business Plan Pro have different but related purposes. The key to bringing them together is being able to show the same categories in Business Plan Pro projections as you have in your QuickBooks bookkeeping. This gives you a powerful tool for planning and management.

Limitations When Using QuickBooks BASIC

The Business Plan Pro QuickBooks import depends on internal capabilities of QuickBooks Pro and Premier versions, which are not available in the QuickBooks Basic version. If you use QuickBooks Basic and want the additional compatibility for your Business Plan Pro, contact Intuit to upgrade your QuickBooks. Contact information is available at www.QuickBooks.com.

Without the upgrade, however, you can still work easily with your QuickBooks data by using the flexibility of Business Plan Pro to match your categories in QuickBooks. Follow the matching chart of account details in the next section and create your own QuickBooks capabilities by adjusting row names to categories.

Matching the Chart of Accounts

Working these two applications together starts with matching the categories so your future plan matches your past results. The import feature sets your categories in both Business Plan Pro and QuickBooks so they match well enough for analysis and management tracking. Figure 12-1 shows the Profit and Loss in QuickBooks. Figure 12-2 shows how this can look almost identical in Business Plan Pro.

FIGURE 12-1: QUICKBOOKS PROFIT AND LOSS

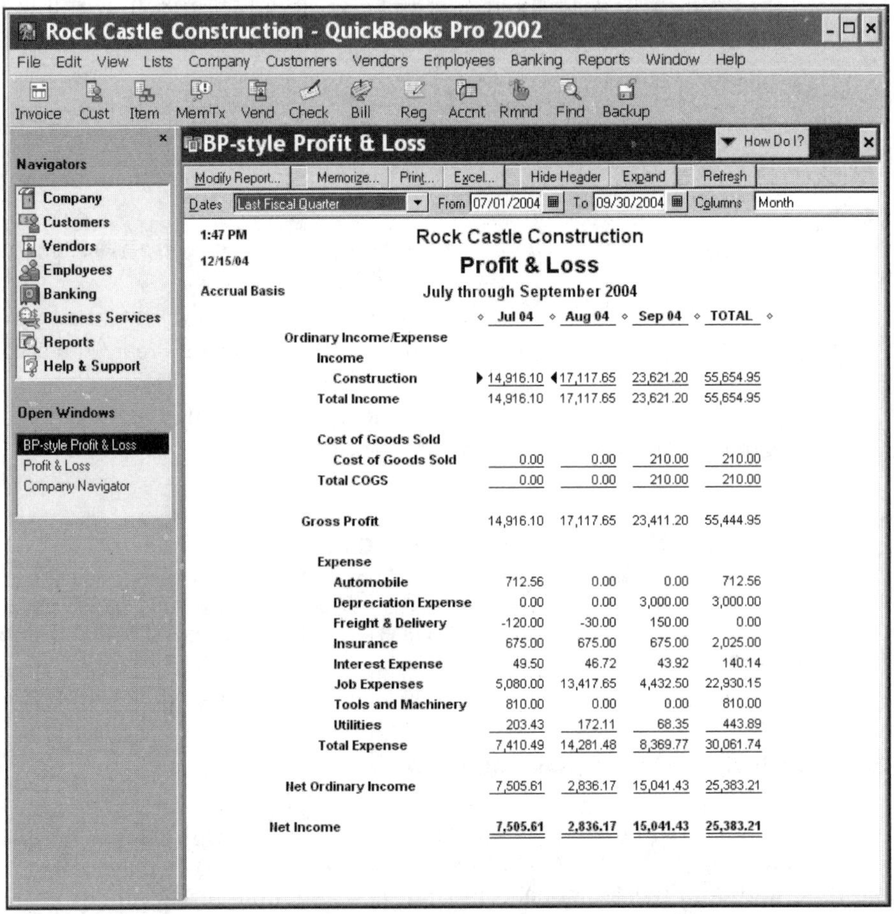

	Jul 04	Aug 04	Sep 04	TOTAL
Ordinary Income/Expense				
Income				
Construction	14,916.10	17,117.65	23,621.20	55,654.95
Total Income	14,916.10	17,117.65	23,621.20	55,654.95
Cost of Goods Sold				
Cost of Goods Sold	0.00	0.00	210.00	210.00
Total COGS	0.00	0.00	210.00	210.00
Gross Profit	14,916.10	17,117.65	23,411.20	55,444.95
Expense				
Automobile	712.56	0.00	0.00	712.56
Depreciation Expense	0.00	0.00	3,000.00	3,000.00
Freight & Delivery	-120.00	-30.00	150.00	0.00
Insurance	675.00	675.00	675.00	2,025.00
Interest Expense	49.50	46.72	43.92	140.14
Job Expenses	5,080.00	13,417.65	4,432.50	22,930.15
Tools and Machinery	810.00	0.00	0.00	810.00
Utilities	203.43	172.11	68.35	443.89
Total Expense	7,410.49	14,281.48	8,369.77	30,061.74
Net Ordinary Income	7,505.61	2,836.17	15,041.43	25,383.21
Net Income	7,505.61	2,836.17	15,041.43	25,383.21

The QuickBooks Profit and Loss is one of its standard reports. This is the condensed Profit and Loss for a fiscal quarter. Note that in this version the categories are collapsed, not expanded.

Some fine tuning was necessary in Business Plan Pro before we imported. For this example, we set the first category to "Automobile" and the last category to "Uncategorized Expenses" to match the QuickBooks accounts (using the Edit > Row Label and Edit > Delete Row features to make those changes).

Figure 12-2 shows the corresponding Profit and Loss table in Business Plan Pro. It was produced by first setting the beginning categories, then importing the data from QuickBooks as explained in the rest of this chapter. The numbers shown are taken from previous results, but multiplied by an assigned growth rate. This is not a statement of past results, but a plan for the future.

FIGURE 12-2: MATCH BUSINESS PLAN PRO WITH QUICKBOOKS

Table	Profit and Loss	Full Columns		↤ ↦			Σ $ %	
H68								
	A	J	K	L	M	N	O
1	**Pro Forma Profit and Loss**						
2		May	Jun	Jul	Aug	Sep	2004
3	Total Income	$9,805	$14,669	$16,408	$18,828	$25,983	$149,791
8	Cost of Goods Sold	$72	$73	$0	$0	$221	$820
9	**Gross Profit**	$9,733	$14,596	$16,408	$18,828	$25,763	$148,970
10	Gross Profit %	99.27%	99.50%	100.00%	100.00%	99.15%	99.45%
19	**Expenses:**						
21	Depreciation	$0	$0	$0	$0	$3,021	$3,021
22	Automobile	$0	$0	$762	$0	$0	$3,346
24	Bank Service Charges	$4	$4	$4	$4	$4	$51
27	Freight & Delivery	$48	$0	($182)	($32)	$161	($102)
29	Interest Expense	$59	$56	$53	$50	$47	$758
30	Job Expenses	$3,533	$916	$5,436	$14,449	$4,743	$41,314
33	Payroll Expenses	$2,129	$2,129	$2,129	$2,129	$2,129	$25,552
36	Rent	$214	$214	$214	$214	$214	$2,568
39	Tools and Machinery	$0	$85	$57	$0	$0	$173
40	Utilities	$12	$13	$14	$12	$5	$102
51							
52	**Total Expense**	$6,000	$3,418	$8,488	$16,827	$10,324	$76,783
53	Gross Profit	$3,733	$11,178	$7,920	$2,002	$15,439	$72,188
65	Net Other Income	$0	$0	$0	$0	$0	$0
66	**Net Profit**	$3,733	$11,178	$7,920	$2,002	$15,439	$72,188
67	**Net Profit/Sales**	38.08%	76.20%	48.27%	10.63%	59.42%	48.19%

The business plan for Rock Castle Construction has the same categories as the QuickBooks bookkeeping chart of accounts. This match makes it easier to work with both programs. NOTE: Some rows with zero values were hidden for this example.

TIPS

Recommended Sequence

Generally it is easier to develop your categories in QuickBooks first, then match them in Business Plan Pro. The QuickBooks categories relate more directly to your bookkeeping needs, and Business Plan Pro imports them as part of the import process.

As you can see in the illustration, the match includes all the major categories on both sides. Even the fiscal year structure matches the QuickBooks example. The example took data included in the QuickBooks distribution disk and accommodated the categories list in Business Plan Pro to make it match. Most of this import process is automatic, but there is some fine tuning to do to match your categories exactly.

The QuickBooks Pro Import

The QuickBooks Pro import process starts in the Plan Setup, as shown in Figure 12-3. You tell the EasyPlan Wizard® you are working with QuickBooks so it can set up a plan to match.

FIGURE 12-3: WIZARD STEP FOR QUICKBOOKS

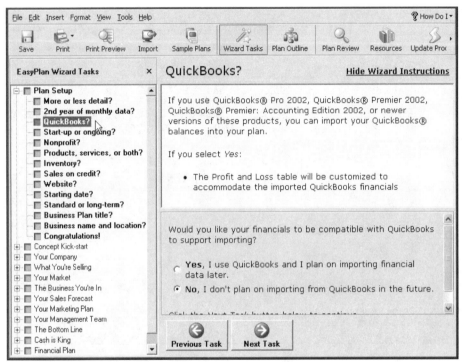

This question in the EasyPlan Wizard lets you modify your plan to work with QuickBooks.

Preparations Before Import

Figure 12-4 shows how categories were modified in Business Plan Pro before importing:

- Set your first and last accounts to match the first and last accounts in QuickBooks. In this example, we set the first row to "Automobile" and the last row to "Utilities."
- Delete any other accounts showing. The import matches values if the category titles match, but does not change the order. "Rent," for example, and "Insurance" are included in the standard new plan with Business Plan Pro. If you do not delete them before importing, they appear out of order after the import.

> **TIPS**
>
> ### QuickBooks Import Matches, but Does not Delete
>
> Business Plan Pro does not delete rows to make your expenses list match the expenses in QuickBooks Pro. To make an exact match, you must delete extra expense rows first, before the import.

FIGURE 12-4: PREPARING PROFIT AND LOSS FOR IMPORT

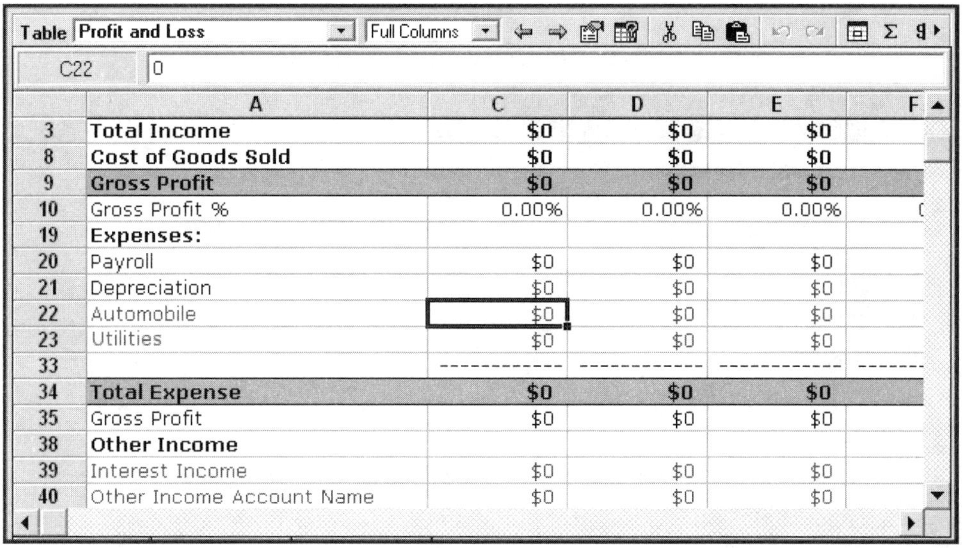

Table	Profit and Loss ▾	Full Columns ▾ ⇐ ⇒ 🖻 📑 ✂ 🗐 📋 ↻ ↺ 回 Σ ¶▸

C22		0

	A	C	D	E	F ▲
3	Total Income	$0	$0	$0	
8	Cost of Goods Sold	$0	$0	$0	
9	Gross Profit	$0	$0	$0	
10	Gross Profit %	0.00%	0.00%	0.00%	0
19	Expenses:				
20	Payroll	$0	$0	$0	
21	Depreciation	$0	$0	$0	
22	Automobile	$0	$0	$0	
23	Utilities	$0	$0	$0	
33		-------------	-------------	-------------	-------
34	Total Expense	$0	$0	$0	
35	Gross Profit	$0	$0	$0	
38	Other Income				
39	Interest Income	$0	$0	$0	
40	Other Income Account Name	$0	$0	$0	▼

For this import example, we set first and last categories to match the first and last categories of the QuickBooks bookkeeping.

The Import Process

The next step is the import process itself. The File > Import command brings up the form shown in Figure 12-5.

FIGURE 12-5: SELECTING QUICKBOOKS IMPORT

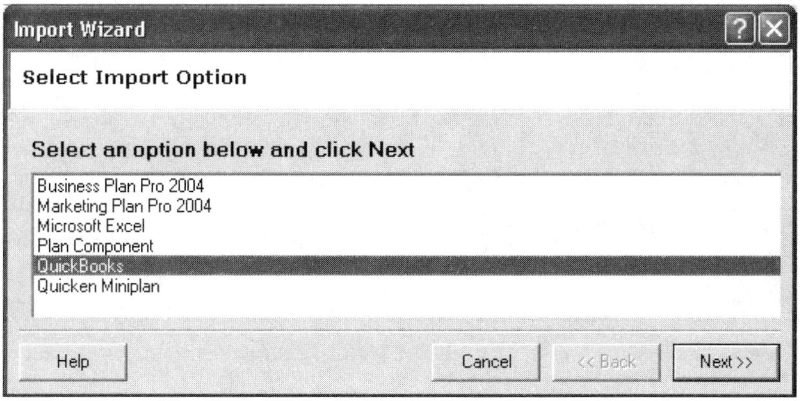

Import Wizard	? X

Select Import Option

Select an option below and click Next

Business Plan Pro 2004
Marketing Plan Pro 2004
Microsoft Excel
Plan Component
QuickBooks
Quicken Miniplan

Help		Cancel	<< Back	Next >>

Select the QuickBooks import option from the input form.

A series of dialog boxes takes you through the import process. Business Plan Pro needs to know how much information you want to import. You have the options shown in the form in Figure

12-6. You can import information for income, which is your sales information; for expenses, and for past balances. This is the first set of choices you can make.

FIGURE 12-6: QUICKBOOKS IMPORT OPTIONS

You have options with QuickBooks import. Choose which information you want to import.

The dialog shown in Figure 12-7 lets you decide whether you want to bring in values from QuickBooks for forecasting purposes, or just account names (categories).

FIGURE 12-7: SETTING IMPORT OPTIONS

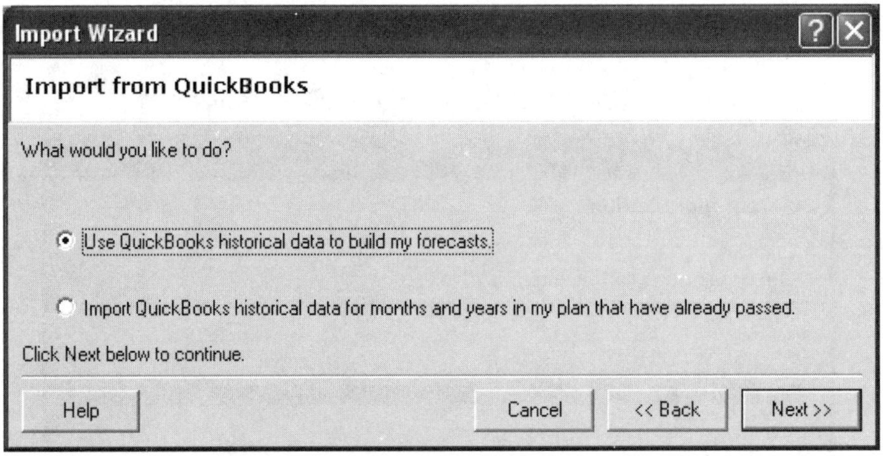

Use this form to set import for either forecasting values or simply account categories.

This is your option. Some people prefer to project past data forward into the future, others prefer to start with no values and set their own. Business Plan Pro includes powerful forecasting tools, such as the Forecaster™ and Row Fill features, to make for easy forecasting.

The QuickBooks import is not a substitute for good forecasting. It does not do data analysis, or technical forecasting. It does, however, take a close approximation of past results and apply any percentage growth you want to set to create future estimates for sales, costs of goods, and expenses.

Setting a Time Frame for Data Import

If you choose to use past data for forecasting, you set the time frame for the forecasting step. The import draws from any 12-month period you specify with the form. Most people choose to import a previous complete fiscal year. That way the months of the calendar match, catching trends related to seasonality. However, this is your choice. Figure 12-8 shows the dialog for setting time frame.

FIGURE 12-8: SETTING IMPORT DATES

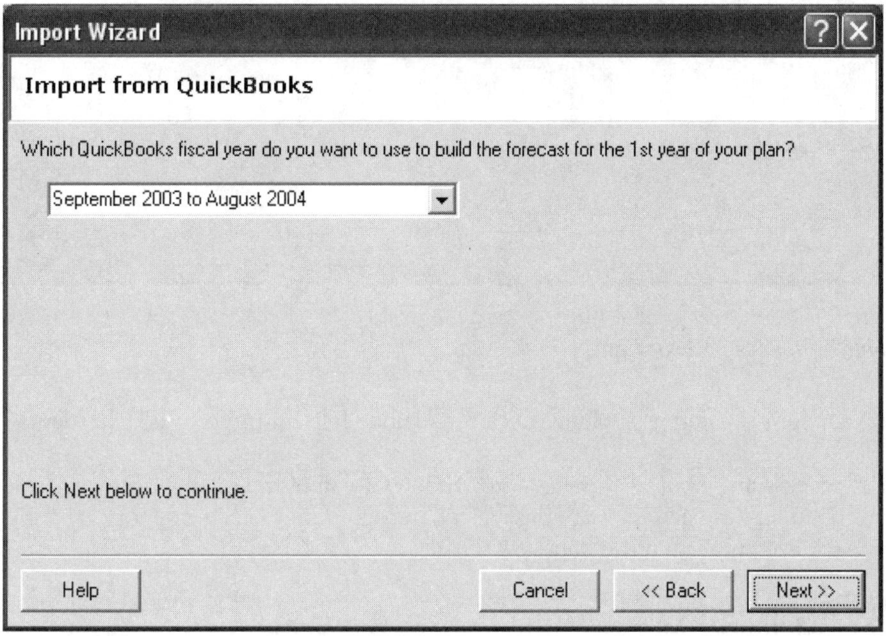

Import Wizard

Import from QuickBooks

Which QuickBooks fiscal year do you want to use to build the forecast for the 1st year of your plan?

September 2003 to August 2004

Click Next below to continue.

Help   Cancel   << Back   Next >>

As the import process continues, you use this form to define the past months for which you want to import your data for forecasting purposes.

Making your Projections

In the next step, if you chose to use past data for forecasting, you set the percentage growth rates to assign to sales, costs of goods, and expenses. Each of these three percentage growth rates is assigned to the entire category of past data, to create future projections.

FIGURE 12-9: SETTING PERCENTAGE GROWTH ESTIMATES

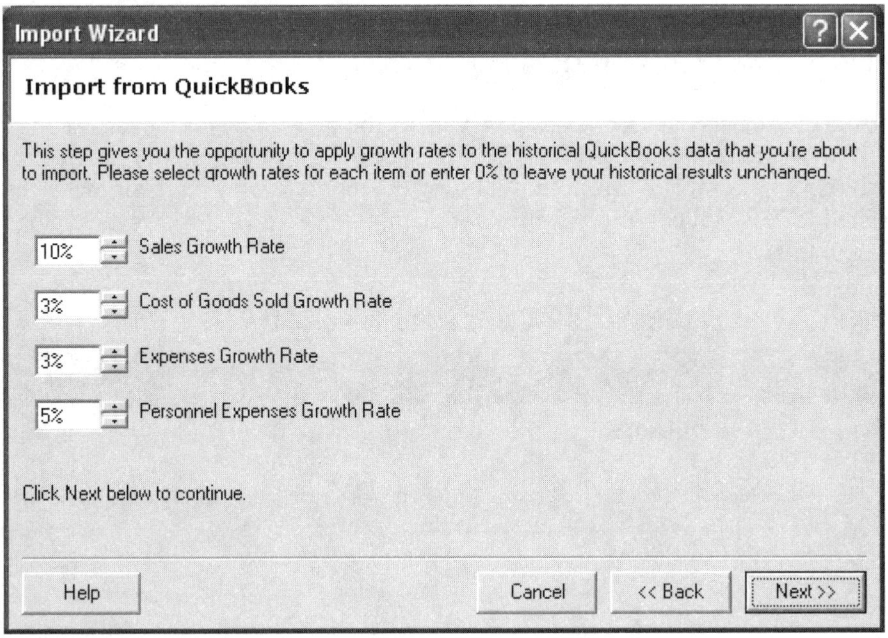

You use this form to set growth rates, as percentages, to convert your past year's QuickBooks data into estimates for your next planning year.

| Help | For step-by-step procedures, click the dialog Help button or the Help menu.

The import process automatically assigns growth rates to all of the relevant categories. It automatically multiplies each month's past result, in each item in each category, by 1 plus the growth rate for each month in the data.

TIPS

QuickBooks Pro Data Import is Not Exact

Business Plan Pro imports QuickBooks Pro data based on what is available in a specific transfer file. Not all monthly details are available. The imported information is useful for forecasting, but is not exact. Payroll, for example, gets only an annual total, so it divides by 12 to estimate monthly amounts.

After the QuickBooks Import

The QuickBooks import affects three tables: the Sales Forecast, the Profit and Loss, and the Past Performance table. It puts your past data and your growth formulas into Sales and Profit and Loss, and your most recent balance into Past Performance.

Sales Forecast

Figure 12-10 shows the Business Plan Pro sales forecast produced by the data and assumptions we use for this example, from Rock Castle Construction. There is only one line for sales ("Construction") and only one for costs of goods in this example because the source file in QuickBooks Pro had only the single categories. You can also see in the example how Business Plan Pro handled the projected 10% growth rate for sales and 5% growth for costs of goods.

Business Plan Pro's handling is intended to make forecasting easier. You can see the growth rate you assigned during input, so it is easy to change. You can also see, by clicking on any cell, the formula that preserves the previous data and assigns a growth rate. In the example, you see the growth rate in the B column. Cell C4 is selected, so the edit bar shows the formula: "=18171.82*(1+$B4)." The 18171.82 is either your previous sales or a close approximation, and the "(1+$B4)" is the application of the growth rate.

FIGURE 12-10: SALES FORECAST AFTER IMPORT

Table	Sales Forecast		Full Columns										Σ $ %
C4	=18171.82*(1+$B4)								

	A	B	C	D	E
1	Sales Forecast				
2	Sales		Oct	Nov	Dec
4	Construction	10%	$19,989	$11,365	$6,147
7	Total Sales		$19,989	$11,365	$6,147
8					
9	Direct Cost of Sales		Oct	Nov	Dec
11	Cost of Goods Sold	5%	$209	$100	$0
13	Subtotal Direct Cost of Sales		$209	$100	$0

The sales forecast after import from QuickBooks puts your growth rates in the second column and applies them to approximate past results from the QuickBooks Pro data.

To make the illustration shown, we used the Format > Row > Hide command to hide leftover rows in the Sales Forecast. The QuickBooks import does not do that automatically.

Profit and Loss

The Profit and Loss already shows in Figure 12-11. The Import settings customize the Profit and Loss to match your QuickBooks. There are some important special situations:

1. QuickBooks Pro puts lines of sales, which it calls income categories, onto the Profit and Loss. Business Plan Pro, however, puts sales and costs of goods sold only, as summary rows, on the Profit and Loss. The detail is in your Sales Forecast.

2. The Business Plan Pro row for payroll remains in the Profit and Loss, but the QuickBooks Pro import ignores it. If you have payroll expenses in your QuickBooks Pro, then your QuickBooks payroll information appears below, in alphabetical order, among the operating expenses. You can choose to stick with QuickBooks compatibility and ignore the Personnel Plan table in Profit and Loss, or to stick with the Personnel Plan and ignore—and delete— the row imported from QuickBooks. You can hide the built-in payroll line from Business Plan Pro, or delete the one from QuickBooks, depending on which option you choose. In the example in Figure 12-11, we chose to hide row 20, which contains the empty payroll information.

FIGURE 12-11: PROFIT AND LOSS AFTER IMPORT

Table	Profit and Loss	▾	Full Columns	▾	← → ☞ 🖳 ✄ 📋 🖺 ↶ ↷ 回 Σ $ %

C22	=712.56*(1+$B22)

	A	B	C	D	E	F	G
1	**Pro Forma Profit and Loss**						
2			Oct	Nov	Dec	Jan	Feb
3	**Total Income**		$19,989	$11,365	$6,147	$4,986	$6,331
8	**Cost of Goods Sold**		$209	$100	$0	$0	$0
9	**Gross Profit**		$19,780	$11,264	$6,147	$4,986	$6,331
10	Gross Profit %		98.95%	99.12%	100.00%	100.00%	100.00%
19	**Expenses:**						
21	Depreciation	7%	$0	$0	$0	$0	$0
22	Automobile	7%	$762	$0	$0	$762	$0
24	Bank Service Charges	7%	$4	$4	$4	$4	$4
27	Freight & Delivery	7%	$0	$0	$0	$0	($96)
29	Interest Expense	7%	$79	$76	$73	$70	$0
30	Job Expenses	7%	$0	$0	$1,070	$1,358	$5,031
33	Payroll Expenses	7%	$2,129	$2,129	$2,129	$2,129	$2,129
36	Rent	7%	$214	$214	$214	$214	$214
39	Tools and Machinery	7%	$0	$0	$0	$0	$0
40	Utilities	7%	$0	$0	$0	$13	$11
51			---------	---------	---------	---------	---------
52	**Total Expense**		$3,189	$2,424	$3,491	$4,551	$7,293
53	Gross Profit		$16,591	$8,841	$2,656	$435	($963)
65	**Net Other Income**		$0	$0	$0	$0	$0
66	**Net Profit**		$16,591	$8,841	$2,656	$435	($963)
67	**Net Profit/Sales**		83.00%	77.79%	43.21%	8.73%	-15.21%

The Profit and Loss table, after import, matches the categories in the QuickBooks Pro accounting data. Note the formula applying growth rates, showing in the edit bar.

3. Depreciation is a set row. Business Plan Pro needs depreciation to calculate cash flow properly. Depreciation must always stay in the same row, or it won't sort properly with the rest of your expenses.
4. Business Plan Pro makes monthly estimates from annual totals for some items. Depreciation, for example, and payroll are available to Business Plan Pro only as annual totals. It takes the totals available from import and divides by 12 to calculate approximate monthly values. This may not be ideal, but in these cases monthly amounts are not available.

The important point is that the business plan can adjust to meet the needs of the bookkeeping; it has sufficient flexibility. Matching the categories makes the information comparable in both.

Past Performance

The QuickBooks import takes the latest available balance and puts it into the Past Performance table. Figure 12-12 shows the latest available QuickBooks balance, from the Rock Castle Construction sample data included with QuickBooks Pro, which is set for a date in December of 2003.

FIGURE 12-12: QUICKBOOKS PRO BALANCE SHEET

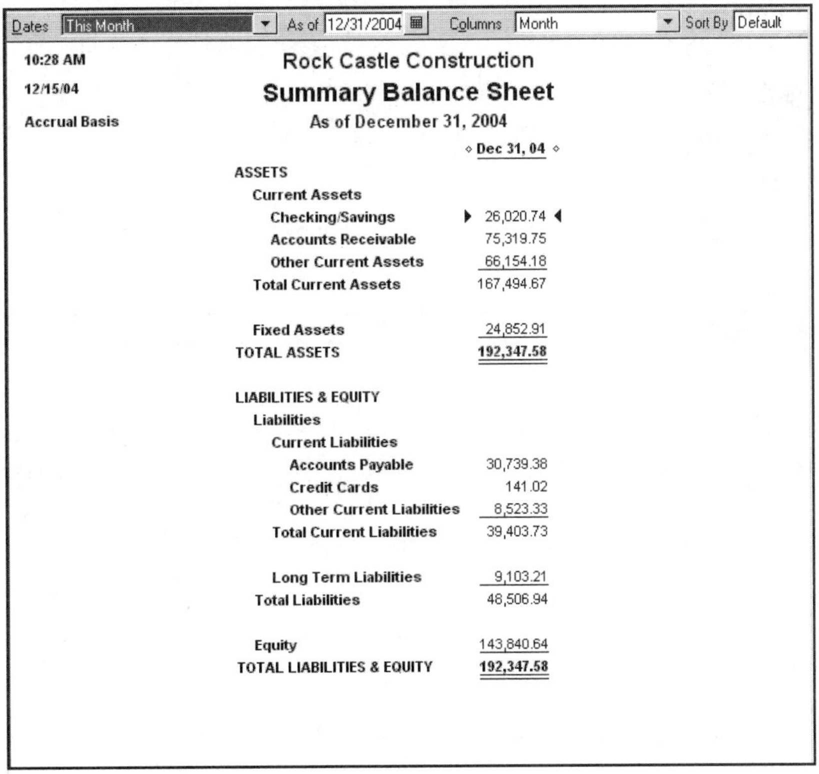

10:28 AM
12/15/04
Accrual Basis

Rock Castle Construction
Summary Balance Sheet
As of December 31, 2004

	Dec 31, 04
ASSETS	
Current Assets	
Checking/Savings	26,020.74
Accounts Receivable	75,319.75
Other Current Assets	66,154.18
Total Current Assets	167,494.67
Fixed Assets	24,852.91
TOTAL ASSETS	192,347.58
LIABILITIES & EQUITY	
Liabilities	
Current Liabilities	
Accounts Payable	30,739.38
Credit Cards	141.02
Other Current Liabilities	8,523.33
Total Current Liabilities	39,403.73
Long Term Liabilities	9,103.21
Total Liabilities	48,506.94
Equity	143,840.64
TOTAL LIABILITIES & EQUITY	192,347.58

The illustration shows the latest balance in the QuickBooks Pro data, at the time of the import to Business Plan Pro.

Figure 12-13, shows the Business Plan Pro Past Performance table after the import. In this case the numbers match exactly. The import catches the main Balance Sheet items as they are in the latest balance.

FIGURE 12-13: PAST PERFORMANCE AFTER IMPORT

Table	Past Performance	Full Columns					
D13	75319.75						

	A	B	C	D
10	**Balance Sheet**			
11	**Current Assets**	2002	2003	2004
12	Cash	$0	$0	$26,021
13	Accounts Receivable	$0	$0	$75,320
14	Inventory	$0	$0	$0
15	Other Current Assets	$0	$0	$66,154
16	**Total Current Assets**	**$0**	**$0**	**$167,495**
17	**Long-term Assets**			
18	Capital Assets	$0	$0	$24,853
19	Accumulated Depreciation	$0	$0	$0
20	**Total Long-term Assets**	**$0**	**$0**	**$24,853**
21	**Total Assets**	**$0**	**$0**	**$192,348**
22				
23	**Capital and Liabilities**			
24		2002	2003	2004
25	Accounts Payable	$0	$0	$30,739
26	Current Borrowing	$0	$0	$141
27	Other Current Liabilities	$0	$0	$8,523
28	**Subtotal Current Liabilities**	**$0**	**$0**	**$39,404**
29				
30	Long-term Liabilities	$0	$0	$9,103
31	**Total Liabilities**	**$0**	**$0**	**$48,507**
32	Paid-in Capital	$0	$0	$27,863
33	Retained Earnings	$0	$0	$115,977
34	Earnings	$0	$0	$0
35	**Total Capital**	**$0**	**$0**	**$143,841**
36	**Total Capital and Liabilities**	**$0**	**$0**	**$192,348**

The Past Performance table shows the latest QuickBooks Pro balances after import.

The result of import is the latest available Balance Sheet from your QuickBooks data. Normally you are developing a plan for the next fiscal year a few months before the end of the present fiscal year. Therefore the latest available balance is a good start for estimating Past Performance.

TIPS   ## Adjust the Past Performance Balance

Business Plan Pro imports the latest available balance for Past Performance. In most cases you use those latest balances to estimate final balances for the year.

Developing Your Plan, After the Import

After the import from QuickBooks, your business plan is ready to go. Continue to develop your projections. Your starting balance is whatever you end up with in Past Performance, and your projected Cash Flow reflects your assumptions for Sales Forecast, Profit and Loss, and Cash Flow. Your plan is ready to go as well as any other plan developed in Business Plan Pro, without the import. Figure 12-14 shows an example of using the Forecaster™ tool, as explained in Chapter 6: Your Plan Tables, to polish the estimates from the original import.

FIGURE 12-14: USING FORECASTER TO DEVELOP PROJECTIONS, AFTER IMPORT

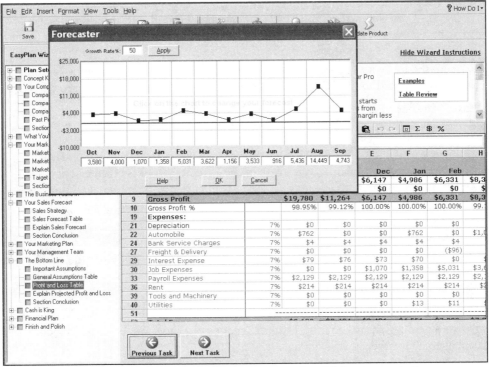

After import from QuickBooks, continue developing your plan. Make your projections as accurate as you can.

Working with the Balance Sheet

The balance sheet in QuickBooks is almost always more complicated than in Business Plan Pro. Consider the Business Plan Pro balance a summarized, streamlined version, ideal for business planning. Do not expect it to be the same as the QuickBooks detailed balance, because the QuickBooks balance depends on exploding into expanding detail. It matches the categories of the QuickBooks Summary Balance Sheet closely.

You should be able to reconcile the two formats by summarizing QuickBooks details with Business Plan Pro. Start with total assets, and divide them first into the summarized categories in Business Plan Pro. Here are some helpful details:

- Cash, in Business Plan Pro, should include all of your business' liquid assets: all checking and savings accounts managed by the business, plus money-market funds, and money in real cash (coins and bills).

- Accounts receivable and inventory are summaries. You do not need to divide them into detail in Business Plan Pro because you have QuickBooks for detailed management.

- Other Current Assets (also known as Short-term Assets) is a holding place for whatever else you have as current assets. For simplification's sake, hold all depreciation for long-term assets (even if you do have current assets that are depreciated, and you do not have long-term assets). Remember, the business plan is for planning purposes, and QuickBooks is for tax reporting and detailed accounting.

- Make sure the totals add up. When in doubt, look at your totals for current assets and long-term assets, adjusted for inflation. Fit the asset base into the Business Plan Pro categories.

Next, make sure your total liabilities match, and then divide them into the Business Plan Pro balance sheet using these hints:

- Accounts Payable are all of your bills due. Include liabilities like credit card balances.
- Current Borrowing is for bank loans, bank lines of credit, accounts receivable financing, inventory financing, and credit card balances if you do not include them in Accounts Payable.
- Other Current Liabilities (a.k.a. Short-term Liabilities) is for all other liabilities that do not fit into the first two categories. This is where you put all interest-free debt, such as loans from founders, or accrued taxes (if you do not have them in Accounts Payable).
- Make sure the liabilities total matches your QuickBooks total. If not, then the numbers are not entered correctly. Business Plan Pro mainly handles totals, so just divide the details into the right categories.

Finally, make the capital match as well. Paid-in Capital is actual money invested. Earnings are current-period earnings, as in the present year. Retained Earnings are whatever is required to make capital equal to assets minus equity.

Appendix A:
Range Names

APPENDIX A: RANGE NAMES

Business Plan Pro *uses named ranges in the tables to simplify reading and working with formulas.*

It is not necessary to know the built-in formulas or the range names; we provide this information for those who would like to know.

Named ranges can be used to create other specialized formulas, as described in more detail in Chapter 10: Advanced Tables.

Range Name   (PV=PREMIER Version Only)   Table and Range

Range Name	(PV=PREMIER Version Only)	Table and Range
accounts_payable		=Balance!$A$18:$AG$18
accounts_receivable		=Balance!$A$6:$AG$6
accumulated_depreciation		=Balance!$A$12:$AG$12
acid_test		=Ratios!$O$55:$AH$55
assets_to_sales		=Ratios!$O$53:$AH$53
average_per_unit_revenue		='Break-even'!$O$6
average_per_unit_variable_cost		='Break-even'!$O$7
cash		=Balance!$A$5:$AN$5
cash_balance_on_starting_date		='Start-up'!$B$18
cash_from_receivables		='Cash Flow'!$A$7:$AG$7
cash_sales		='Cash Flow'!$B$6:$AG$6
cash_spending		='Cash Flow'!$C$23:$AG$23
collection_days		=Ratios!$A$38:$AH$38
collection_days_estimator	PV	='Cash Pilot'!$A$3:$AN$3
cost_of_unit_sales		='P&L'!$A$4:$AN$4
CP_CollectionDays	PV	='Cash Pilot'!$C$3
CP_InventoryTurns	PV	='Cash Pilot'!$C$5
CP_PaymentDays	PV	='Cash Pilot'!$C$4
current_borrowing		=Balance!$A$19:$AG$19
current_interest_rate		=Assumptions!$A$4:$AG$4
depreciation		='P&L'!$A$22:$AN$22
direct_cost_of_sales		='P&L'!$A$4:$AG$4
dividend_payout		=Ratios!$O$57:$AH$57
dividends		='Cash Flow'!$A$35:$AG$35
earnings		=Balance!$A$28:$AG$28
estimated_monthly_fixed_cost		='Break-even'!$O$8
general_and_administrative_payroll		='P&L'!$A$20:$AG$20
general_and_administrative_percent		='P&L'!$A$30:$AG$30
gross_margin		='P&L'!$A$9:$AG$9
gross_margin_percent		='P&L'!$A$10:$AG$10
include_negative_taxes		='P&L'!$AD$54:$AG$54
include_negative_taxes_2nd_year		='P&L'!$AC$54

Range Name   (PV=PREMIER Version Only)   Table and Range

Range Name	(PV=PREMIER Version Only)	Table and Range
include_negative_taxes_first_year		='P&L'!$O$54
interest_expense		='P&L'!$A$40:$AG$40
inventory		=Balance!$A$7:$AG$7
inventory_purchase		=Assumptions!$A$14:$AG$14
inventory_purchased_this_period	PV	='Cash Pilot'!$A$26:$AG$26
inventory_turnover		=Ratios!$O$39:$AH$39
inventory_turnover_estimator	PV	='Cash Pilot'!$A$5:$AG$5
inventory_used_this_period	PV	='Cash Pilot'!$A$23:$AG$23
long_term_assets		=Balance!$A$11:$AG$11
long_term_interest_rate		=Assumptions!$A$5:$AG$5
long_term_liabilities		=Balance!$A$23:$AG$23
long_term_liabilities_principal_repayment		='Cash Flow'!$A$32:$AG$32
monthly_sales_breakeven		='Break-even'!$O$3
monthly_units_breakeven		='Break-even'!$O$2
net_cash_flow		='Cash Flow'!$A$38:$AG$38
net_other_income		='P&L'!$A$51:$AG$51
net_profit		='P&L'!$A$52:$AG$52
net_profit_margin		=Ratios!$O$33:$AH$33
net_worth		=Balance!$A$31:$AG$31
new_accounts_payable		=Assumptions!$A$13:$AN$13
new_current_borrowing		='Cash Flow'!$A$13:$AG$13
new_investment_received		='Cash Flow'!$A$18:$AG$18
new_long_term_liabilities		='Cash Flow'!$A$15:$AG$15
new_other_liabilities_interest_free		='Cash Flow'!$A$14:$AG$14
other_liabilities_principal_repayment		='Cash Flow'!$A$31:$AG$31
other_current_liabilities		=Balance!$A$20:$AG$20
paid_in_capital		=Balance!$A$26:$AG$26
past_capital_assets		=Past!$D$18
past_performance_accounts_payable		=Past!$D$25
past_performance_accounts_receivable		=Past!$D$13
past_performance_accumulated_depreciation		=Past!$D$19
past_performance_cash		=Past!$D$12

Range Name	(PV=PREMIER Version Only)	Table and Range
past_performance_collection_days		=Past!$D$7
past_performance_current_borrowing		=Past!$D$26
past_performance_earnings		=Past!$D$34
past_performance_gross_margin		=Past!$D$4
past_performance_gross_margin_percent		=Past!$D$5
past_performance_inventory		=Past!$D$14
past_performance_inventory_turnover		=Past!$D$8
past_performance_long_term_liabilities		=Past!$D$30
past_performance_operating_expenses		=Past!$D$6
past_performance_other_current_assets		=Past!$D$15
past_performance_other_current_liabilities		=Past!$D$27
past_performance_paid_in_capital		=Past!$D$32
past_performance_payment_days		=Past!$D$39
past_performance_sales		=Past!$D$3
payment_days_estimator	PV	='Cash Pilot'!$A$4:$AG$4
payments_on_accounts_payables	PV	='Cash Pilot'!$A$18:$AG$18
payroll		=Personnel!$C$67:$AN$67
payroll_expense		=Assumptions!$A$11:$AN$11
Payroll1		=Personnel!$C$3:$AN$3
Payroll2		=Personnel!$C$11:$AN$11
Payroll3	PV	=Personnel!$A$39:$AN$39
Payroll3GA	PV	=Personnel!$C$30:$AN$30
Payroll3OTH	PV	=Personnel!$C$36:$AN$36
Payroll3P	PV	=Personnel!$C$18:$AN$18
Payroll3SM	PV	=Personnel!$C$24:$AN$24
Payroll4	PV	=Personnel!$A$63:$AN$63
Payroll4GA	PV	=Personnel!$C$55:$AN$55
Payroll4OTH	PV	=Personnel!$C$60:$AN$60
Payroll4P	PV	=Personnel!$C$45:$AN$45
Payroll4SM	PV	=Personnel!$C$50:$AN$50
percent_equity_acquired	PV	='Investment Analysis'!$N$9
pilot_accounts_payable_balance	PV	='Cash Pilot'!$A$69:$N$69

Range Name	(PV=PREMIER Version Only)	Table and Range
pilot_accounts_receivable_balance	PV	='Cash Pilot'!$A$13:$AG$13
pilot_inventory_balance	PV	='Cash Pilot'!$A$27:$AG$27
plan_month		=Assumptions!$A$3:$AN$3
principal_repayment_of_current_borrowing		='Cash Flow'!$A$30:$AG$30
production_payroll		='P&L'!$5:$5
profit_before_int_and_taxes		='P&L'!$A$39:$AG$39
profit_before_interest_and_taxes		='P&L'!$A$39:$AG$39
purchase_long_term_assets		='Cash Flow'!$A$34:$AG$34
purchase_other_current_assets		='Cash Flow'!$A$33:$AG$33
retained_earnings		=Balance!$A$27:$AG$27
sales		='P&L'!$A$3:$AG$3
sales_and_marketing_percent	PV	='P&L'!$A$18:$AG$18
sales_of_long_term_assets		='Cash Flow'!$A$17:$AG$17
sales_of_other_current_term_assets		='Cash Flow'!$A$16:$AG$16
sales_on_credit		=Assumptions!$A$12:$AG$12
sales_on_credit_percent		=Assumptions!$A$7:$AG$7
sales_tax_vat_hst_gst_paidout		='Cash Flow'!$A$29:$AG$29
sales_tax_vat_hst_gst_received		='Cash Flow'!$A$12:$AG$12
sales_units_directcosts	PV	='Sales Forecast'!$A$41:$AG$44
sales_units_sales	PV	='Sales Forecast'!$A$28:$AG$31
salesunits	PV	='Sales Forecast'!$A$32:$AG$32
salesvalues		='Sales Forecast'!$A$5:$AG$5
startup_accounts_payable		='Start-up'!$B$36
startup_current_assets		='Start-up'!$B$21
startup_current_borrowing		='Start-up'!$B$37
startup_current_liabilities		='Start-up'!$B$39
startup_inventory		='Start-up'!$B$19
startup_long_term_assets		='Start-up'!$B$23
startup_long_term_liabilities		='Start-up'!$B$41
startup_loss_at_startup		='Start-up'!$B$44
startup_other_current_assets		='Start-up'!$B$20
startup_other_current_liabilities		='Start-up'!$B$38
startup_total_assets		='Start-up'!$B$24

Range Name	(PV=PREMIER Version Only)	Table and Range
startup_total_capital		='Start-up'!$B$45
startup_total_investment		='Start-up'!$B$33
startup_total_liabilities		='Start-up'!$B$42
subtotal_cash_from_operations		='Cash Flow'!$A$8:$AG$8
subtotal_cash_received		='Cash Flow'!$A$19:$AG$19
subtotal_cash_spent		='Cash Flow'!$A$36:$AG$36
subtotal_current_liabilities		=Balance!$A$21:$AG$21
subtotal_direct_cost_of_sales_units	PV	='Sales Forecast'!$A$45:$AG$45
subtotal_direct_cost_of_sales_values		='Sales Forecast'!$A$10:$AG$10
subtotal_spent_on_operations		='Cash Flow'!$A$25:$AG$25
tax_rate		=Assumptions!$A$6:$AG$6
taxes_incurred		='P&L'!$A$41:$AG$41
total_assets		=Balance!$A$14:$AG$14
total_capital		=Balance!$A$29:$AG$29
total_cost_of_sales		='P&L'!$A$8:$AG$8
total_current_assets		=Balance!$A$9:$AG$9
total_expense		='P&L'!$A$29:$AG$29
total_general_and_administrative_expense	PV	='P&L'!$A$29:$AG$29
total_liabilities		=Balance!$A$24:$AG$24
total_liabilities_and_capital		=Balance!$A$30:$AG$30
total_long_term_assets		=Balance!$A$13:$AG$13
total_operating_expenses		='P&L'!$A$38:$AG$38
total_other_expense		='P&L'!$A$50:$AG$50
total_other_income		='P&L'!$A$45:$AG$45
total_other_operating_expenses		='P&L'!$A$35:$AG$35
total_sales_and_marketing_expense	PV	='P&L'!$A$17:$AG$17
total_startup_expenses		='Start-up'!$B$15
total_unit_sales	PV	='Sales Forecast'!$A$19:$AG$19
valuation_earnings_multiple	PV	='Investment Analysis'!$B$15:$S$15
valuation_sales_multiple	PV	='Investment Analysis'!$B$16:$S$16

This page intentionally blank.

Appendix B:
Collaboration

APPENDIX B: COLLABORATION

Business Plan Pro® PREMIER *version includes a unique email-based collaboration tool. You can use it with plan development teams to share the process. Collaboration allows you to send and receive portions or components of a plan, with tracking of who modified, and when. You can choose when to accept a received portion of a plan, and whether to accept it and override what is there, on a component-by-component basis.*

Details on how to use collaboration are included in the main Help in the application. This appendix is a basic review of when and why to use it.

Collaborative Planning (PREMIER version)

As soon as a business plan involves more than a single person, it should become a collaborative effort. Teams implement plans, so teams should develop plans.

Normally a team includes different people with different skill sets and different responsibilities. The classic entrepreneurial team includes a leader, a numbers or finance oriented person, a sales and/or marketing oriented person, and a production person. The ideal business plan for a team like this is a plan developed jointly by team members.

Figure B-1 shows the main form for Business Plan Pro collaborative planning.

FIGURE B-1: COLLABORATION MAIN FORM

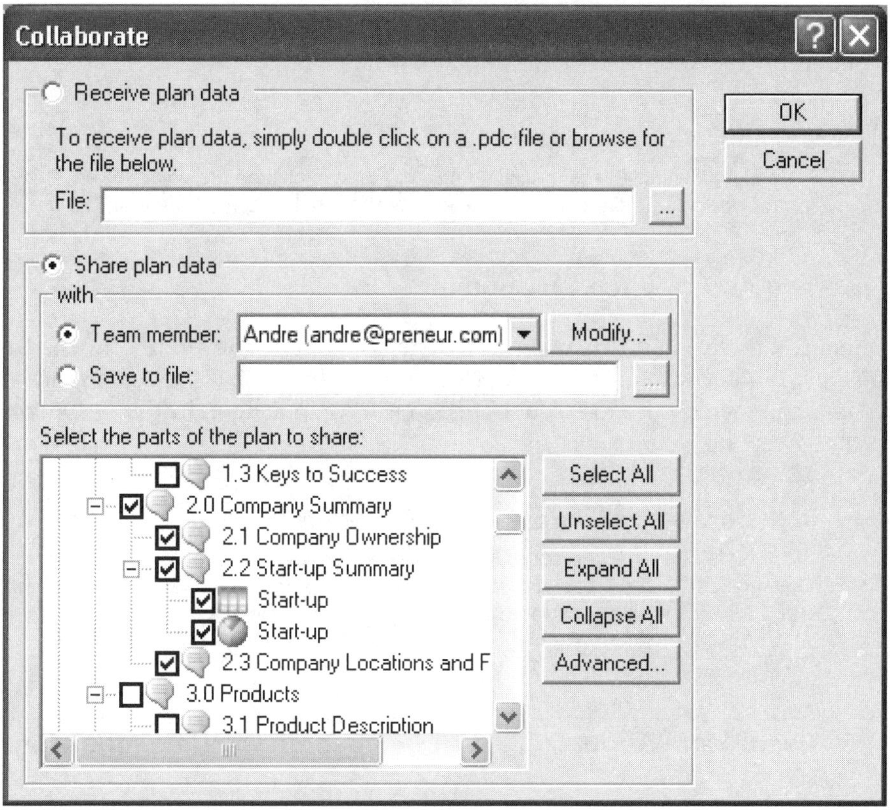

The collaboration form lets you manage team members, send and receive email collaboration, and save topics or other components to specific files. Note how on this form one team member receives topics, a table, and a chart in the Company chapter of this plan.

Help   For step-by-step procedures, click the dialog Help buttons or the Help menu.

Email Collaboration (PREMIER version)

The unique collaboration feature of Business Plan Pro uses the favorite tool for business communication known for file sharing and real-world teamwork—email. Email does not require posting to anybody's Web or Internet site, or additional security measures. Email is as private as your email server and email management.

Manage Team Members

As explained in detail in Help, use the main Collaboration form to manage team members' names and emails. You can add as many team members as you like.

Select Plan Components to Share

Select plan components (topics, tables, and charts), select team members to receive them, and send them the files. They will receive a file in their email.

TIPS

Collaboration Uses the Plan Outline

The collaboration list uses the Plan Outline. You can collaborate on tables or topics not currently part of the printed plan. Select them from the bottom of the Plan Outline.

Receive and Accept Each Component

As a team member receives a collaboration file, there is an opportunity to track each component for date modified, and by whom. The person who receives the email collaboration can preview the component and then choose to accept or reject each component individually. Optionally, he or she can also accept all, or reject all.

TIPS

Collaboration vs. Import/Export Component

You can also export a component, send it to somebody else, then they import it. The difference between collaboration and export-import is tracking modifications and replacing. Importing adds the component to your plan, duplicating what is there, if necessary. Collaboration replaces what is there, if you accept the collaborative component.

?	To Learn More About...	Search the Help Index for...
	Collaboration	Collaborate, Plan Components

Appendix C:
Import and Export Components

APPENDIX C: IMPORT AND EXPORT COMPONENTS

Business Plan Pro® PREMIER *version includes the ability to build and share components of a plan, such as add-on tables with business-specific details. This is called export.*

Both PREMIER *and* Standard versions *can import exported components. Some examples of these components are:*

- *Company-specific sales and expense forecasts.*

- *Industry-specific add-on worksheets, or sales or expense listings.*

- *Past or previous data, for use as a basis for forecast.*

- *Extra years in months, or quarters for more complex plans.*

Export Component (PREMIER version)

Business Plan Pro PREMIER version can export a component of a plan—text topic or table—so that it can be imported into another plan. Use the File > Export command. The Export Wizard (previously illustrated in this manual) guides you through the process. The discussion here is about common or suggested uses of this facility:

- Companies spreading business planning and forecasting responsibilities can create a standard form for Sales Forecast or Profit and Loss, for example, then have dozens or hundreds of people import that form for their own plans.
- Franchisors can create blank master forms for Sales Forecast and Profit and Loss, etc. The tables are left with the numbers blank, so prospective franchisees can make their own projections (less legal liability).
- Business plans requiring additional years in months or quarters can export important statements (e.g., Sales Forecast, Profit and Loss, Cash Flow, Balance Sheet) and then import them back for duplicates to use for the additional time frames.
- Content experts can create components containing their special expertise: planning forms for nightclub businesses, or bed and breakfast inns, for instance.
- Consultants can export their preferred formats for tables, for example, and share them with consulting clients.

| Help | For step-by-step procedures, click the dialog Help buttons or the Help menu.

Import Component

An exported component from Business Plan Pro PREMIER version can be imported into either Standard or PREMIER. This facilitates work between consultants and clients, plan experts and planning satellite sites, franchisee and franchisor, etc. The Import Wizard, accessed from the File > Import command, guides you. Imported components appear at the bottom of the Plan Outline. They do not replace existing topics or tables. Details of how to use this feature are in the online help.

TIPS

Collaboration vs. Import/Export Component

You can also export a component, send it to somebody else, then they import it. The difference between collaboration and export-import is tracking modifications and replacing. Importing adds the component to your plan, duplicating what's there, if necessary. Collaboration replaces what's there, if you accept the collaborative component.

?

To Learn More About...	Search the Help Index for...
Import/Export Components	Import, Export, File menu
Collaboration	Collaborate, Plan Components, File menu

This page intentionally blank.

Index

I

V

W

This page intentionally blank.